Understanding and Treating Patients in Clinical Psychoanalysis

Understanding and Treating Patients in Clinical Psychoanalysis: Lessons from Literature describes the problematic ways people learn to cope with life's fundamental challenges, such as maintaining self-esteem, bearing loss, and growing old. People tend to deal with the challenges of being human in characteristic, repetitive ways. Descriptions of these patterns in diagnostic terms can be at best dry, and at worst confusing, especially for those starting training in any of the clinical disciplines. To try to appeal to a wider audience, this book illustrates each coping pattern using vivid, compelling fiction whose characters express their dilemmas in easily accessible, evocative language. Sandra Buechler uses these examples to show some of the ways we complicate our lives and, through reimagining different scenarios for these characters, she illustrates how clients can achieve greater emotional health and live their lives more productively.

Drawing on the work of Dostoevsky, Tolstoy, Munro, Mann, James, O'Connor, Chopin, McCullers, Carver, and the many other authors represented here, Buechler shows how their keen observational short fiction portrays self-hurtful styles of living. She explores how human beings cope using schizoid, paranoid, grandiose, hysteric, obsessive, and other defensive styles. Each is costly, in many senses, and each limits the possibility for happiness and fulfillment.

Understanding and Treating Patients in Clinical Psychoanalysis offers insights into what living with and working with problematic behaviors really means through a series of examples of the major personality disorders as portrayed in literature. Through these fictitious examples, clinicians and trainees, and undergraduate and graduate students can gain a greater understanding of how someone becomes paranoid, schizoid, narcissistic, obsessive, or depressive, and how that affects them, and those around them, including the mental health professionals who work with them.

Sandra Buechler is a training and supervising analyst at the William Alanson White Institute. She is also a supervisor at Columbia Presbyterian Hospital's internship and postdoctoral programs, and a supervisor at the Institute for Contemporary Psychotherapy. Her publications include *Clinical Values: Emotions that Guide Psychoanalytic Treatment* (Routledge, 2004), *Making a Difference in Patients' Lives: Emotional Experience in the Therapeutic Setting* (Routledge, 2008), and *Still Practicing: The Heartaches and Joys of a Clinical Career* (Routledge, 2012).

PSYCHOANALYSIS IN A NEW KEY BOOK SERIES
DONNEL STERN
Series Editor

When music is played in a new key, the melody does not change, but the notes that make up the composition do: change in the context of continuity, continuity that perseveres through change. Psychoanalysis in a New Key publishes books that share the aims psychoanalysts have always had, but that approach them differently. The books in the series are not expected to advance any particular theoretical agenda, although to this date most have been written by analysts from the Interpersonal and Relational orientations.

The most important contribution of a psychoanalytic book is the communication of something that nudges the reader's grasp of clinical theory and practice in an unexpected direction. Psychoanalysis in a New Key creates a deliberate focus on innovative and unsettling clinical thinking. Because that kind of thinking is encouraged by exploration of the sometimes surprising contributions to psychoanalysis of ideas and findings from other fields, Psychoanalysis in a New Key particularly encourages interdisciplinary studies. Books in the series have married psychoanalysis with dissociation, trauma theory, sociology, and criminology. The series is open to the consideration of studies examining the relationship between psychoanalysis and any other field—for instance, biology, literary and art criticism, philosophy, systems theory, anthropology, and political theory.

But innovation also takes place within the boundaries of psychoanalysis, and Psychoanalysis in a New Key therefore also presents work that reformulates thought and practice without leaving the precincts of the field. Books in the series focus, for example, on the significance of personal values in psychoanalytic practice, on the complex interrelationship between the analyst's clinical work and personal life, on the consequences for the clinical situation when patient and analyst are from different cultures, and on the need for psychoanalysts to accept the degree to which they knowingly satisfy their own wishes during treatment hours, often to the patient's detriment.

Vol. 24
Understanding and Treating Patients in Clinical Psychoanalysis: Lessons From Literature
Sandra Buechler

Vol. 23
The Interpersonal Tradition: The Origins of Psychoanalytic Subjectivity
Irwin Hirsch

Vol. 22
Body-States: Interpersonal and Relational Perspectives on the Treatment of Eating Disorders
Jean Petrucelli (ed.)

Vol. 21
The One and the Many: Relational Approaches to Group Psychotherapy
Robert Grossmark & Fred Wright (eds.)

Vol. 20
Mended by the Muse: Creative Transformations of Trauma
Sophia Richman

Vol. 19
Cupid's Knife: Women's Anger and Agency in Violent Relationships
Abby Stein

Vol. 18
Contemporary Psychoanalysis and the Legacy of the Third Reich: History, Memory and Tradition
Emily A. Kuriloff

Vol. 17
Love and Loss in Life and in Treatment
Linda B. Sherby

Vol. 16
Imagination from Fantasy to Delusion
Lois Oppenheim

Vol. 15
Still Practicing: The Heartaches and Joys of a Clinical Career
Sandra Buechler

Vol. 14
Dancing with the Unconscious: The Art of Psychoanalysis and the Psychoanalysis of Art
Danielle Knafo

Vol. 13
Money Talks: In Therapy, Society, and Life
Brenda Berger & Stephanie Newman (eds.)

Vol. 12
Partners in Thought: Working with Unformulated Experience, Dissociation, and Enactment
Donnel B. Stern

Vol. 11
Heterosexual Masculinities: Contemporary Perspectives from Psychoanalytic Gender Theory
Bruce Reis & Robert Grossmark (eds.)

Vol. 10
Sex Changes: Transformations in Society and Psychoanalysis
Mark J. Blechner

Vol. 9
The Consulting Room and Beyond: Psychoanalytic Work and Its Reverberations in the Analyst's Life
Therese Ragen

Vol. 8
Making a Difference in Patients' Lives: Emotional Experience in the Therapeutic Setting
Sandra Buechler

Vol. 7
Coasting in the Countertransference: Conflicts of Self Interest between Analyst and Patient
Irwin Hirsch

Vol. 6
Wounded by Reality: Understanding and Treating Adult Onset Trauma
Ghislaine Boulanger

Vol. 5
Prologue to Violence: Child Abuse, Dissociation, and Crime
Abby Stein

Vol. 4
Prelogical Experience: An Inquiry into Dreams & Other Creative Processes
Edward S. Tauber & Maurice R. Green

Vol. 3
The Fallacy of Understanding & The Ambiguity of Change
Edgar A. Levenson

Vol. 2
What Do Mothers Want? Contemporary Perspectives in Psychoanalysis and Related Disciplines
Sheila F. Brown (ed.)

Vol. 1
Clinical Values: Emotions That Guide Psychoanalytic Treatment
Sandra Buechler

Understanding and Treating Patients in Clinical Psychoanalysis

Lessons from Literature

Sandra Buechler

LONDON AND NEW YORK

First published 2015
by Routledge
27 Church Road, Hove, East Sussex, BN3 2FA

and by Routledge
711 Third Avenue, New York, NY 10017

Routledge is an imprint of the Taylor & Francis Group, an informa business

© 2015 Sandra Buechler

The right of Sandra Buechler to be identified as author of this work has been asserted by her in accordance with sections 77 and 78 of the Copyright, Designs and Patents Act 1988.

All rights reserved. No part of this book may be reprinted or reproduced or utilised in any form or by any electronic, mechanical, or other means, now known or hereafter invented, including photocopying and recording, or in any information storage or retrieval system, without permission in writing from the publishers.

Trademark notice: Product or corporate names may be trademarks or registered trademarks, and are used only for identification and explanation without intent to infringe.

British Library Cataloguing in Publication Data
A catalogue record for this book is available from the British Library

Library of Congress Cataloging in Publication Data
Buechler, Sandra.
Understanding and treating patients in clinical psychoanalysis: lessons from literature/Sandra Buechler.
pages cm.—(Psychoanalysis in a new key book series)
1. Psychoanalysis and literature. I. Title.
PN56.P92B85 2015
616.89'17—dc23
2014019288

ISBN: 978-0-415-85646-1 (hbk)
ISBN: 978-0-415-85647-8 (pbk)
ISBN: 978-1-315-74506-0 (ebk)

Typeset in Times New Roman
by Swales & Willis Ltd, Exeter, Devon, UK

Printed and bound in Great Britain by
TJ International Ltd, Padstow, Cornwall

For Daphne, Isaac, Eva, Phoebe, their parents, and George

Contents

	Introduction	1
1	Schizoid Relating	10
2	Paranoid Processing	27
3	Humiliated Suffering	44
4	Grandiose Posturing	57
5	Hysterical Bargaining	70
6	Obsessive Controlling	82
7	Anguished Grieving	98
8	Depressive Self-Harming	113
9	Generative Aging	124
	Index	138

Introduction
Characters in Fiction as Templates for Clinical Assessment and Treatment

> I am a sick man... I am a spiteful man. No, I am not a pleasant man at all. I believe there is something wrong with my liver. However, I don't know a damn thing about my liver; neither do I know whether there is anything really wrong with me.
>
> Dostoevsky (1972, p. 107)

Thus begins Dostoevsky's great short story "Notes from the Underground." The reader is immediately drawn into a push-pull relationship with this cantankerous, bitter old man. We feel what it is like to be with him, not just through his descriptions of interpersonal events, but also through skirmishes the underground man creates with the reader. We enter into his world, with its bitter grudges, nursed for decades. Caught up in his endless debates, we feel the claustrophobia of a life spent in hiding from society.

No one can portray human dilemmas more vividly than the best fiction writers. In their imagined worlds, we meet characters struggling with the whole gamut of life's possibilities. We watch as some triumph over seemingly impossible obstacles while others sink beneath their weight. We have a ringside seat as they show us how they cope.

For the past 15 years, I have taught a course called "Psychopathology: Issues of Diagnosis, Entity, Process, and Character" at the William Alanson White Institute of Psychiatry, Psychoanalysis, and Psychology. The course is given to candidates in our four-year program, leading to a Certificate in Psychoanalysis. Generally, candidates enter this program with prior training in one of the mental health professions and are experienced clinicians. Together with my co-teacher, Gurmeet Singh Kanwal, M.D., I discuss some of the ways people cope with the challenges of being a person. We identify a number of fundamental human dilemmas and some frequently recurring attempts at solutions. Diagnosis names and describes some of the ways, however faulty, people try to deal with life.

Over the years, I have found that short stories portray these patterns of coping more vividly than any other medium. Unlike a novel or memoir, they can be read in their entirety within a week, making them ideal for teaching purposes. The skill of accomplished writers renders them more compelling than most case descriptions. When I ask for feedback at the end of each term, many confirm that the short stories brought the coping patterns alive. Many other texts describe personality disorders, but they rarely communicate with the stunning clarity of an outstanding work of fiction.

In this book, I have steered clear of the voluminous debates about differences between the concepts of character and personality, as well as the controversies that swell around the utility of diagnostic categorization. For interesting discussions of some of these issues, I recommend a lively book by Edgar Levenson, M.D. (1991), as well as the work by Adam Phillips wittily titled *Going Sane: Maps of Happiness* (2005). Nancy McWilliams (2011) contributed an excellent, thorough, and extremely helpful text; it should be read by any serious student of the subject. David Shapiro (1965, 1984, 1989) has made extremely significant contributions. For a fascinating discussion of problems with the concept of pathology, I suggest a volume called *What's Normal? Narratives of Mental and Emotional Disorders* (Donley & Buckley, 2000).

My approach is to focus on the ways people tend to grapple with their troubles. Thus, when I use a term like *paranoid*, I intend it to be understood as an adjective rather than as a noun. So, for example, Bessy, in I. B. Singer's story "The Key" (1999), uses paranoid strategies to deal with her anxieties (see chapter 2). I don't think of Bessy as "a paranoid," though I understand that in some contexts we have to use the term this way. Insurance companies want a diagnosis that fits their schemas, so, with them, we have to categorize. But in this book, I try to get to the heart of what it means to cope with life using paranoid, schizoid, obsessive, hysteric, depressive, and narcissistic defensive patterns. From short stories and clinical experience, I also cull some ways people deal with grief and aging. Characters in fiction vividly and memorably "speak" about their efforts to live fulfilled lives. As students of human nature, we do well to listen closely.

Seven of the book's nine chapters address schizoid, paranoid, shame-prone, grandiose, hysteric, obsessive, and depressive styles of coping. Two others (chapters 7 and 9) focus on specific human challenges: bearing profound grief and dealing with the process of aging. In each chapter, I first let the characters speak for themselves; that is, I summarize and quote from an array of stories that illustrate a pattern of dealing with the human condition. Some of these patterns are described more fully below.

Each of the first eight chapters then moves to a section on treatment. I do not intend these sections to provide a "cookbook." Rather, they are attempts to name some of the difficulties I have regularly encountered in my own clinical work with people who repetitively deal with their anxieties in obsessive ways, schizoid ways, and so on. The chapters on grief and aging treat these as experiences that occur in every life. What do they ask of us? What can we learn from fictional characters about ways of bearing these challenges with sufficient fortitude?

This book can be understood as a series of "interviews" of fictional characters. I ask them what they can tell me about their ways of dealing with their lives; they tell me stories of how they lost, or regained, or retained their balance in the face of life's dilemmas. The conclusion of each chapter considers one of my favorite questions: *Who* does the clinician need to be in order to help someone with this coping style? When I ask this question in class, I emphasize the word *who* and point out that I did not ask what we need to say or do, but rather, who we need to be. All of my writing (2004, 2008, 2012) rests on the premise that the personhood of the clinician is a key factor in treatment. Our "clinical values," such as hope, courage, and curiosity, shape how we work with everyone we treat. But in each chapter, I suggest some human qualities that I think are particularly relevant to treating the people considered in that section.

Throughout this book, I have used the word *patient* for simplicity's sake, since it is the term I grew up with, analytically speaking. I have used *treatment* interchangeably with *psychotherapy* and *analysis*. I do not intend this as a statement that these processes are the same, but what I do mean to imply is that, regardless of the mode of treatment, the practitioner will be faced with some regularly occurring difficulties in the work with people who cope obsessively, or hysterically, and so on.

The first chapter brings schizoid coping to the fore. We get an extremely vivid portrayal of this way of life in Mary E. Wilkins Freeman's "A New England Nun" (1965). The "nun" in the title is not actually a member of a religious order. If she has a religion (aside from an ordinary, conventional belief in God), it is solitude. She lives a pared-down life, communicating with her vegetable garden and her dog. Her "fiancé" spends decades pursuing his fortune in far-off lands. When he finally comes home, expecting them to be married, how will she cope? Will she be drawn into his embrace? Or will she remain encircled by the careful stitches of her embroidery?

In Wilbur Daniel Steele's "How Beautiful With Shoes" (1952), Guy de Maupassant's "Looking Back" (1952), Irwin Shaw's "Main Currents of American Thought" (1952), Dostoevsky's "Notes from the Underground" (1972), Sartre's "The Wall" (2002), and so many other stories, someone tells us what it is like to live a socially and emotionally restricted life. What can we learn about the human condition from these characters? How can they help us understand the solitary life?

The second chapter highlights paranoia. Sam, Bessy's husband in I. B. Singer's story "The Key" (1999), is long dead. Bessy lives or, rather, exists in an apartment on New York's Upper West Side. Danger lurks everywhere. Her neighbors wait for opportunities to rob, rape, utterly unhinge her. Strangers conspire to confuse her. Banks calculate how to divest her of her money. Supermarkets are designed to dizzy her with their incessant glare. Everyone is against her or, at the very least, indifferent. And then, there's her body. It won't do as she wills. It buckles and bulges, betraying her at every turn. Taming it takes every ounce of strength she can muster.

To go outside, to shop for food, is a monumental undertaking. Preparations include extra locks and other security measures to hold the predators at bay. Her enemies' every move must be anticipated and thwarted.

Then, suddenly, disaster strikes. Even after following every ritual, with every device in place, Bessy is beset by evil forces. They break her key, leaving her locked out of her sanctuary. The familiarity of routine is gone, perhaps forever. She is at the mercy of every passerby. Will they take advantage of this opportunity to torture her? Will she die, alone, homeless, weak, undefended?

Bessy is not the only fictional character acutely aware of lurking danger. In "The Door" (1952), E. B. White evokes our fear of appearances, and how they may differ from reality. In Conrad Aiken's truly chilling tale "Silent Snow, Secret Snow" (2002), we listen in as a 12-year-old child descends into a paranoid state. A similar fate awaits the protagonist of Gogol's masterpiece, "The Diary of a Madman" (1960). From these characters and others, we can get a sense of why some become excessively afraid of life itself.

The third chapter describes the life of those particularly vulnerable to narcissistic injury. Thomas Mann's great short story "Little Lizzy" (1972) portrays a downtrodden, overly compliant man who literally dies of shame. What causes someone to sink to this level of contempt for himself? Vivid expressions of low self-esteem abound in the short stories of Dostoevsky, such as his "The Meek Girl" (1989). Sherwood Anderson, in "Death in the Woods" (1988), shows us a woman, worn down by years of caring for others, with no thought for her own life. This tragic story illuminates how little entitlement a human being can have. Mann, Dostoevsky, and many other authors provide shattering portraits of people who see themselves at the lowest rung of society and cannot bear it. The third chapter asks if there is any way to salvage demolished self-esteem.

At the other end of the spectrum, some people flaunt inflated senses of self-regard. The characters described in chapter 4 exude grandiosity. Thomas Mann's great story "The Dilettante" (1997) illustrates, with stunning insight, the relationship between grandiosity and depression. Versions of the Icarus myth, where those who believe themselves to be high and mighty are shot down, abound in literature. While some cultures might read these endings as just punishments for hubris, our own might explain them differently. We understand that the drive to be an exception, to live outside normal limits, carries with it a vulnerability to the forces of "gravity," in several senses of the word.

Literature can help us fully grasp the relationship between low self-esteem, depression, and grandiosity. In stories such as "The Dilettante," and "The Blood of the Walsungs" (1997) Mann portrays what it is like for those who hold themselves as superior to fall from their pedestals. Studying these works of fiction can be rewarded with an enhanced understanding of both high and low self-regard. For example, we watch the protagonist in Willa Cather's moving story "Paul's Case" (2002) head toward suicide, as his sense of superiority crumbles.

The fifth chapter looks at those who can be seen as "hysterics." Most often, it is women who are portrayed as emotionally labile and intense. Countless heroines, from the wife in Charlotte Perkins Gilman's "The Yellow Wallpaper" (1994) to John Steinbeck's Elisa in "The Chrysanthemums" (1952), help us understand how soaring emotion can result from a person's effort to live within the confines of a stifling role. Edith Wharton gives a brilliant explanation in "The Other Two" (1952): Mrs. Waythorn has found it a little too easy to adjust to being with different men. Wharton looks at her through her current husband's eyes: "Her pliancy was beginning to sicken him. Had she really no will of her own . . . She was 'as easy as an old shoe' . . . a shoe that too many feet had worn. Her elasticity was the result of tension in too many different directions" (p. 217). What a succinct statement of Mrs. Waythorn's characteristic interpersonal pattern! We can learn a great deal about what has been called "hysteria" from these characters.

In "Molloy" (1955), Beckett gives us a character whose efforts at control can engender nervous laughter. Chapter 6 looks at people who cope with life obsessively. What if, along with Beckett's character, we lose track of which sucking-stones we have already sucked, and suck one of them twice? Heaven forbid! In "Father Wakes Up the Village" (1952), Clarence Day gives us Clare, whose ice *must* be delivered in exactly the right way or all hell really does break loose. Melville's "Bartleby the Scrivener" (1954) can be read as a cautionary tale about the conflict between what one is expected to do and the impulse to rebel. What if we would rather not do as we are told? Compliance versus rebellion is the issue at the heart of these characters' dilemmas. They illustrate how limiting this conflict can become. In his great poem "East Coker" (1943), T. S. Eliot poignantly expresses the urge to control life by knowing all there is to know, and how that eventually "falsifies." Each of these authors has portrayed an aspect of the obsessive dilemma. Trying to control life too much itself creates the very havoc we are desperately striving to avoid.

From my perspective, James Agee's *A Death in the Family* (2009) remains one of the most poignant stories ever written. This autobiographical work won the Pulitzer Prize for literature in 1958, three years after its author's death. Grief and shock war for ascendance as Mary suffers the sudden loss of her beloved husband. At first, Mary is numb from the paralyzing dislocation of the news of his fatal accident. But gradually, she begins to understand how life will never be the same. Each separate realization of what it will mean to live the rest of her life without him stabs her, penetrates the numbness, until grief overcomes shock. Nowhere in literature have I found a more affecting portrait of grief's passages. Our initial refusal to recognize its enormity postpones, but does not diminish, our suffering; we then begin to apprehend how the loss will affect our mornings, our Sundays, our New Years. Gradually, we are battered into resignation. Eventually, we give in to sorrow. Portrayals of grief in fiction are far more vivid than anything in our analytic literature. When King Lear (Shakespeare, 1972) repeats the word *never*, he expresses, in that one word, the unbearable shock of forever losing the daughter he so deeply loves. Our losses can coalesce and form a landslide that carries us down to depths of abject sorrow. We grieve for the lives we have almost had, had and lost, and never known. Can grief be treated? Should it be? Should we aim to diminish it, or are we more helpful if we aim to accompany it? What can exacerbate and/or prolong grief, so that it takes on a life of its own? This is the subject of chapter 7.

"All through life that piece of crape had hung between him and the world; it had separated him from cheerful brotherhood and woman's love, and kept him in that saddest of all prisons, his own heart, and still it lay upon his face, as if to deepen the gloom of his darksome chamber, and shade him from the sunshine of eternity" (Hawthorne, 1952, p. 498). Thus did Nathaniel Hawthorne describe the protagonist in his story "The Minister's Black Veil." The eighth chapter explores the terrain of that prison of the heart. Many authors have charted it. It is the asylum of Dickens' Miss Haversham in *Great Expectations* (1996); the world inhabited by those, like William Styron (1992), for whom the darkness has become visible. Depression can also take addictive forms, as it does in Sherman Alexie's funny and tragic "What You Pawn I Will Redeem" (2008).

Depression is both like and unlike grief, as Freud (1917) and countless others have suggested. As in grief, something has been lost, but in depression, the loss is more fully interior. One has lost one's own light. I believe that shame often plays a key role. While an exterior loss may have contributed, the depressed person mourns him or herself. This death in the midst of life transfixes us, like specimens caught in amber. Depression's paralysis can make movement monumentally, impossibly effortful. Should we signal to the depressed that their suspension of life is temporary, as Styron (2001) advises?

> A tough job, this calling "Chin up" from the safety of the shore to the drowning person is tantamount to insult, but it has been shown over and over again that if the encouragement is dogged enough—and the support equally committed and passionate—the endangered one can nearly always be saved. (p. 122)

Or is it better to heed depression as a signal that there is something to address, as Stringer (2001) suggests?

> [W]hat we call depression isn't really a disorder at all but, like physical pain, an alarm of sorts, alerting us that something is undoubtedly wrong; that perhaps it is time to stop, take a time-out, take as long as it takes, and attend to the unaddressed business of filling our souls. (pp. 112–113)

As friends, family, or therapists of people who are depressed, should we try to persuade the sufferer that life can be better, or that the pain will pass, or should we aim to alleviate the loneliness by sharing in it?

The last chapter asks, in effect, how gently we should go into this good night. Aging can be experienced as a pitiless series of unmitigated losses. We can lose our faculties at a slow, agonizing, relentless pace or with terrifying speed. We can lose family, friends, and the habits of a lifetime. Our life's purpose can become as blurry as small print in a darkened room. Should we fight to keep change as gradual as possible? Do we make fools of ourselves if we try to work, love, lust, keep up with the younger, fitter, and more savvy? Is it better to embrace the changes, let the hair go gray, fade from the work place, linger over lunch, and take up golf? Regarding this dilemma, T. S. Eliot's (1930) Prufrock is one of my favorite spokespersons. He forthrightly asks whether he should wear his trousers rolled, and whether he should risk being "almost ridiculous" by daring to eat a peach. Knowing that the mermaids will never again sing for him, he asks what is left. He can remember their songs and imagine what lucky, younger people are still experiencing. But he knows that this, like so much else, is over for him.

Some of the characters who speak to us in this chapter weigh in on the side of gracefully embracing aging, while others fight, literally, to the death. Some give poignant voice to the struggle to find meaning in their lives. A beautiful example of this is Margaret, the old aunt in Mary Lerner's story "Little Selves" (1999). Like the most dedicated patient in an analysis, Margaret yearns to recover and communicate her previous identities before she dies. A similar striving impassions the protagonist in Willa Cather's "Neighbor Rosicky" (1994), who finds great joy in trying to pass on a sense of his life's meaning.

Perhaps the most poignant stories about aging portray the feeling of having missed the boat. If we let ourselves down by failing to take advantage of opportunities when they occurred, we suffer as both betrayer and betrayed. Nowhere is this terrain more movingly explored than in Henry James' "The Middle Years" (1992). This is the story of an author who feels he has allowed it to happen that he will never reach his fullest potential. The protagonist pleads with life to give him "an extension" of time, so he can correct his mistakes, but to no avail.

In this final chapter, I explore stories of aging gracefully, aging bitterly, raging against the fading of the light, and finding new ways of seeing. What can these stories contribute to our ability to help others, and ourselves, with the process of growing old? And, more generally, what can the stories throughout this book teach us about coping, and helping others cope, with the human condition?

References

Agee, J. (2009). *A death in the family.* New York: Penguin Books.
Aiken, C. (2002). Silent snow, secret snow. In A. H. Bond (Ed.), *Tales of psychology: Short stories to make you wise* (pp. 142–163). St. Paul: Paragon House.
Alexie, S. (2008). What you pawn, I will redeem. In J. Kelly (Ed.), *The seagull reader stories* (pp. 8–29). New York: W. W. Norton & Company.
Anderson, S. (1988). A death in the woods. In P. S. Prescott (Ed.), *The Norton book of American short stories* (pp. 220–230). New York: W. W. Norton & Company.
Beckett, S. (1955). *The unnamable: Part of trilogy including Molloy and Malone dies.* New York: Alfred A. Knopf.
Buechler, S. (2004). *Clinical values: Emotions that guide psychoanalytic treatment.* Hillsdale, NJ: Analytic Press.
Buechler, S. (2008). *Making a difference in patients' lives: Emotional experience in the therapeutic setting.* New York: Routledge.
Buechler, S. (2012). *Still practicing: The heartaches and joys of a clinical career.* New York: Routledge.
Cather, W. (1994). Neighbor Rosicky. In A. W. Lidz (Ed.), *Major American short stories* (pp. 301–326). New York: Oxford University Press.
Cather, W. (2002). Paul's case. In A. H. Bond (Ed.), *Tales of psychology: Short stories to make you wise* (pp. 220–244). St. Paul: Paragon House.
Day, C. (1952). Father wakes up the village. In M. Crane (Ed.), *Fifty great short stories* (pp. 315–321). New York: Bantam Dell.

De Maupassant, G. (1952). Looking back. In M. Crane (Ed.), *Fifty great short stories* (pp. 175–180). New York: Bantam Dell.
Dickens, C. (1996). *Great expectations*. London: Penguin Classics.
Donley, C., & S. Buckley. (2000). *What's normal? Narratives of mental and emotional disorders*. Kent, OH: Kent State University Press.
Dostoevsky, F. (1972). Notes from the underground. In D. Magarshack (Trans.), *The best short stories of Dostoevsky* (pp. 107–241). New York: The Modern Library.
Dostoevsky, F. (1989). The meek girl. In D. McDuff (Trans.), *Uncle's dream and other stories* (pp. 253–296). New York: Penguin Books.
Eliot, T. S. (1930). *Selected poems*. New York: Harcourt.
Eliot, T. S. (1943). *Four quartets*. New York: Harcourt.
Freeman, M. E. W. (1965). A New England nun. In M. Crane (Ed.), *Fifty great American short stories* (pp. 108–123). New York: Bantam Dell.
Freud, S. (1917). Mourning and melancholia. In J. Strachey (Ed. & Trans.), *The standard edition of the complete works of Sigmund Freud* (Vol. 14, pp. 237–258). London: Hogarth Press.
Gilman, C. P. (1994). The yellow wallpaper. In A. W. Lidz (Ed.), *Major American short stories* (pp. 286–300). New York: Oxford University Press.
Gogol, N. (1960). The diary of a madman. In A. R. MacAndrew (Trans.), *The diary of a madman and other stories* (pp. 7–29). New York: New American Library.
Hawthorne, N. (1952). The minister's black veil. In M. Crane (Ed.), *Fifty great short stories* (pp. 494–500). New York: Bantam Dell.
James, H. (1992). The middle years. In J. C. Oates (Ed.), *The Oxford book of American short stories* (pp. 171–190). New York: Oxford University Press.
Lerner, M. (1999). Little selves. In J. Updike & K. Kenison (Eds.), *The best American short stories of the century* (pp. 7–18). New York: Houghton Mifflin Company.
Levenson, E. (1991). *The purloined self: Interpersonal perspectives in psychoanalysis*. New York: Contemporary Psychoanalysis Books.
Mann, T. (1997). The blood of the Walsungs. In *Little Herr Friedemann and other stories* (pp. 159–186). London: Minerva.
Mann, T. (1997). The dilettante. In *Little Herr Friedemann and other stories* (pp. 36–62). London: Minerva.
Mann, T. (1997). Little Lizzy. In *Little Herr Friedemann and other stories* (pp. 70–85). London: Minerva.
McWilliams, N. (2011). *Psychoanalytic diagnosis: Understanding personality structure in the clinical process*. New York: Guilford Press.
Melville, H. (1994). Bartleby the scrivener. In A. W. Lidz (Ed.), *Major American short stories* (pp. 135–167). New York: Oxford University Press.
Phillips, A. (2005). *Going sane: Maps of happiness*. New York: HarperCollins.
Sartre, J-P. (2002). The wall. In C. Neider (Ed.), *Great short stories of the masters* (pp. 387–405). New York: Cooper Square Press.
Shakespeare, W. (1972). *King Lear*. In *The Arden edition of the works of William Shakespeare*. London: Methuen Drama.
Shapiro, D. (1965). *Neurotic styles*. New York: Basic Books.
Shapiro, D. (1984). *Autonomy and rigid character*. New York: Basic Books.
Shapiro, D. (1989). *Psychotherapy of neurotic character*. New York: Basic Books.
Shaw, I. (1952). Main currents of American thought. In M. Crane (Ed.), *Fifty great short stories* (pp. 471–482). New York: Bantam Dell.

Singer, I. B. (1999) The key. In J. Updike & K. Kenison (Eds.), *The best American short stories of the century* (pp. 493–503). New York: Houghton Mifflin Company.
Steele, W. D. (1952). How beautiful with shoes. In M. Crane (Ed.), *Fifty great short stories* (pp. 361–383). New York: Bantam Dell.
Steinbeck, J. (1952). The chrysanthemums. In M. Crane (Ed.), *Fifty great short stories* (pp. 337–347). New York: Bantam Dell.
Stringer, L. (2001). Fading to gray. In N. Casey (Ed.), *Unholy ghost: Writers on depression* (pp. 105–114). New York: HarperCollins.
Styron, W. (1992). *Darkness visible.* New York: Vintage Books.
Styron, W. (2001). From *Darkness visible.* In N. Casey (Ed.), *Unholy ghost: Writers on depression* (pp. 114–126). New York: HarperCollins.
Wharton, E. (1952). The other two. In M. Crane (Ed.), *Fifty great short stories* (pp. 201–221). New York: Bantam Dell.
White, E. B. (1952). The door. In M. Crane (Ed.), *Fifty great short stories* (pp. 348–353). New York: Bantam Dell.

Chapter 1

Schizoid Relating

Mare, or Amarantha, is the passive, becalmed main character in William Daniel Steele's heart-rending story "How Beautiful With Shoes" (1952). When we first meet her, going through the motions on her family's farm, doing her chores as though hypnotized, moving through one dazed day after another, she is trying to avoid the attentions of her betrothed. But soon a stranger, a "loony" who is poetically passionate about Mare, kidnaps her. She is terrified. The "loony," Humble Jewett, is being hunted down by her fiancé, and half the rest of the town. Meanwhile Humble, who has trapped Mare in an old farmhouse, confesses to her that he has never really lived, or loved, until now. When she is finally rescued, and Humble is killed, all she can do is sit in her house and stare at the wallpaper. Her *feet* know her shoes hurt, but *she* doesn't know it. Her mother asks her if her poor feet are dead, as though intuiting that, in fact, for her daughter a familiar kind of death has returned. Mare wonders if only "loonies" feel passion. When her fiancé visits, expecting her to resume their business as usual, she finds a kind of passion in her determination to keep him at bay, slamming the door in his face and wanting only to be left alone. No matter how crazy Humble was, he felt her, touched her, wanted her. He was alive. He was poetry, intensity, passion, worship. When he died, Mare resisted going back to sleepwalking, though she also cried because she knew that her beautiful feet were doomed to plod unrecognized through the rest of her days.

Mare's emptiness, at the two ends of the story, expresses schizoid depression. She functions behaviorally but is disconnected from herself. The person suffering from schizoid depression doesn't see the point of living. She feels nothing intensely and seems to be an observer of her own life, getting through it, rather than living it. She does what is expected of her, dully, carefully, dutifully. She knows something is missing from her life. It tastes bland, as though the spices were accidentally left out. She observes others and tries to copy their recipe, but it never comes out right. Here are some aspects of schizoid living as I understand it (for a discussion of some pertinent literature, see Buechler, 2002):

- Muted, camouflaged emotionality; it is as though the feelings are all there, but hidden and without intensity;
- A need to keep functioning, no matter what it takes;

- An ability to forge stunted, but serviceable, relationships with others;
- An unacknowledged, vivid fantasy life, or dream life, that profoundly contrasts with relatively sterile external relationships.

In Mary E. Wilkins Freeman's story "A New England Nun" (1965), Louisa Ellis lives a narrow life, but within its confines it is graced with dainty delicacy. Her china is just so, as is her sewing basket. For 15 years, she has been engaged to Joe Dagget. Joe spent most of that time in Australia, making his fortune. They had agreed to marry upon his return. Now, with him back, the wedding date is one week away. Neither would even think of disappointing the other. But when they are together, the rough and ready Joe feels confined, like a bull in a china shop. And Louisa experiences him as disrupting her calm, ordered world. She feels she must be loyal and go through with the marriage, but she realizes that, years ago, her feet "had turned into a path, smooth maybe under a calm, serene sky, but so straight and unswerving that it could only meet a check at her grave, and so narrow that there was no room for anyone at her side" (p. 114). Louisa mourns as she imagines what it will be like to leave her possessions and live with Joe and his mother. She foresees disorder and confusion taking the place of her life of quiet harmony.

A chance encounter tells Louisa that Joe is struggling with attraction to another woman. She finds a way to break the engagement, much to their mutual relief. That night, alone, she cries a little, but the next morning she feels like a queen newly restored to her rightful place. As she thinks about her future, "She gazed ahead through a long reach of future days strung together like pearls in a rosary, every one like the others, and all smooth and flawless and innocent, and her heart went up in thankfulness . . . Louisa sat, prayerfully numbering her days, like an uncloistered nun" (p. 123).

Louisa epitomizes the schizoid's deal with life: Live small but safe. Constrict relationships, adventure, and feeling. Nest. Pour your love into the inanimate. Live in a painting by Chardin, and polish the silverware to a high sheen. Love sameness. Cling to it. Forgo surprise. Keep your blood pressure steady. No thrills, but, also, no shocks. Make your future into a succession of days just like the past and the present. Louisa worships her tea set and pours her soul into every hem she sews. Her passion is spent in avoiding the experiences most of us would call passionate. In exchange for these sacrifices, Louisa achieves a height from which she can survey her world in utter peace. She is like a nun, forsaking most worldly pleasures, but she has not married Christ, or anyone else, except, in a sense, her static world. She is as devoted as any nun, as loyal, observant, industrious, caring. She has gained equilibrium and a pleasant life. She depends only on herself, and on the sun to come up every morning. She will never know powerful, full-blooded desire. She has invested all her resources in a bank account that yields small but steady returns.

There are many versions of the schizoid bargain. Some are much less extreme than Louisa's. We see people inhabiting only a limited range of their potential, blending in, or, as I would suggest, "blanding" in with their interpersonal surround. We notice subtly muted affects, limited dependence, passion felt mostly in observing the passions of others. There are legions of human beings who experience life at a remove. They may cry the hardest at a sad movie, since it is in this form that they can allow themselves to feel the tragic dimension of life. They are the onlookers, observers, on the rim.

Henry James, certainly one of the finest chroniclers of schizoid lives, has given us a precise picture of them in his story "The Tree of Knowledge" (1954). We are introduced to Peter, who exists in a delicately balanced relationship with his artist friend, Morgan Mallow, and Morgan's wife. Peter is described as "a man who had reached fifty, who had escaped marriage, who had lived within his means, who had been in love with Mrs. Mallow for years without breathing it" (p. 201). Morgan is a sculptor of statues who thinks himself a genius but who, in Peter's opinion, lacks genuine talent. However, in this paragon of schizoid compromise situations (for a discussion of this term, see Guntrip, 1969), Peter must keep mum about this judgment, and much else.

The subtle balance is threatened by Lance, the Mallows' son, who is thinking of following in his father's footsteps. Peter senses that this might somehow upset the applecart. He tries to pressure Lance: "Well, we're so right—we four together—just as we are. We're so safe. Come, don't spoil it" (p. 206). Peter is afraid of change. For years, he has joined with Mrs. Mallow to oversee Lance's development. This project has brought them together in countless ways. Lance's wish to go to Paris, pursue art, and become a master like his father confronts Peter with difficult choices. Does he confess to Lance that Morgan's genius has been exaggerated, to keep all the interpersonal balances intact?

Surely, this confession would unleash disaster. When Lance guesses the truth on his own, he manages to have time alone with Peter to wonder "how the deuce then for so long you've managed to keep bottled" (p. 213). This is just what an analyst might ask. Peter confesses his fears to Lance and gets him to promise never to reveal the secret of Morgan's mediocrity.

But the threat of change grows greater as his father pressures Lance to make a success like his own, lecturing him from on high about the road to fame and fortune. Mrs. Mallow recognizes the strain this places on Lance and comes to him privately to tell him she does recognize her husband's limitations. Lance believes that Peter cares about his mother so much that he has done everything to spare her from disillusionment. What Lance doesn't fully understand is Peter's personal stake in keeping the status quo.

Peter's relationships with Lance and his parents could be read out of Guntrip's (1969) description of schizoid compromises. They share some intimacy, but no one is able to be their full selves. Peter doesn't have his own partner or child, but he does get a portion of Morgan's family, in return for his pretense that he admires Morgan's work, and his limited expression of his passion for Morgan's wife. He sees truth and change as his enemies, to be deeply feared. This makes Peter's position precarious. I think it is implied that it is ultimately untenable, although this is not spelled out. But the fragile tissue of lies has been rent, and it seems likely to be eroded further in the future.

Sometimes a limited schizoid relationship seems to work, at least for a while. This is the case in Bobby Ann Mason's short story "Shiloh" (2008). Leroy used to drive a truck, and his wife, Norma Jean, worked in the Rexall drugstore. Leroy did long hauls, so he was away from home about half the time, until four months ago, when he had a highway accident that changed their lives. Now Leroy is at loose ends, staying at home and occupying himself with craft "projects." Norma Jean makes it all too clear that she yearns to have more time to herself again. At an outing they take together, Norma Jean tells Leroy that she wants to leave him, not because he has done anything wrong, but just because she can't have people, like Leroy and her mother, around her so much. Leroy is frantic. He realizes that he doesn't understand his marriage at all. He doesn't know why it seemed to work before and why it has stopped working now. He thought his wife would be happier with him home more, but instead, she is miserable. Norma Jean doesn't really understand her own feelings, but she knows she isn't happy. Their inability to "get" each other is succinctly described in just a few lines of dialogue, "'Didn't I promise to be home from now on?' he says. 'In some ways, a woman prefers a man who wanders,' says Norma Jean. 'That sounds crazy, I know'" (p. 178). The story ends with Leroy literally hobbling to try to catch up with his sprinting wife: "Now she turns toward Leroy and waves her arms. Is she beckoning to him?" (p. 279). Leroy can't grasp how to approach a woman who passionately wants to be left alone. Norma Jean can only bear bouts of relating interrupted by stretches of rejuvenating peace. Like Louisa (see above), she is an onlooker, happiest watching life at a bit of a remove.

Unlike Norma Jean and Louisa, the anti-hero in Dostoevsky's "Notes from the Underground" (1972) extravagantly protests against his outsider status, but also fervently clings to it. His nose is permanently out of joint. He complains that he is not invited to join his old schoolmates for a farewell dinner, but dreads the social contact when he does attend. He mutters in a corner, refusing to share the merriment, but also refusing to leave.

The "Notes" are reflections 20 years after the events in the story. They are a loner's resentful account of feeling snubbed by people he loves to snub. He certainly would never want to be a part of a club that would have him as a member. But, along with his infinite irritation, there are moments of exquisite yearning. He allows himself a brief fantasy about an officer who refused to acknowledge his existence: "Oh, how wonderfully we should have got on together! He would have protected me by his rank of an army officer, and I would have enlarged his mind by my superior education and—well—by my ideas, and lots of things could have happened" (p. 156).

But, for the underground man, "lots of things" happen mainly in his fantasies and dreams. He passes most of his time watching from the sidelines, full of criticism and equally full of longing. He spends months engineering a brief encounter with the officer, hoping to force a moment of mutual regard. He squanders his last rubles to join the farewell dinner, fully realizing what a miserable evening it will be. Going one step further, as if to prove to himself that he is not fit for human company, he follows the group to a house of prostitution. With Lisa, a struggling runaway assigned to him by the madam, he attempts flickers of connection but then feels compelled to destroy any hope of intimacy.

Dostoevsky has so beautifully captured the schizoid dilemma, that I have often found myself juxtaposing the anti-hero's words with passages from Guntrip (1969). For example, for Guntrip, the schizoid person has renounced relationships but still needs them: "There is a constant oscillation between hungry eating and refusal to eat, longing for people and rejecting them" (p. 31). Similarly, Dostoevsky's anti-hero describes his periodic bouts of social activity:

> I was never able to spend more than three months of dreaming at a time without feeling an irresistible urge to plunge into social life. To me, plunging into social life meant paying a call on the head of my department, Anton Antonovich Setochkin. He was the only permanent acquaintance I have had in my life. (p. 164)

Guntrip sees the schizoid person as caught in a perpetual dilemma, needing human connection but believing his love to be fundamentally dangerous. In Guntrip's words, "love made hungry is the schizoid problem and it rouses the terrible fear that one's love has become so devouring and incorporative that love itself has become destructive" (p. 24). Dostoevsky's character describes his certainty that his love would inevitably hurt the prostitute, Lisa: "Could I make her happy? Had I not learnt today for the hundredth time what I was really worth? Should I not torture her to death?" (p. 238). Ultimately, the underground man has to destroy connection because, in his experience, it threatens to overwhelm him and to make others suffer.

When I was a candidate, my first analytic supervisor, Ralph Crowley, M.D., described schizoid functioning as living in the head, using real events in the outside world as furniture for the life of the mind. Guntrip (1969) calls this "introversion." The underground man calls it a solution: "But I had a solution which made up for everything, and that was to seek salvation in all that was 'sublime and beautiful,' in my dreams, of course. I would give myself up entirely to dreaming" (p. 161). The most vivid feelings are experienced in fantasies and dreams, not in real life. Dostoevsky's anti-hero explains that the vivid dreams made actual relationships unnecessary:

> But how much love, good lord, how much love I used to experience in those dreams of mine . . . there was so much of it, so much of this love, that one did not feel the need of applying it in practice afterwards; that would indeed have been a superfluous luxury. (p. 163)

Guntrip describes schizoid functioning as regressed: "The schizoid person at bottom feels overwhelmed by the external world, and is in flight from it both inwards and, as it were, backwards, to the safety of the womb" (p. 44). The underground man sees himself as having retreated to a "little corner." He hides "in that conscious burying oneself alive for grief for forty years" (p. 110).

For Guntrip, the quintessential schizoid feeling is a sense of futility. This is the essence of schizoid depression. There is just no point in going on. Thus, this type of depression is an expression of utter despair. Dostoevsky's character is constantly shadow boxing with his own sense of being meaningless. Nothing really counts and no one really matters, which means that his own life has no worth. Spitefully, he destroys the prostitute's hope that their contact could have significance for them both. He tells her that all he wants is peace, that to be left alone he would "sell the whole world for a farthing. Is the world to go to rack and ruin or am I to have my cup of tea? Well, so far as I'm concerned, blow the world so long as I can have my cup of tea" (p. 232).

For me, the most poignant moment in the story occurs just after this hateful speech. Lisa sees through it to his suffering. She tries to embrace him, and for one heart-wrenching moment, he lets himself sob, "They—they won't let me—I—I can't be good!" (p. 234). But the moment passes, and he crushes her by trying to pay her for her "services," once again reducing the meaning of their intimacy to a business exchange. He just can't let it matter any more than that. In a schizoid state, the world is empty and the self is hollow. The only substance exists in dreams. The underground man insists on keeping it that way.

How does someone become schizoid? Of course, there is no definitive answer to this question. McWilliams (2011) highlights two routes: an early life threatened by over-stimulating adults and an empty, bleak life deprived of interpersonal connection. Although these alternatives are opposite, it makes emotional sense to me that, in either case, the child does not develop faith that others will usually increase, rather than decrease, his or her security. In both cases, the threat of traumatic engulfment is present. The child who is over-stimulated may be traumatically deluged by intense reactions to other people's needs, while the under-stimulated child may be overwhelmed by his or her own towering, unmet need. Either way, emotional intensity becomes something to avoid rather than seek, or, as I would put it, affectively "less is more." Schizoid maneuvers hold out the promise that if we will want less, feel less, connect less, expend less effort interpersonally, invest less in the external world, we will be rewarded with relative peace and security. Emotional withdrawal is, in a sense, the ultimate power of the powerless. It can be an elegant solution, but it comes at a monumental price.

The magic of Guy de Maupassant's story "Looking Back" (1952) is that it compresses the life of a schizoid man into five pages. The Abbe Mauduit is visiting an old friend and her three grandchildren. She asks him why he became a priest rather than choosing to have a wife and family. He explains that he was made to be a priest. When his friend remains puzzled, he told her a story from his adolescence. He was terribly shy, easily wounded, always on the defensive. He became extremely self-protective and avoided social life. He hid from everyone, and lived "in the prison of my own thoughts" (p. 178). Only one creature broke through his isolation: his dog, Sam. Sam was killed in an accident the teenager witnessed but was helpless to avert. It was then that he realized that he was not well equipped for the slings and arrows of outrageous fortune. In his own words, "I was without physical desires or ambition, so I decided to sacrifice the possibility of happiness to the certainty of suffering" (p. 180). He vowed to devote himself to serving others, soothing their sorrows and sharing their joys. This way, he could experience feelings at bearable intensities. Looking back, he believes "[I] could never have endured the sorrow with which I come into contact every day had it been my own" (p. 180). He concludes that his choice was right, since he was not made to live in this world.

The priest eloquently expresses the idea that, to some people, less is more. Less involvement with others means less risk of being demolished by their rejections, accidents, and other exigencies. Less emotion means fewer moments of joy, but also fewer pangs of heartache. Less ventured, less gained, but also, less lost. The priest lives a life once removed. Its colors are muted, its sounds at soft decibels. Perhaps like many in the clinical professions, he lived largely through others. The schizoid compromise turns the burners down. Fewer sparks fly, but there is less likelihood of being consumed by the flames.

Alice Munro gives us another portrait of the life histories of schizoid people in her story "Visitors" (1991). Mildred and Wilfred, a retired couple, just fit into their modest home, in a literal sense. They are grossly overweight people, with separate bedrooms that take up most of the house, except for a strategically placed television set that allows them to share a space without interacting. But three visitors disrupt this low-key domestic bliss. Wilfred's brother Albert, Albert's wife, Grace, and Grace's sister, Vera, come for a visit. It is the first time in 30 years that Wilfred has seen his brother, so Wilfred and Mildred are determined to go all out to make them comfortable. "Going all out" means, here, that they give up one of their bedrooms, and, therefore, they have to sleep in the same bed. Munro describes (pp. 200–201) the ensuing delicate balance:

> They were lying on their backs. They both heaved, and turned to face the outside. Each kept a courteous but firm hold on the top sheet. "Is it whales that can't turn over when they get up on the beach?" Mildred said. "I can still turn over," said Wilfred. They aligned backsides. (p. 180)

Thus, even in such close quarters, each tries to preserve separate space by turning away from the other. But, at the same time, their backsides communicate the wordless adjustments they have to make in order to share space harmoniously.

Mildred and Wilfred married in late middle age, each having been alone until that point. Mildred, an only child, had spent most of her adult life in a relationship with her married boss. Wilfred's mother died within hours of his birth. He lived with his aunt until, when he was 12, she died. From then on, Wilfred worked, moving from one temporary job and home to another.

Wilfred tries to entertain the visitors with stories of his life, but they are curiously lifeless. Like still life paintings, each portrays a moment in time, preserved exactly as it was first experienced. For example, there was the time Wilfred drove through a terrible blizzard, utterly determined to get to a scheduled dart game. Mildred, who has heard the story countless times, registers that the words never vary. Wilfred doesn't relive his history, or reflect on it, but merely recites it. My own fantasy is that Wilfred died along with his mother, in some sense, or, perhaps, was never born, from a psychic standpoint.

I have always considered schizoid functioning as the earliest form of defense. In a sense, it has always been there. Like any other absence of something, the failure to look toward other people for safety and connection has existed from the beginning. I picture schizoid functioning as amoeba-like. It moves away from others, in an emotional version of a smooth fox trot. Like Mildred's and Wilfred's backsides, two people may seem to connect, since they do align themselves to each other, but their very connection is also an avoidance of more full-bodied relating. In Guntrip's (1969) language, this halfway relating would be a schizoid compromise.

And yet, we see glimpses of feelings that threaten to break through. On the first night after the visitors leave, Mildred is awakened by Wilfred's crying in his sleep. Even though he was not making any noise or moving, "she knew that he was lying beside her on his back with tears welling up in his eyes and wetting his face" (p. 216). As I read it, Mildred's thorough acceptance of Wilfred enables her to understand his limitations. In the dark, she reflects on other times Wilfred had cried. On the occasions when he consented to explain why he was crying, "the reason had seemed to her very queer, something thought up on the spur of the moment, or only distantly connected with the real reason. But maybe it was as close as he could get" (p. 216). Like the schizoid person who allows himself to feel great sorrow about the human condition while watching a film, but can't fully respond to his own sorrows, Wilfred usually masks the real sources of his most profound feelings. But Mildred intuitively catches on to this.

And then, for one exceptional moment, Wilfred nearly connects with what he really feels: "'Albert and I will probably never see each other again,' said Wilfred, in a loud voice with no trace of tears, or any clear indication of either satisfaction or regret" (p. 216). In the night, in the nearness of a wife who loves him to the extent of her own ability to feel, Wilfred comes close to the gulf between himself and other people, and the potentially overwhelming need, loss, and loneliness that have so profoundly shaped his experience from the very beginning of his life. Can Wilfred ever really be known? As I see it, even Mildred experiences him as a mystery, a vast jigsaw puzzle she can never solve because some pieces will always be withheld.

From my perspective, Jean-Paul Sartre illustrates the link between cut-off emotions and schizoid depression exceptionally vividly. In his superb story "The Wall" (2002), Sartre imagines the thoughts of three prisoners condemned to be shot the next morning. The narrator, Pablo, and his cell mates, Tom and

Juan, are imprisoned for being anarchists. Most of the details concerning their actual political activities are not specified. Tom is a heavy man, who tries to stay warm in the freezing cell by exercising. Juan is a young man, whose brother is a militiaman, but who loudly proclaims his own innocence at every opportunity. When their sentence is read, and it is clear they will die, he fights tears, unlike the other two. Pablo says he would have pity for the boy, if pity didn't horrify and disgust him. Pablo passes the time watching the circle of light made by an oil lamp. He suddenly realizes that, in the midst of winter in a freezing cell, he is sweating; he hadn't been aware of it for an hour, but when he felt the sweat he knew he was afraid to die.

Tom feels he needs to imagine exactly what being lined up and shot will be like, in order to face it bravely: "I'll think how I'd like to get inside the wall. I'll push against it with my back . . . with every ounce of strength I have, but the wall will stay, like in a nightmare" (p. 394). Both Tom and Pablo already feel pain where they imagine the bullets will enter them, but they both try to ignore the pain and go on, as if it didn't exist.

Pablo is glad he is with two men he didn't care about: "I liked that better, anyhow; with Ramon I might have been more deeply moved. But I was terribly hard just then and I wanted to stay hard" (p. 395). Pablo keeps himself awake, so as not to lose hours of life. He wants to be fully awake when they kill him: "I didn't want to die like an animal. I wanted to understand" (p. 397).

A doctor offers to transmit a message to the prisoners' loved ones. Pablo declines the offer, and Tom reminds him of how much he had previously wanted to see his girlfriend.

Pablo hates that Tom knows anything about him and derides himself for having lost control and confided his feelings to Tom the previous night. He begins to feel disconnected from his body, as if it were the body of someone else: "I had the impression of being tied to an enormous vermin" (p. 399).

For one second, as Juan weeps, Pablo wants to feel pity for himself, but that doesn't last. He says to himself that he wants to die cleanly, without pity. Even while he is jolted by each shot he hears as he waits for his turn to die, he stays outwardly calm. The soldiers try to intimidate Pablo into revealing the whereabouts of Ramon, an important activist. They offer Pablo his life in exchange for information about Ramon. He thinks it over and decides not to give information, not out of loyalty to Ramon, but because it doesn't matter which one of them dies. His friendship for Ramon "had died a little while before dawn at the same time as my love of Concha, at the same time as my desire to live" (p. 403). Nothing matters. Pablo tells himself to be obstinate, stubborn, and a feeling of gaiety spreads through him. Officers come for him and he "looked at them with curiosity, as insects of a very rare species . . . It was a farce" (p. 403). At the very end, Pablo thinks he is giving them a false lead, but, by mistake, he leads them to Ramon, whom they kill. When Pablo realizes what happened, he laughs until he cries.

I see Pablo as largely succeeding in walling off his feelings, his connection to his body, and his connections to other people. For me, this is the wall that the title alludes to. Pablo believes that if he walls off caring for his own life and the lives of others, he can have a death that is "clean" of weakness. To do this, he has to become an observer of others and of his own body. He detaches as fully as he can, and whenever he "slips" and feels something, he pushes himself against that inner wall until he is numb again. To stay strong he has to eradicate pity, love, and all meaningfulness. Pablo is willing an estrangement with his own body, as well as with his fellow inmates. Losing touch with himself, he is unaware of his own sweat, so it feels as if his body is suffering an attack. I think of people I have treated who react to their anxiety in a similar way. One woman was so cut off from her feelings that when she felt the symptoms of anxiety, she thought she was having a heart attack. In this state, everything becomes unreal, and Pablo's own body feels like an albatross or, in Sartre's words, an enormous vermin.

If human feeling, and even human sensation, is walled off, the inevitable result is futility. Nothing matters enough to motivate exerting effort. Why bother? Pablo has destroyed every connection that makes him human. Ironically, although at the end of the story we don't know whether he remains alive, we do know that, in a sense, he no longer exists as a human being. Striving so hard not to die like an uncomprehending animal, he has inadvertently done just that.

Jack London's "To Build A Fire" (1965) is a story of what can happen when solitary self-reliance is glorified. The protagonist is called, simply, "the man," perhaps a reference to how much his identity is built around his conception of manliness. The man is walking in the extreme cold, in snowy terrain, with only his wily dog for companionship. He has ignored the advice of an old-timer, who told him not to go out alone in weather this cold. At first, through sheer determination, he seems to be able to think his way through the situation. Remembering the old-timer's advice, he gloats: "Those old-timers were rather womanish, some of them, he thought. All a man had to do was to keep his head; and he was alright. Any man who was a man could travel alone" (p. 275). But a series of his own mistakes and some bad luck work against him. When his painstakingly nurtured and essential fire goes out, he is shocked. He feels as though he just heard a sentence of death. But then he makes himself grow calm. And from that point on, he wages war against the freezing cold, his increasing paralysis, and, most of all, his own rising panic. When he can't get his fingers to obey him and light the fire he so desperately needs, he acknowledges that the old-timer was right. And yet he still tries to ignite twigs and cherish a flame that he now knows spells the difference between his life and death.

Perhaps London means it symbolically when the man loses all physical sensation as he battles against his psychological feelings. Like Sartre's character Pablo (see above) in his fight not to feel weak fear, he ends up succumbing to total paralysis. After beating down his panic for the last time, he resolves to meet death with dignity (again, perhaps like Pablo). Since he was going to freeze, he "might as well take it decently" (p. 283). It is then that he "leaves" himself altogether, to join the men who would find his frozen body the next day: "He did not belong with himself any more, for even then he was out of himself in the snow. It certainly was cold, was his thought. When he got back to the States he could tell the folks what real cold was" (p. 283). He imagines telling the old-timer: "You were right, old hoss; you were right" (p. 283). The man dies, and the dog, unencumbered by any willful urges except the will to live, trots off in the direction of the camp and its blazing fires.

The man stubbornly pits himself against the idea that he needs anyone. He sees need itself as a form of weakness. Need is the problem, and gutsy, manly determination is the solution. He is the ultimate loner, facing down adversity with only his own brain and stamina. In contrast to the dog, the man is handicapped by his *idea* of himself, as being able to control Nature. He has fatally cut himself off, from any dependence on others, from his own sensations and feelings, and finally, from his own identity, and so he freezes to death.

Carson McCullers' story "The Sojourner" (1954) is another portrait of a loner. John Ferris has just attended his father's funeral and is in New York on his way back to his home in Paris. He catches sight of his ex-wife, Elizabeth, and runs after her, but fails to catch up. He finds her number, and they arrange for him to come to dinner the following night. Looking through his address book, which contains the numbers of many old lovers, Ferris experiences a disembodied sense of danger, somewhat akin to fear. This moment presages the rest of the story. How much time has gone by while Ferris was not paying attention? Whom has he lost touch with? How can we bear the fragile nature of our connections with others, and the fragility of our own hold on life?

Ferris's body tells him he is deeply disturbed by seeing Elizabeth. This is the only way he knows his feelings, since, otherwise, he is not in close touch with them. But his wildly beating heart and damp hands announce to Ferris that he is unhinged. So he does what comes naturally. Although it is still morning, he pours himself a drink.

In my experience, as I have already noted, it is not uncommon for someone schizoid to hear news about his feelings via bodily disturbances. I think of this as a kind of desperation on the part of emotions that have to go to extreme lengths to be recognized. Quieting these suddenly erupting affective disturbances with substances is also a frequent pattern. People take a drink, or pop a Valium, just to "get through" today, promising themselves they won't make a habit of it. But that is exactly what they do.

The terrible and wonderful thing about schizoid strategies is that, up to a point, they work smoothly. And then, with riveting intensity, something seems to crack, revealing a shocking lapse. I am always reminded of pop art paintings of startled women suddenly realizing they left the baby on the bus. Ferris is shocked by his own sense of urgency. When did he lose track of time and of the fact that his life is going by in isolated, impermanent episodes? When did he start forgetting to build a life that coheres? When did he disconnect from his deep feelings about Elizabeth?

As he prepares to meet Elizabeth and Bailey, her new husband, and their two children, Ferris still has the feeling he has forgotten something important and necessary. This is so true! Disconnected from himself, he has not begun to fathom what this meeting means to him. He has "forgotten" to know himself.

As Ferris meets Elizabeth's new husband and two rosy children, he realizes he is an outsider in this home, as in all others. He feels utterly extraneous, not only here, but everywhere. Ferris wonders why he accepted the dinner invitation in the first place. He suffers with the sense that his is a flimsy life lacking any solid foundation. Ferris leaves, but the next day he is overcome with envy and regret when he contrasts the stability and continuity of Elizabeth's family life with the transitory impermanence of his own. As the story ends, Ferris succumbs to terror and sorrow as he acknowledges that he has wasted his life.

Elizabeth, her family, and, above all, the passage of time, are rooted, real. They don't disappear, even when a significant amount of vodka is consumed. They still exist, connected to each other and to themselves. They have substance, whereas Ferris is peeping at a picture of a family through a keyhole. Their lives have dimensions, but his is flat, a still life series. He has a collection of quickly posed photos, whereas they are gathering a family album. At those moments when he realizes what he is missing, Ferris panics. He feels like he is dying when he vaguely senses that he is just a sojourner, visiting other peoples' lives but forgetting to lay a foundation and build a life of his own.

In "Main Currents of American Thought" (1952), Irwin Shaw contrasts a writer's impulse-laden fantasy life with his plodding, over-burdened reality. Andrew is a writer for hire, who gets paid by the page for turning out adventure stories. His characters live on the brink of disaster, buffeted by intense rages, murderous schemes, and terrifying pledges of vengeance. But in real life, Andrew lives with his mother, trembles at the threatening sound of her vacuum cleaner, and is afraid to commit to his girlfriend. He is eternally bored, permanently tired, churning out stories at the opposite pole from his mundane existence. Andrew lives and breathes futility. Asking himself how long he will be able to bear his life, he imagines his future as a bleak and depressing trudge toward a death he will be powerless to avert.

Andrew can see marriage only as an added financial responsibility, another undue burden life thrusts upon your shoulders that ends up weighing more than you think. When Andrew's girlfriend brings up marriage, he lets this chance slip by. All the while, what is going on in his head is the question of how his fictional characters will escape *their* dangers. He dismisses his girlfriend's plea on the telephone with a mechanical goodbye, wishing her luck.

Andrew wades through his days, shouldering financial responsibilities for his parents and sister, until, one day, he can't take it. For the schizoid person who usually holds in his feelings, intense emotion can burst out, erupting rather than flowing. When his mother asks him for more money for a dress for his sister, Andrew explodes in frustration and resentment. But, of course, Andrew is quickly ashamed of his emotional outburst and ends up apologizing and giving his mother the money. The storm passes as suddenly as it appeared. Moving slowly, Andrew quietly takes his usual place. The story closes with the poignant and surprising detail that Andrew is only 25 years old. By giving us this fact in the last line of the story, the author makes Andrew's spiritual death even more poignant.

It is fascinating to me that, in a paper I wrote (2002) about my treatment of a schizoid patient, some extremely similar issues arose. I had not yet read Shaw's short story, so I could not compare his protagonist with my patient. The patient was the eldest of three siblings and had played the role of the big brother all his life. When his father asked him to help his siblings financially he readily complied, hiding his rising anxiety about his own financial pressures. Much like Andrew in Shaw's story, my patient did not feel entitled to prioritize his own needs. Much of the time, he didn't even register them. Like Andrew, his intense emotions occasionally burst out against his conscious wishes, feeling more like an explosion than self-expression. Had anger erupted when his father asked for the money, my patient would have quickly apologized, much as Andrew did in the story. When intense feeling is prohibited, we can settle into a lifeless stasis, in treatment as well as in other relationships. We waft through sessions, gliding seamlessly, seeming to connect but really just missing each other. None of the characters in Shaw's story truly know each other. Like my patient and his father, they usually carefully navigate around each other. Of course, my patient brought his navigational skills to our work, as well. I think he needed me to have the courage to agitate rather than navigate, which I eventually did.

The dull glide of inauthentic selves maneuvering past each other is admirably portrayed in Tolstoy's masterpiece, "The Death of Ivan Ilych" (1886/1982). Ivan Ilych is an examining magistrate in a small town. He lives a personal and professional life dedicated to keeping exertion at a minimum. His day is littered with petty power struggles and routine official business. Nothing really happens, until he "stumbles" while arranging furniture. Life goes on around him, but he has now slipped into a private hell, from which he knows he won't ever emerge. Something terrible is wrong with him. He longs for someone to understand and explain it to him. The thought that creeps up is that he didn't live as he should have. Very gradually, Ivan realizes that he is dying from the false, mechanical way he lived his life:

> "Maybe I did not live as I ought to have done," it suddenly occurred to him. "But how could that be, when I did everything properly?" he replied, and immediately dismissed from his mind this, the sole solution of all the riddles of life and death, as something quite impossible. (p. 273)

Ivan fights against this awareness, but, eventually, must succumb to it. At night he reviews his life, and in the morning he sees his own falseness mirrored in the bloodless attention to form of his doctor and his wife: "In them he saw himself—all that for which he had lived—and saw clearly that it was not real at all, but a terrible huge deception which had hidden both life and death. This consciousness intensified his physical suffering tenfold" (pp. 276–277).

But Tolstoy ends his story on a note of hope. Much as might happen in a good treatment, Ivan is transformed by an insight that is deeply felt as well as profoundly comprehended. At last, he understands that he can transform his death into a final gift to those he cares about. He feels sorry for his family and sees his death as their release. Once that happens, he becomes matter-of-fact about his pain, and "sought his former accustomed fear of death and did not find it. 'Where is it? What death?' There was no fear because there was no death. In place of death there was light" (p. 279).

Can the (emotionally) dead awaken? Can form recede and make way for substance? Can people touch, when they have spent their lives honing avoidance? For most of the characters in these stories it is too late. But for Tolstoy's Ivan Ilych, there is just enough light.

For me, the poet Rilke (1934) captures the essence of the truncated schizoid life. He describes our lives as like larger or smaller rooms, noting that some of us "know only a corner of their room, a place by the window, a strip of floor on which they walk up and down. Thus they have a certain security" (p. 68). In a Faustian bargain, the person gains temporary peace but trades away vibrant life without even understanding what has been lost. We all make this bargain to some degree. At times, we try to protect ourselves by not caring. Rather than risk hurt, we hunker down, and retreat to the more manageable internal world. Asking for less becomes so ingrained that subjectively we are not aware of doing it. Whereas the financial wizard drives a hard bargain, asking the impossible to set the stage for a favorable compromise, interpersonally the schizoid uses the opposite strategy. Requesting little, he often gets exactly what he asked for.

Treatment

When I teach, my favorite question is, "Who do we have to be, to help this patient?" It is important to me that I ask who we need to be, rather than what we need to do. In this final section of the chapter, I discuss some aspects of who the clinician needs to be when working with people whose functioning is prevailingly schizoid.

My basic suggestion is that, in these situations, the clinician needs to be especially attuned to fluctuations in his or her own schizoid tendencies, as well as the patient's. That is, for example, we need to notice when we feel like just getting through the session, going through the motions, but not really living it. It is vital for us to be people who can notice when our emotions become muted and flat, and we feel a resistance to expending effort. With this patient, do we fall into an uncharacteristically dull, deadened state? We should observe when we don't feel like relating to the patient (a version of "less is more"). When we see this patient, do we feel a sense of despair about the profession in general, or about the probable outcome of this treatment? Does futility permeate the atmosphere? Does it feel as though two demoralized people are confronting each other, with at least one of them, the analyst, often feeling fraudulent for taking the fee?

We should note it if we become unusually detached, observing but not really participating in the work. It is important to be aware of times when we choose to "play it safe," opting to avoid saying things that might intensify our own and/

or the patient's emotional responses. It sometimes happens that the treatment itself plays a role in the patient's schizoid compromises, and it is important to register our own feelings if this is occurring. For example, if a patient stays in a relationship that is unsatisfying by supplementing it with the treatment, is this a "schizoid compromise"? Is the patient forming a "half way" relationship with each of us, thereby getting just enough of his dependency needs met so that he can muddle through his life? Whether or not we think this is an acceptable outcome, we need to be aware of the part we might be playing in it.

Our own tendencies to avoid "rocking the boat" may be recruited with patients who use schizoid defensive strategies (and other patients as well, of course). It is important to note these pulls, as well as any feelings in ourselves that our "love is dangerous." It can be very helpful to recognize when our countertransferential feelings become known to us through signals from our bodies; when we notice our hands shaking before we know we are afraid or develop a headache before we realize we are tense or angry, this is important information. The way I tend to put it is that we have entered "schizoid territory." I am very aware of the limitations of spatial metaphors, but I don't know a better way to say that, in the presence of strong schizoid pulls from the patient, my own schizoid aspects tend to come to the fore.

In other words, I think an important part of our equipment as clinicians is our ability to operate like tuning forks, picking up the vibrations, so to speak, occurring between ourselves and our patients. In this chapter, I am illustrating some characteristics of schizoid pulls, in the hope that it will help us all recognize them in sessions.

But it is equally important, and probably even more frequent, that we might respond to schizoid pulls with "anti-schizoid" or contrasting impulses. Do I feel lonely and hungry for *more* contact? Am I overly active, expending more effort than usual? Do I run after the patient, fearing he or she will leave treatment, finding excuses to e-mail or call between sessions?

In a paper on the analyst's experience of loneliness (Buechler, 1998), I focused on what it is like to treat a patient who acts as though nothing in his life really matters. In one example, a 17-year-old, depressed, withdrawn young man showed little investment in the treatment, so the analyst, who was my supervisee, felt himself to be uncomfortably alone. The analyst found himself making unusually structuring suggestions about how the patient might use the session, coming close to telling him what to talk about, in order to prevent prolonged silences in which both participants might wonder why they are meeting.

Since we all read each other's emotional expressions to sense what is happening interpersonally, the schizoid patient, rather like the unresponsive infant or caregiver, doesn't give his or her partner feedback about how interventions are being received. In discussing the analyst's loneliness in this situation, I likened it to trying to work in a vacuum, sending messages in bottles into an expanse of sea, or trying to play tennis when the ball doesn't come back. Under these circumstances, our own loneliness will be tinged with whatever extreme separateness and isolation means to us personally. We vary in how much human responsiveness we each need. The analyst of the schizoid patient is likely to find out just where he or she stands on this continuum. For some of us, a patient's schizoid distancing may be too difficult for us to bear, while for other clinicians, it is too comfortable to notice. Of course, both of these extremes are problematic.

When I sense myself in "schizoid territory," I pay special attention to my own state of passion, courage, curiosity, and involvement in the work. I notice how much the session seems to matter to me and to the patient. I note whether or not I think about the patient between sessions. Of course, I focus on the same questions about the patient's participation in our work.

Whatever is passionate contrasts with schizoid detachment and, therefore, makes it more obvious. Elsewhere (Buechler, 2004, 2008), I have spelled out the uses the analyst can make of contrasts. Here, I will note that sometimes our own very alive presence itself begins the process of both participants experiencing and eventually recognizing the patient's schizoid functioning. For the sake of clarity, verbal interpretations are necessary at some point, but I believe that *how we live the basic schizoid issues in the session* sets the stage for subsequent verbal interpretation.

For someone schizoid, any intensity can make clearer what is usually absent. If I find myself extremely eager to reschedule sessions, it gives me the opportunity to voice this countertransference and to get into how we each relate to expending effort for the treatment. Similarly, if I find myself unusually uninterested in rescheduling, I could notice that out loud and get into similar territory. In other words, what seems to me most important is not whether or not our own schizoid tendencies are recruited, but whether or not we can *notice* their presence or absence. If we deeply enter schizoid territory in the session with the patient, we can use that experience to profoundly understand the patient's state of mind and, eventually, interpret it verbally. If our own "anti-schizoid" pulls are recruited, we will contrast with the patient's way of being and make it more palpable, thus paving the way for eventual verbal interpretation. However easily we enter schizoid territory in a session, we can use this experience in the service of the treatment, provided we are able to stay in touch with it.

Our own schizoid layers may prompt us to enter a profession that fosters relationships that are intimate but limited in many ways. We may, for our own schizoid reasons, be drawn toward work that allows us to feel life's joys and sorrows one step removed. Although we must enter our patients' worlds, we only stay for 45 minutes at a time. To the extent that we are schizoid, we may try to make our work our whole lives, thus avoiding the intensity of a more fully engaged personal life.

But it is our job to notice our own pulls toward schizoid functioning when they occur and to wonder about them, sometimes aloud. When we lean in or lean away, when we feel our love to be dangerous or non-dangerous, we need to be curious about our reactions. They are about us, about the patient, and about our work. When we are working with a prevailingly schizoid person, our own tendencies toward or away from schizoid functioning are more relevant than usual. I wrote about this state of mind in a paper on the treatment of a schizoid patient:

> But I feel that when I am in the presence of a detached, deadened schizoid patient I can actively search for the fighter in me. I can ask myself where she is today. I can remember her previous battles and their outcomes. I can think about those who have fought for life in my presence and, sometimes, on my behalf. I can recall moments, including some with my own supervisors and analysts, that have communicated their spirited intensity and determination to live every moment, in treatment as elsewhere, to its fullest. (Buechler, 2002, pp. 496–497)

References

Buechler, S. (1998). The analyst's experience of loneliness. *Contemporary Psychoanalysis*, 34, 91–115.
Buechler, S. (2002). More simply human than otherwise. *Contemporary Psychoanalysis*, 38, 485–497.
Buechler, S. (2004). *Clinical values: Emotions that guide psychoanalytic treatment.* Hillsdale, NJ: Analytic Press.
Buechler, S. (2008). *Making a difference in patients' lives: Emotional experience in the therapeutic setting.* New York: Routledge.
De Maupassant, G. (1952). Looking back. In M. Crane (Ed.), *Fifty great short stories* (pp. 175–180). New York: Bantam Dell.
Dostoevsky, F. (1972). Notes from the underground. In D. Magarshack (Trans.), *The best short stories of Dostoevsky* (pp. 107–241). New York: The Modern Library.
Freeman, M. E. W. (1965). A New England nun. In M. Crane (Ed.), *Fifty great American short stories* (pp. 108–123). New York: Bantam Dell.
Guntrip, H. (1969). *Schizoid phenomena, object relations, and the self.* New York: International Universities Press.
James, H. (1954). The tree of knowledge. In R. P. Warren & A. Erskine (Eds.), *Short story masterpieces* (pp. 201–217). New York: Dell.
London, J. (1965). To build a fire. In M. Crane (Ed.), *Fifty great American short stories* (pp. 264–284) New York: Bantam Dell.
Mason, B. A. (2008). Shiloh. In J. Kelly (Ed.), *The Seagull reader stories* (pp. 265–280). New York: W. W. Norton & Company.
McCullers, C. (1954). The sojourner. In R. P. Warren & A. Erskine (Eds.), *Short story masterpieces* (pp. 322–333). New York: Dell.
McWilliams, N. (2011). *Psychoanalytic diagnosis: Understanding personality structure in the clinical process.* New York: Guilford Press.
Munro, A. (1991). Visitors. In *The moons of Jupiter* (pp. 198–216). New York: Vintage.
Rilke, R. M. (1934). *Letters to a young poet.* New York: W. W. Norton & Company.
Sartre, J-P. (2002). The wall. In C. Neider (Ed.), *Great short stories of the masters* (pp. 387–405). New York: Cooper Square Press.
Shaw, I. (1952). Main currents of American thought. In M. Crane (Ed.), *Fifty great short stories* (pp. 471–482). New York: Bantam Dell.
Steele, W. D. (1952). How beautiful with shoes. In M. Crane (Ed.), *Fifty great short stories* (pp. 361–383). New York: Bantam Dell.
Tolstoy, L. (1886/1982). The death of Ivan Ilych. In A. Maude & L. Maude (Trans.), *The raid and other stories* (pp. 228–280). New York: Oxford University Press.

Chapter 2

Paranoid Processing

For Bessie, the terrified old woman in I. B. Singer's short story "The Key" (1999), the world has become a minefield. Bessie's husband, Sam, is long dead. She lives or, rather, exists in an apartment on New York's Upper West Side. Danger lurks everywhere. Her neighbors wait for opportunities to rob, rape, utterly unhinge her. Strangers conspire to confuse her. Banks calculate how to divest her of her money. Supermarkets are designed to dizzy her with their incessant glare. In Bessie's view, everyone is against her or, at the very least, indifferent. In reality, it is Bessie who despises her neighbors, but she is unable to see the role of projection in her experience. And then there's her body. It won't do as she wills. It buckles and bulges, betraying her at every turn. Taming it takes every ounce of strength she can muster.

To go outside, to shop for food, is a monumental undertaking. Preparations include extra locks and other security measures to hold the predators at bay. Her enemies' every move must be anticipated and thwarted.

Then, suddenly, disaster strikes. Even after following every ritual, with every device in place, Bessie is beset by evil forces. "They" break her key, leaving her locked out of her sanctuary. The familiarity of routine is gone, perhaps forever. Her profound insecurity turns a mishap (her door key breaks) into a catastrophe, threatening her very existence. Bessie is at the mercy of every passerby. Will they take advantage of this opportunity to torture her? Will she die, alone, homeless, weak, undefended?

As is true throughout this book, in this chapter I discuss a style of coping available to all of us when threatened, although some people rely on it more often than others (see the Introduction for a discussion of how I use diagnostic terminology). We all have some potential to become somewhat like Bessie, if the context is conducive to it. Some of us revert to being a version of Bessie under most circumstances, whereas for others, it would take extraordinary events to bring out our paranoid proclivities.

In his poem, "The Second Coming" (1968), Yeats paints the landscape of disintegration:

> Things fall apart; the centre cannot hold;
> Mere anarchy is loosed upon the world . . . (p. 479)

When chaos reigns, why should we expect good to triumph over evil? More likely, "The ceremony of innocence" will be "drowned," since, in the midst of upheaval,

> The best lack all conviction, while the worst
> Are full of passionate intensity. (p. 480)

Some of us spend most of our lives waiting for all hell to break loose. The expectation that disaster lurks around every corner might not be conscious, or formulated, in Donnel Stern's (1997) sense of the word. But it can be discerned. Those who live in constant dread search earth, sky, and every face for harbingers of their inevitable doom. They narrow their sights and hunker down, hoping to survive. Their terror of some form of death is ironic, since they no longer live, in the fullest sense of the word. They exist, holding their breaths, tensing their bodies, scanning, anxiously waiting.

I. B. Singer's Bessie exemplifies the fearful expectations that form a component of paranoid dysfunction. What experiences are sufficient to transform a predominantly neutral world into enemy territory? What makes some of us hypervigilant, always expecting and often creating our own downfall? Some characters in fiction vividly portray the suffering inherent in paranoia. Here are some of its components, as I understand them:

- The sense of profound inadequacy. A feeling of being fundamentally insufficient to navigate the world readies us to experience life as exquisitely dangerous.
- The tendency to externalize blame. Trying to capture its reflexive, automatic nature, I call this an "allergy" to blame.
- The use of projection as a central defense. Because one's own hostility is often projected, this makes the world feel dangerous. It also makes one feel like a victim, at the mercy of others. The locus of control is external, which limits a sense of hope about changing things, since control is in the hands of others.
- Perception of other people (and life itself) as either purely good or purely bad. Loss of the ability to see ambiguity and ambivalence.
- A truncated capacity for curiosity and surprise. An inability to perceive paradoxes. The need for an airtight theory that explains all one's experience. A kind of false clarity. This threatens reality testing, because reality has to be distorted to fit the theory. An inability to see a hypothesis as just a hypothesis and hold it lightly. The paranoid person feels certain about the causes of their suffering, and demands that others share their point of view.
- Confusion about how much to trust other people.
- Preoccupation with assessing the motives of others.
- An unshakable belief that appearances deceive, that a benign surface (of a person or a situation) camouflages a malignant reality.
- A predominant feeling of being suspended in purgatory. Life now is an antechamber to the hell that inevitably awaits us. Therefore, it is necessary to be hypervigilant in order to pick up signs of approaching disaster.

- Feeling targeted because of special qualities that make others eager to destroy us.
- An inability to bear risk. Difficulty differentiating small from larger risks, and the avoidable from the unavoidable.
- Delusional or nearly delusional thinking that may be logical, in itself, but rests on one false premise.

The stories discussed in the remainder of this chapter illustrate these components of paranoia. What can help someone living in paranoid purgatory? The final section of this chapter addresses clinicians attempting to treat those suffering from this dysfunction. Who do we have to be in order to have an impact on people gripped, ultimately, by a fear of life itself?

In Charlotte Perkins Gilman's fascinating story "The Yellow Wallpaper" (1994), John controls every aspect of his wife's life, ostensibly in an effort to avoid her becoming over-stimulated. Consciously, he believes this will keep her well, but the reader may view his motives as less benign. As McWilliams (2011, chapter 10) suggests, paranoid people can have real enemies. Being caged in by John propels his wife's gradual slide toward madness.

As she begins to sink into a world of phantoms, she "sees" a woman behind bars who is obviously herself. As her confusion mounts, she becomes more and more desperate for an explanation. Why can't she think clearly? When she has obeyed John's dictates, why does she still feel terrible? Surely John, who is a doctor as well as her husband, can't be wrong about what is best for her. There must be some other, all-inclusive explanation. At last she comes to it: "Perhaps it is the paper" (p. 295). There is a secret in the wallpaper, and it alone can tell her the root cause of her confusion and misery. Everything will be understood once the wallpaper's secret is penetrated. There will be no more need to wonder, to flail in confusion, to suspect John or anyone else. All her sensations will make perfect sense. She merely has to direct her attention to the wallpaper and concentrate with all her might. Just as some people come to a "realization" that they are Christ or Napoleon and this explains all their mysterious experiences, John's wife feels relieved, at first, to discover the source of all her troubles. But her relief is short-lived. The wallpaper begins to smell. Now she is tortured by fantasies of escape. But there is no way out. She is as trapped by her own paranoid thinking as she was imprisoned by the regimen imposed on her by her husband.

"The Yellow Wallpaper" has an interesting back story. According to Patrick McGrath (writing in the *New York Times Book Review*, June 30, 2013, p. 31, in an essay entitled, "Method to the Madness"), Gilman was a feminist, a philosopher, a socialist, and an activist. This story emerged from her experience of having been subjected to a "rest cure," prescribed to treat her "hysteria." Gilman was deprived of books, work, and all other stimulation for three months. She felt that she saved her sanity by resuming her writing. McGrath's research suggests to him that Gilman wrote the story partially to try to convince the psychiatric community that this nineteenth-century form of treatment was unacceptable. I think Gilman's experience can serve as a cautionary tale for us as clinicians. We should guard against an uncritical acceptance of what current culture considers "pathological." We should also maintain a healthy skepticism about the role our professional culture plays in reinforcing those norms.

Gogol's masterpiece "The Diary of a Madman" (1960) provides another frame-by-frame portrayal of a downward slide. Step by step, Gogol's protagonist sinks into a paranoid delusional world. It is of note that this story was first published in 1835; well before psychoanalytic explorations of this subject, it illustrates the profound sense of inadequacy, projection, mounting distrust, and gradual loss of reality testing that underlie a paranoid decline.

The "hero" of this story is a poor, disgruntled Russian clerk who falls hopelessly in love with Sophie, a woman way above his station. When we first meet him, he is musing about the advantages and disadvantages of his meager post. He chances to come across Sophie, the beautiful young daughter of the director of his department. His first words, "Oh God, I'm lost, lost forever" (p. 8), turn out to be prophetic. From that point on he is obsessed with his desire to know if he stands a chance with her. Unable to make any contact, the clerk is startled when he thinks he hears her dog and another dog chatting. At this point, he is still able to question his perceptions and wonder how this could possibly be true. The next day, taking advantage of an opportunity, he runs into Sophie (almost literally!). After an hour, he is unceremoniously asked to leave the premises.

A month later, the Chief of the Division calls him to task:

> What do you fancy you are? Don't imagine I can't see what you're up to. I know you are trailing after the Director's daughter. Just look at yourself—what are you? Just nothing. You haven't a penny to your name. Look in the mirror. How can you even think of such things? (p. 11)

At this point, the clerk is understandably indignant, but also unbearably aware that there is a basis for the chief's conclusions. A mere clerk, he feels that he really is an inadequate nobody and of no interest to Sophie. He fantasizes about what goes on between Sophie and the others in her set but is unable to enter into any conversations with them. He would give anything to see into her boudoir, but because of his lowly status, this will never be. Beginning to project his own motives, he imagines that all the other clerks have similar preoccupations with Sophie but still reviles himself for his sexual thoughts about her.

As is often true when a paranoid delusion is first formulated (Sullivan, 1956), for Gogol's clerk, everything suddenly seems clear, as he becomes more and more convinced that the dogs really *are* having conversations, and it is by overhearing their chatter that he *can* enter into Sophie's world. At this point, the clerk feels rather like Sophie's lap dog, invisible to her as a sensitive, dignified being and willing to follow her anywhere for the crumbs of attention she might deign to spare him. He yearns to know Sophie's thoughts, but the only creatures who walk around her freely are the dogs. If only they would share what they hear, he could have access to Sophie's exalted realm.

It is here that reason gives way, and paranoid thinking is solidified into a delusional form. The clerk goes to the home of one of the dog owners and asks for the letters he believes the dogs exchange, so he can read about their observations of Sophie. In the pieces of paper he receives, which he thinks are the dogs' letters to each other, the clerk "reads" all his own feelings of sexual hunger and unfulfilled longing. He also thinks they are talking derogatively about him, making fun of him, saying that he looks like a scarecrow or a "turtle caught in a bag" (p. 19).

Now the clerk begins to suspect a plot against him, perpetrated by his Division Chief: "For some reason, that man has sworn undying hatred for me and he is trying to harm me, to harm me every minute of the day and night" (p. 19). In the airtight way that paranoid delusions work, it is all beginning to make sense. There is a plot against him, conceived out of some sort of jealousy and designed to take advantage of his vulnerabilities. But if only he could be something other than a clerk! Then Sophie would pay attention to him, and everyone else would be respectful.

Reading about political problems in Spain, he hits upon the final piece to his puzzle. He is not a clerk, after all, but the King of Spain. At this point, he loses track of time, and the entries in his diary have unrealistic dates. As Sullivan (1956) described a century later, when the delusion settles into the paranoid person's mind, suddenly everything makes perfect sense. The clerk exclaims, "Now I see everything clearly, as clearly as if it lay in the palm of my hand" (p. 22).

Finally, the clerk goes to Sophie's home, marches into her boudoir, and announces to her that "she couldn't even imagine the happiness awaiting her and that, despite all our enemies' intrigues, we would be together" (p. 23).

The clerk's mind is taken over by fantasies of the Devil and a determination to be recognized as the King of Spain. He rips up his own coat to make a royal mantle for himself. At this point, he is taken to an asylum, which he imagines to be Spain's royal court, although after he is cruelly mistreated, he wonders if he has fallen into the hands of the Inquisition. The story ends with a poignant plea to be saved from the torture he is undergoing. Imagining his mother's presence, he begs:

> What have I done to them? Why do they torture me so? What do they want from me? What can I give them? I have nothing to give. I have no strength. I cannot bear this suffering, my head is on fire, and everything goes around me in circles. Save me! (p. 28)

The clerk has to escape from his unbearable feelings of being judged as an inferior human being. Escaping shame and guilt about his sexual longings by projecting them onto dogs, he nonetheless identifies with them and enters the dogs' world. He must have some theory about what is really going on beneath surface civilities. Why is he unacceptable to Sophie? His perceptions are more and more skewed as he attempts to create an airtight theory. Maybe it is a plot. Maybe he is really exalted and the King of Spain. Maybe there is a secret that will explain it all and forever alter his status from a contemptible nonentity to a revered monarch.

The need to penetrate behind the surface and beneath the secrets to underlying explanations drives Paul, the 12-year-old protagonist of Conrad Aiken's truly chilling story, "Silent Snow, Secret Snow" (2002). When we first meet Paul, he is becoming obsessed with a private world: "Nor was it only a sense of possession—it was also a sense of protection. It was as if, in some delightful way, his secret gave him a fortress, a wall behind which he could retreat into heavenly seclusion" (p. 142).

One morning, Paul begins constructing his private world by lying in bed and concentrating on the arrival of the postman. But he doesn't hear the first steps of the postman's approach. How could this be explained? Paul concludes it must have snowed during the night, and the snow was muffling the usual sounds. But when he looks out the window, there is no snow to be seen. Which to believe, his eyes looking at reality, or his mind imagining snow? Paul opts for the latter, understanding his snowy blanketed world as his miraculous, private, utterly peaceful refuge.

Desperate to pin down details about his new world, Paul listens intently each subsequent morning for exactly when he first hears the postman's steps. Is it at the first house on his block or the second? Paul is obsessed with getting every detail exactly right. He knows he is living in an alternate universe, apart from everyone around him, and he is glad:

> When he found, each morning, on going to the window, after the ritual of listening, that the roofs and cobbles were as bare as ever, it made no difference. This was, after all, only what he had expected. It was even what pleased him, what rewarded him: the thing was his own, belonged to no one else. (p. 146)

The silent, secret snow blankets Paul's private haven.

And yet, Paul is obliged to continue daily life. He tries to carry on, holding his secret close, revealing it to no one. Sometimes he longs to drop the pretense and cease carrying on a double life, but he feels he must keep the secret: "At whatever cost to himself, whatever pain to others" (p. 148). He wants to avoid unnecessary pain to Mother and Father who are, after all, very nice. But some pain is inevitable. The experience cannot be communicated. Mother and Father are increasingly worried about Paul and want to pry the secret out of him. He doesn't want to hurt them but vows to be resolute in protecting his special world.

Within his world's parameters, Paul flirts with reality. He imagines looking in at his own window and seeing himself lying in bed. Is he the observer or the observed? Has he actually left his bed at all, since that first morning when he discovered the secret? There is just enough danger in these unsettling thoughts to suit him: "No fairy story he had ever read could be compared with it—none had ever given him this extraordinary combination of ethereal loveliness with a something else, unnamable, which was just faintly and deliciously terrifying" (p. 152). Paul taunts himself with questions. How can he be *sure* of the sequence of what actually happens?

And then we learn that, while Mother and Father may *seem* very nice, there is a harsher reality beneath the surface. When the parents call in a doctor, who tries to trick Paul into revealing his preoccupation, the darker side of the adult world is revealed. An "inquisition" begins. The doctor feigns friendship, trying to pry Paul's secret from him. The child feels all their eyes probing him: "it was as if one had been stood up on a brilliantly lighted stage, under a great round blaze of spotlight; as if one were merely a trained seal, or a performing dog, or a fish dipped out of an aquarium and held up by the tail" (p. 155). And then Paul hears his father's all too familiar warning, punishing, cruel voice. Feeling cornered, Paul tries to tell them a little about the snow, hoping that will satisfy them. But it doesn't. It is as if they smell his blood. Father becomes more menacing, and Mother more directly challenging. Paul sees "that all three of them were watching him with an extraordinary intensity—staring hard at him—as if he had done something monstrous, or was himself some kind of a monster" (p. 159). He runs from them, retreating into his bed and visions of the snow. The snow promises that it will take the place of everything else, and he won't see much in its white expanse. Just then, his peace is shattered by his mother, who rushes in, grabs and violently shakes him. He tells her that he hates her and she should go away. This is where Paul truly commits to his private world. The hissing snow promises to tell him "'a very small story—a story that gets smaller and smaller—it comes inward instead of opening like a flower—it is a flower becoming a seed—a little cold seed—do you hear?'" (p. 160). Paul lets himself be lost in a story that moves backward. Unlike the complicated world of the adults, the snow's story is simple, peaceful, and predictable. Like a baby wrapped in comfort, Paul sleeps under the protective blanket of his own, private snow.

E. B. White's story "The Door" (1952) brings the reader across a threshold and directly into paranoid territory. We are forced to experience the confusion and disorientation the narrator describes. Familiar words are altered just enough to startle us. Experiments on rats seem to be replicated with humans. But are they really replications, or is the narrator mad? Rats are taught to jump at the square card with the circle on it, which has food behind it. Then one day, the "Professor" plays a trick on a rat and changes the card. The rat continues to jump, because the change is impossible for the rat to comprehend. It then acts erratically in its frustration, convulsing and running around, until it settles into a quieter but more pliant, surrendered state.

The rat is trapped by its own expectations. It is battered by its own unwillingness to give them up. When we lose all hope that we can bring about a favorable outcome, we stop caring about what happens. The narrator (and then the reader) is led to wonder whether the rat is enduring a process meant to imitate the stages of a human life. Is there a Machiavellian sorcerer arousing our youthful expectations, only to dash them and watch us knock ourselves senseless against a metaphoric stone wall?

The narrator reflects that, all his life, he has been confronted with situations that can't be solved. He concludes that it must be deliberate. He kept jumping at cards that wouldn't give way. At first, he suffered "young bewilderment." His wounds really hurt, forever after, and yet, it was impossible not to keep jumping. When we are young, we build a life, and it seems as though there will be food behind the cards if we can only knock them down. So we plan, work hard, and get fooled into thinking we can predict (and thereby control) the future. And then, one day, the game changes on us. When that happens, it would be better to be lobotomized, because it's better to simply not know than have to experience hopes being lost – in other words, ignorance is bliss. At the very end, the narrator thinks he has escaped through the door but, of course, he soon feels the ground shifting underfoot. He has taken his illusions (or delusions) with him.

The story itself is like a rat's maze. Phrases recur with disturbing, jarring resonances. What seems like a straight line from one event to another becomes a circle. Familiar words morph slightly. The reader, like the narrator, is seduced into expectations that are met at first and then contradicted. We don't just read this story. We enter it. We live it. We feel knocked senseless, become passive, cease caring, and succumb to whatever happens.

Contagious paranoia is vividly portrayed in Sartre's great short story, "The Room" (1963). We first meet Mme. Darbedat, an elderly sufferer from an unknown but highly debilitating illness, and her brutish husband as he prepares to visit their married daughter, Eve. While I imagine there is much the husband and wife see differently, they vehemently agree that Eve has made a terrible marriage. Eve's husband, Pierre, is a sick man who is draining her of life. Nevertheless, out of duty, M. Darbedat will visit her, and try to persuade her to free herself by committing Pierre to an institution.

The parents fear that Eve will join her husband in his psychotic state, and they do have cause for concern. Eve hides her own ambivalence about her life with Pierre beneath an exquisitely solicitous attitude toward him. She is supremely dedicated to catering to his every whim.

M. Darbedat is portrayed as an energetic, determined, and sometimes ruthless man, who will say whatever he thinks will advance his argument. The author broadly hints at his more than fatherly interest in Eve, his preference for Eve over his wife, and his disturbance at the thought that Eve and Pierre have a sexual union. So, for many reasons, M. Darbedat is set on convincing Eve that Pierre would be "better off" committed to institutional care, and she would be "better off" returning home.

Pierre is described as sensitive, beautiful, and ensconced in his own world. Early in the father's visit, Pierre rejects the fork sitting next to his plate, declaring that he has been warned not to use it. M. Darbedat grows increasingly agitated as the visit progresses, as does the reader (or, at least, this reader).

Father and daughter have a private conversation, in which, with blunt, cruel logic, he tries to persuade Eve to bring Pierre to a hospital and begin her own life anew. He does everything he can to frighten her about the future, choosing to create powerful images of misery with little concern for their wrenching impact. He predicts that Pierre's condition will decline, and he will soon be like a beast. He justifies his harsh words with the thought that bluntness might cut through Eve's stubborn loyalty to Pierre. To himself, M. Darbedat thinks of Pierre as no longer a human being.

Eve, who has her own painful conflicts about caring for Pierre, sees her father as the epitome of the "normal," vain, selfish, thoughtless masses. So, after the visit, when Pierre tells Eve that normal people, like her father "don't know how to take hold of things; they grab them" (p. 207) it sounds correct, until he takes his thoughts further, wondering why "they" sent the father. Pierre reflects: "If they wanted to know what I'm doing all they have to do is read it on the screen" (p. 208). He goes on to gloat that while "they" have power, they make mistakes, and he never makes any.

When Pierre questions her about her conversation with M. Darbedat, Eve decides to tell him that her father wants Pierre locked up, preferring to tell him the truth, since when she lies to him she feels superior to him, which horrifies her. Pierre's reaction is to declare that walls have no effect on him, since he can get through them.

What follows is a description of Eve's excruciating interior dialogue with herself. She hates the part of herself that is "normal" like her father and believes that Pierre sees this aspect of her and hates her for it. She doesn't think like her father but can't entirely accept Pierre's world view either. She reflects to herself that sometimes she thinks she is going mad, and it seems to me that she wants to go completely crazy, if only to end the agonizing debates that fill her mind.

Meanwhile, Pierre (who calls Eve Agatha, for unexplained reasons) announces that he likes her but can't trust her. He believes that a wall separates them, declaring that it was easier for them to love each other in Hamburg. Eve is able to be clear that he is wrong about that, at least, since they had never been to Hamburg.

And then, Pierre mournfully announces that the statues are coming. Pierre is frightened of the statues, and Eve realizes that she is frightened of Pierre. She tries to comfort herself that Pierre only hears the statues and doesn't actually see them.

Their nights together are increasingly lonely for Eve. Pierre, horrified of contact, never kisses or touches her. His nightly experience is terrifying: "at night they touched him—the hands of men, hard and dry, pinched him all over; the long-nailed hands of women caressed him" (p. 212). Eve wants to be close to Pierre, enter his mind, and believe in the presence of the statues, but Pierre insists on separateness: "My lovely devil-woman. You disturb me a little, you are too beautiful; that distracts me" (p. 215). As the story closes, Eve is haunted by fears about the future, wondering how she will cope as her father's predictions come true, and Pierre's condition deteriorates. For, after all, she believes that her father is right.

I sometimes think of the father as making some of the mistakes typical of a misguided clinician who is trying to badger a patient to renounce a paranoid system of thought. M. Darbedat has an airtight theory of what is happening. There is as little room for doubt in his mind as there is in his son-in-law's mind. Both have certainty and a passionate need for others to corroborate their thinking. Agreement is equated with loyalty, and disagreement is betrayal. While the father is not psychotic, he uses logic like a sledgehammer, to try to force Eve into a corner. He wants to *make* her see the reality that Pierre is terribly sick, and the "sane" thing to do is to free herself by committing him.

Like Bessie in the I. B. Singer story (above), Pierre feels everyone is against him, sees people in black or white terms, projects his own hostility and prejudice, can't trust the motives of others, and believes that danger lurks beneath seemingly benign exteriors. Also, like Bessie, he feels targeted and fails to see his part in creating his own purgatory. Pierre is clearly more delusional, but some of his patterns of thought overlap with Bessie's and illustrate a paranoid way of experiencing the world. It is a closed system of thought with no room for doubting one's perceptions or imagining there might be other perspectives. But Bessie is still capable of change, while Pierre is sinking into a more and more delusional state.

Eve is caught in a terrible dilemma. She is attracted and repulsed by Pierre's terrifying, nightmarish world. But she is equally ambivalent about "normal" life, at least as it is represented by her self-absorbed father.

Like Eve, a clinician can get caught up in the question of how far to follow a paranoid person into their way of thinking in order to "save" them. Should we prove ourselves "loyal" by seeming to agree? But, then, aren't we confirming that the paranoid person is right to distrust us, since they really *can't* trust us to mean what we say? If we pretend to go along with their theories, what we show on the surface *really is different* from what is beneath it. But if we differ, we fear losing the patient. Sometimes, we wonder if there is a way to keep the patient in treatment and also hold on to our own integrity, for our own sakes as well as in the interest of the therapeutic relationship.

The contrast between the surface and what lies beneath is central to another story by Conrad Aiken (see above, for his story "Silent Snow, Secret Snow"). Titled "Impulse" (1954), this is a tale about how suddenly and completely life can change and our terrifying helplessness and estrangement from each other become all too apparent.

Michael plans an ordinary night with three buddies, playing cards and drinking. It promises to give him temporary respite from unpaid bills and marital dissatisfaction with his wife, Dora. On a lark, after the game, he decides to give in to an impulse and steal something. It is an experiment. He wants to find out if stealing gives him any real satisfaction. He steals a safety-razor set from a drugstore and gets caught by a detective. He tries to get someone to vouch for him, but his resentful wife and self-protective friends refuse. He wants to shout. This is absurd! He is still Michael! He just wanted to see what would happen! No one pays any attention to his version of the story. Dora's voice on the phone is chillingly, shockingly cold and calculating. Is she really that bitter? Do they know each other at all? He knows the rhythm of her hand, combing her hair at night, but does he know her heart? Doom closes in around him. Is it possible that his whole life will change because of a momentary impulse? That everyone will betray him by silently abandoning him to the arms of the law? Has he really always been totally alone but ignorant of it?

In court, Michael and Dora stare at one another as if they are strangers. Her half-hearted testimony that he is not very dependable damages his case, and he is led off to jail. A week later, she serves him for divorce, taking the children. Michael has plenty of time to reflect. He comes to this conclusion:

> This was what life was. It was just as meaningless and ridiculous as this; a monstrous joke: a huge injustice. You couldn't trust anybody, not even your wife, not even your best friends. You went on a little lark, and they sent you to prison for it, and your friends lied about you, and your wife left you . . . (p. 13)

Beneath displays of friendship and intimacy, beneath the ties that seem to bind, Michael watches his life ebb away and learns how little he really matters to anyone. Like Pierre in Sartre's story (above), the people who are against Michael really do exist. Because he is constructing an airtight belief system that externalizes all blame, can we say that Michael is paranoid, or is he just embittered? It seems to me that Michael shows us how complicated these distinctions can be.

Treatment

Throughout this book, I ask who we need to be in order to treat someone with the difficulties I am describing. More specifically, in this section, I address the personal qualities, talents, and skills the clinician most needs in order to cope well with someone suffering from intense paranoid anxiety. Who would we need to be in order to successfully treat I. B. Singer's Bessie or Conrad Aiken's Paul?

In a general sense, I suggest we need to be comfortable with our own limitations. The analyst of the paranoid patient has to be able to accept having a very limited grasp of the patient's problems and the treatment's goals. The work requires comfort with long periods in which it isn't clear that treatment is having a positive impact or, perhaps, any impact at all. In addition, I think there are particular personal strengths involved in being able to bear the constant risk of being categorized as an enemy. We have to be able to contain the patient's projections relatively non-defensively. Courage, determination, and a firm sense of our own positive therapeutic motivations are requirements. It is a tall order! In what follows, I detail these qualities more fully.

1   *The clinician treating paranoia needs a great deal of humility about what can be accomplished in treatment.* I think Otto Will (1961) most gracefully expressed the limits of our impact on the life of someone suffering from paranoia. He suggested that we should aim to help the patient find the strength to go on. In other words, we can't "cure" paranoia. The patient will not become the person he or she could have become without the advent of paranoid anxiety and coping patterns. We can help patients face what can't be known and better bear life's inherent uncertainties. Our work should contribute to the patient's overall sense of security. But the patient has already suffered losses that won't be repaired and must be mourned. We can help the patient mourn if we ourselves can accept the limits of what can be accomplished.

2 *We need enough self-acceptance and professional and personal confidence to be able to bear being seen as posing a threat by being incredibly naïve.* Even when we evince the humility described above, we can seem too hopeful to the paranoid patient. In paranoid thinking, hope is an enemy, tempting them to let down their guard and become more vulnerable to injury. For example, Ruth, one of my patients, adamantly insists on maintaining her vigilance against hopefulness about her husband's career. If I cite reasons to be hopeful, she responds as though I were a dangerous temptress. If she became hopeful, she might relax her vigil. My optimism shows I am a sucker and, therefore, a danger to her.

Elsewhere (Buechler, 2004), I have characterized paranoia on a continuum with the capacity to bear being surprised. Paranoia is a search for more certainty about the future than we mortals can have. Ruth wants to be sure she doesn't get disappointed by expecting her husband to succeed and then feeling like a fool when he fails. Interestingly, sometimes in sessions I find myself making pronouncements and feeling embarrassed about them as soon as the session is over. Why did I need to sound so sure of myself? Whether we are talking about Ruth, her husband, or other topics, why do I become such a know-it-all? I think the paranoid need for certainty may itself be "contagious," in a sense.

Another way to say this is that, in a paranoid world, having any degree of confidence seems to require knowing the score in advance. Ruth feels if she "knows" her husband won't succeed, she is safe from disappointment. But I am also relying on "knowing the score." I label her "defensive," just as she labels her husband a "loser." Each of us is reaching for certainty about another person by putting him or her in a neat box.

Hopefully, I can see this parallel and give voice to it. It does not feel easy to do, but I may be able to break through my own stultifying, pigeonholing tendencies. In the long run, I think this will be of benefit to both of us, but in the short run, this situation elicits some anxiety in me. What if I try to help Ruth relax about her husband's financial life and then he really fails in some catastrophic way? She may then feel that instead of helping her become better armed, I coaxed her into letting down her guard. It won't be the first time I am accused of seducing someone to relax their guard. The accusation is uncomfortably familiar. Furthermore, no matter what happens, she may envy my own hopefulness. I may be told (not for the first time) that my optimism must mean that (unfairly) in my own life I have had better luck than Ruth has had. I am likely to be seen as the "fool," the naïve child who hopes when a sensible adult would be wary. I imagine being asked how someone so naïve dares to occupy the position of a mental health professional. Uncomfortable with being accused (again!) of leading people astray, I am likely to fall into my own version of paranoia. That is, I will try (too hard) to predict life in advance and seem as though I know what I am doing.

I wonder how much my gender affects what it is like for me to be accused of being too hopeful. Sometimes I feel doubly condemned. I know I will be seen as not only a cockeyed optimist, but also a superficial, empty-headed, scatter-brained woman. I think that, in a paranoid climate, hope is always derided. But my gender may play some role in how my patient and I experience my attitude.

One form my "dangerous" optimism often takes is my hope that the patient will eventually feel able to venture out into the world and trust someone. Even my implicit wish that the patient will trust me, to some appreciable degree, can pose a threat from the patient's point of view. Even though the patient may be very unhappy, it is an unhappiness they already know and have survived. In paranoid territory, things may be terrible, but they are predictably terrible. No one can be fully trusted, but that guarantees that no one truly shocks or disappoints. When the therapist enters this territory, we usually hope that the paranoid suspicious rules can be suspended and gradually changed. We want to prove we are an exception, to show the patient that someone *can* be trusted, that we can be trusted. We hope to make human relating feel possible and safe for the patient. All this is well-intended, but for the paranoid patient, it can create rather than solve a problem. Now, in addition to a frightening world, the patient has to contend with the temptation presented by the therapist. Invited to see new possibilities, the patient often fights to preserve what is painful but familiar. When as therapists we evoke the urge to venture out into the world, we can seem to the patient like their chief threat, rather than their chief ally.

3 *To treat paranoia, we need sufficient comfort with living in a world of absolute good and evil and with the constant threat of being labeled as the enemy.* To work with someone suffering from paranoid anxiety, I think we have to have a firm belief that we are in touch with our motives to a reasonable degree, although of course we are human and have unconscious feelings. Then, at least, if the patient accuses me of malevolence, I will be able to become curious about it, rather than either defensively denying the accusation or reflexively agreeing with it. When I am inhabiting this territory with a patient, it sometimes helps me to remember that even when I have done something hurtful I am not evil incarnate, and there may be ways to atone as well as valuable insights we both can gain from this experience. Another way to say this is that since the patient is "allergic" to blame (Buechler, 2004, 2008, 2012) and uses projection as a major defensive strategy, the clinician will sometimes have to withstand being the target of intense projected rage.

4 *The clinician needs an ability to bear the patient's externalizing of control, with its many consequences for the patient's life and for the treatment.* In paranoid thinking, cause and blame are equated, and the patient feels he is neither the cause of events that happen to him, nor is he to blame. This avoids self-blame, but the price of this is to feel one is living in a world over which one has no influence. In what I like to call an "allergic response to blame" (see above), the paranoid person sees himself as the recipient of the impact of others. The heavy price of this is that he loses the realistic hope we can have when we face the part we are playing in the creation of our own lives. Recognizing our own participation allows us to make choices and, potentially, changes. In paranoia, this realistic hope has been lost.

This, of course, limits what the patient can expect from treatment. In fact, if we imply that the treatment can be of any help, a paranoid patient may hear us as *blaming them for their suffering*. If they could potentially change the situation, they must be responsible for it. That can make us feel at cross purposes with the patient. Sometimes, I think, we have to accept the grave limitations on the impact of the work that defensive externalization creates. It is very hard to work with paranoid patients, because the patient often tries to maintain tight control over what the clinician is allowed to focus on in the session. Treatment sometimes requires us to try out new ideas by, for example, asking the patient, "What comes to mind when you think about your brother?" The paranoid person has trouble with such open-ended questions. They need to know just where they are going *before* they get there, so they can make sure nothing bad will happen.

As already mentioned, the person who is paranoid often projects his own aggression, seeing the world as hostile, rather than the self as angry. This, again, avoids self-blame but at a heavy cost. There is often a central nightmare, a fear of something that, in some sense, has already happened. The patient who greatly fears financial bankruptcy already suffers emotional and spiritual poverty, but he may not see the connection between these things. The person who is terrified of being alone and psychotic may, in some sense, have already lived through something like that in early infancy. Sitting with someone who is terrified a horrible trauma will recur but feels helpless to prevent it (in part because he can't see his own part in creating it) can take a great deal of stamina and determination on the clinician's part.

5   *It is necessary for us to have an ability to bear being the object of intense scrutiny, most especially scrutiny about our emotional reactions and motives.* The treatment of someone suffering from paranoid anxiety often puts us in the spotlight. The patient cross-examines us about the meaning of our every reaction or absence of reaction. If we object to the scrutiny, that itself will be scrutinized. Our relative comfort with our own exhibitionistic tendencies may be required. Some of us may feel we like the spotlight too much, while others may dread it. Either way, the clinician will be analyzed by the patient, sometimes to a potentially uncomfortable degree.

6   *We need to be comfortable holding our theories lightly.* As already mentioned above, we have to be able to recognize the limitations of our theories about human functioning in general and about this patient in particular. That is, we must not be too rigidly fixed on making the patient see himself as we see him. We have to be people capable of a light touch. The patient may well pressure us to give him *the answers* to his life's mysteries. We must not feel too much pressure to deliver what he wants. But we also must not be condemning him for wanting it. We can want to understand the patient and his mysteries, but we must not *have* to understand, or, just like the patient, we will feel too much urgency about making a theory explain everything. If something happens that does not conform to our theories about the patient, we must be able to take

in the new information and adjust the theory. Just as Sullivan (1956) saw the patient's health as a function of the ability to learn from new experience, we, as clinicians, need to be able to learn from new, unpredictable experiences with the patient.

7   *It is essential to be able to bear the challenge of living in what I call the "invisible court"* (Buechler, 2012). A married, middle-aged woman comes into her session agitated about her weekend. She tells me that her husband, a very busy professional, spent much of the weekend working. At one point, she said to him, "I am so worried about you. You look tired. Are you depressed?" Her husband sensed there was a criticism hidden beneath her concern. He said something like, "Don't tell me how to live my life." She got offended and began an exhausting inner debate. Should she leave him alone or continue to try to engage him? Is he avoiding her, hiding in his work, really dissatisfied with the marriage? Here we can see them both involved in guessing each other's motives, that is, both are asking what is *really* going on under the surface? What does the other person really mean?

In our session, it doesn't stop there. The patient continues her inner debate: "Shouldn't he take time off, rest, take care of himself? Is he not interested enough in me for our marriage to last? My friend and her husband take weekend trips together. Isn't balance part of health in life?"

I tell my patient that I think it is as though she were arguing her case, last night with her husband and also during the session, in what I call the "invisible court." She has a particular view of the reality. Her view is that her husband should want to spend more time with her. She expresses some of her feelings to him, but most of the time she is rather indirect about how her own needs play a role in her position. But inwardly, she articulates many reasons why his behavior should be different. It is as though she were in a courtroom, arguing a case for her husband being more focused on spending time with her.

To some degree, I believe we all carry around an invisible court and argue in favor of our own personal vision of reality. But in paranoia, the need for others to accept our vision is more intense. The paranoid person urgently requires that the other accepts his point of view as the only possible point of view. He sees his point of view as the truth, not just "a" truth. In the invisible court, arguments are never settled. How the partner was unkind, how the boss was unfair, is endlessly replayed. It is as though the patient believes if he proves in the invisible court that he has been unjustly treated, life will stop being adversarial. The paranoid person does not really believe he can change his life, but he somehow feels if he could "win" in "court," *life would have to change for him.*

This can be problematic in treatment, where the clinician can feel controlled by the patient's need to be right. Clinicians can feel they have two equally problematic choices: to act as though they blindly accept the patient's views, and thereby sacrifice their freedom to independently think for themselves, or to sometimes differ with the patient and risk losing the patient altogether. This can be very challenging, especially for relatively inexperienced clinicians, unsure of themselves and wanting to keep every patient who comes to them. But it is always difficult, even for the more seasoned analyst.

I close with a quotation from Adam Phillips (1995):

> The psychoanalyst and her so-called patient share a project. The psychoanalyst, that is to say, must ask herself not Am I being a good analyst (am I wild enough, am I orthodox enough, have I said the right thing)? But, What kind of person do I want to be? There are plenty of people who will answer the first question for her. Faced with the second question, there may be terrors but there are no experts. (p. xvii)

Perhaps more than with any other patients, when we work with people who defend themselves in paranoid fashion, we have to be unusually able to face terrors and unusually able to accept that, in many senses, we are not experts.

To return to the question at the outset of this section, who would we need to be to treat I. B. Singer's Bessie or Conrad Aiken's Paul? Let's imagine that someone persuades Bessie to see a therapist before the incident in which her key broke. She is an old widow, burdened by physical limitations, unable to accept the realities of aging, frightened by the bewildering world around her, projecting evil intentions on her neighbors, intensely prejudiced against those whose racial and ethnic backgrounds differ from her own, seeing threat everywhere, and desperately trying to keep the world at bay. She comes in for her first session, where we usually explore the reasons for seeking treatment. Perhaps she says she wants to "understand" why her neighbors are against her and why her landlord is plaguing her. But we soon see that Bessie isn't really trying to "understand," but rather to try her case in the "invisible court" and find the neighborhood guilty as charged. Who do I have to be to have any chance to help Bessie?

It is easier to see who I can't be. If I am caught up in my own outrage at her prejudices, I probably wouldn't recognize their meaning as attempts to defend against profound threats to her survival. If I am too worried about whether Bessie is about to add me to her list of enemies, I might become too anxious to work creatively. If I need to "figure her out," label her, and predict her, my security needs are likely to prevent me from sufficiently contrasting with her paranoid certainties. In other words, I won't be able to hold my theories lightly enough to make her clutching of her own theories palpable to both of us. It seems likely to me that, at some point, Bessie will wonder about my motives, and I will need a firm grip on my own sense of self.

Most of all, I would suggest, I need to be able to look past Bessie's rage and hear the sorrow. Bessie has lost her world, her youth, and her familiar surround. But by far her greatest loss is Sam's absence from her life and the loss of all the love and security they gave each other. Her life has lost its flavor and its meaning. It has no priorities, other than the necessity to breathe, eat, and sleep, so as to breathe, eat, and sleep tomorrow.

The clinician who can help Bessie is someone who can accompany mourning. I explore this capacity in many of the subsequent chapters of this book. But, for now, I suggest that to help Bessie I would have to be able to sit with her, as she remembers herself with Sam. Without trying to control the pace of her mourning, I would have to be able to witness it.

References

Aiken, C. (1954). Impulse. In R. P. Warren & A. Erskine (Eds.), *Short story masterpieces* (pp. 1–14). New York: Dell.
Aiken, C. (2002). Silent snow, secret snow. In A. H. Bond (Ed.), *Tales of psychology: Short stories to make you wise* (pp. 142–163). St. Paul: Paragon House.
Buechler, S. (2004). *Clinical values: Emotions that guide psychoanalytic treatment.* Hillsdale, NJ: Analytic Press.
Buechler, S. (2008). *Making a difference in patients' lives: Emotional experience in the therapeutic setting.* New York: Routledge.
Buechler, S. (2012). *Still practicing: The heartaches and joys of a clinical career.* New York: Routledge.
Gilman, C. P. (1994). The yellow wallpaper. In A. W. Lidz (Ed.), *Major American short stories* (pp. 286–300). New York: Oxford University Press.
Gogol, N. (1960). The diary of a madman. In A. R. MacAndrew (Trans.), *The diary of a madman and other stories* (pp. 7–29). New York: New American Library.
McGrath, P. (2013). Method to the madness. *New York Times* book review, June 30, 2013, p. 31.
McWilliams, N. (2011). *Psychoanalytic diagnosis: Understanding personality structure in the clinical process.* New York: Guilford Press.
Phillips, A. (1995). *Terrors and experts.* Cambridge, MA: Harvard University Press.
Sartre, J-P. (1963). The room. In F. R. Karl & L. Hamalian (Eds.), *The existential imagination* (pp. 192–217). Greenwich, CT: Faucet Publications.
Singer, I. B. (1999) The key. In J. Updike & K. Kenison (Eds.), *The best American short stories of the century* (pp. 493–503). New York: Houghton Mifflin Company.
Stern, D. B. (1997). *Unformulated experience: From dissociation to imagination in psychoanalysis.* Hillsdale, NJ: Analytic Press.
Stilman, L. (1960). Afterword. In A. R. MacAndrew (Trans.), *The diary of a madman and other stories* (pp. 223–238). New York: New American Library.
Sullivan, H. S. (1956). *Clinical studies in psychiatry.* New York: W. W. Norton.
White, E. B. (1952). The door. In M. Crane (Ed.), *Fifty great short stories* (pp. 348–353). New York: Bantam Dell.
Will, O. A. (1961). Paranoid development and the concept of the self: Psychotherapeutic interventions. *Psychiatry*, 2, 74–86.
Yeats, W. B. (1968). The second coming. In F. B. Millet, A. W. Hoffman, & D. R. Clark (Eds.), *Reading poetry* (pp. 479–480). New York: Harper & Row.

Chapter 3

Humiliated Suffering

Thomas Mann was acutely aware of how someone can judge themselves as superior to average people but also feel vastly inferior. Several of Mann's stories can be read as studies of the relationship between low self-esteem and grandiosity. In "The Hungry" (1997), Mann gives us a portrait of an artist who generally sees himself as a superior being, but also feels unworthy of the joys available to the merely average. Detlef, an artist, watches his fellow audience members at a concert. He is especially keen to observe "little laughing, dancing, chattering Lily" (p. 105) and her companions. Thinking of how ordinary they are, he reflects on his power to use words to reshape them any way he likes. Defiantly, he silently exults that he can expose their foolish joys to the world. But then, suddenly, pure longing takes over, and he yearns "just once to drink in magic draughts the bliss of the commonplace" (p. 104).

Detlef can't bear to remain in the theater and abruptly leaves. On the way to his carriage, he encounters a starving, shivering outcast. He realizes that the outcast looks at him with the same combination of envy and disdain that he just directed toward Lily's companions. Which one of us is above the others? Who is the superior and who the inferior? Detlef is able to come to the realization that "we are all brothers we creatures of the restlessly suffering will, yet we do not recognize ourselves as such. Another love is needed, another love" (p. 107).

Many characters in literature and people in everyday life spend much of their time trying to stave off feelings of their inferiority. Shame, or a sense of insufficiency, is a key aspect of their sense of themselves. While, theoretically, we can assume that grandiosity is unconsciously at play, in their conscious experience they frequently suffer the pangs of low self-esteem. Shame shadows them, making every new experience another proof of their fundamental inadequacy and worthlessness. In this chapter I highlight people who *present themselves* as shamefully lacking in self-esteem. I deal with their treatment in the second part of the chapter. The next chapter, on narcissism, will include discussion of the relationship between deficits in the sense of self and over-entitled grandiosity. Although the shame-prone and the grandiose both suffer from a lack of clarity about their worth, and although when we see one of these syndromes we can assume the other lurks, I discuss them in separate chapters to make it clear that their *initial self-presentations*, in fiction and in the consulting room, can radically differ.

James Joyce provided an eloquent example of low self-regard in his touching story "Araby" (2002). A young boy falls hopelessly in love with a neighbor. At last, she speaks to him, asking if he plans to go to the "Araby" bazaar. He vows to go and bring her back a present. After overcoming obstacles, he finally gets there, only to find everything closing. Although it is not his fault, he defines himself by this failure. Adding to his misery is the sense that his mission was foolish and prideful: "Gazing up into the darkness I saw myself as a creature driven and derided by vanity; and my eyes burned with anguish and anger" (p. 204). He is ashamed he could not win the neighbor's attention, and, even more, ashamed that it mattered so much.

The utter humiliation of the main character in Mann's story "Little Lizzy" (1997) is almost unbearable for me to read. Jacoby is an extremely obese lawyer, married to a much younger, beautiful woman, Amra. Jacoby is extravagantly self-effacing, most especially when he is in the presence of his wife. Mann astutely observes that Jacoby's over-obligingness was forced, that "its true source was an inward insecurity and cowardice—the impression it gave was not very pleasant. A man who despises himself is a very ugly sight" (p. 71).

Seemingly as an impulsive prank, Amra decides to totally, publicly humiliate him. She talks him into wearing an absurd costume and singing and dancing at a party. Jacoby's strength gives out and, in the middle of his song, he collapses and dies. It is as though Jacoby literally dies of shame.

In a sense, people die of shame every day. They are willing to kill or die themselves because someone insulted their family, or their country, or their religion. They commit suicide rather than face the shame of bankruptcy, or failure in school, or work, or love. They kill themselves when a bully threatens to expose their shameful secrets. Some of us take our time dying of shame, spreading it out over a lifetime, while others exit abruptly, but dying of shame is as old as humankind.

We die of shame when something happens that displays, for all the world to see, a shortcoming we believe we suffer from. I don't think we die of shame unless we *agree* with the indictment. I believe we have to collaborate in being shamed, or it doesn't have the power to make us suffer.

Anna, the adoring wife of a self-important hussar in Mann's story "A Gleam" (1997), is forced to watch her husband dance with a very beautiful young woman. Anna wears the smile expected of her, but we, the readers, know that she is dying inside. Anna is acutely self-conscious, with a "constitutional fear of putting people out" and a "constitutional yearning to be like them and have them love her" (p. 138). Her husband, Baron Harry, is just as in love with himself as she is. And for Anna, that is part of his charm: "His vanity hurt her—and yet she loved it! How sweet to feel how handsome he was, how young, splendid, and bewitching! The infatuation of those other women would bring her own to a fever pitch" (p. 139). Harry's flirtations make sense to Anna because they express his preference for women of greater worth than his wife. Harry's strutting gives Anna her only chance to shine in public, if only through reflected glory. But the price is tremendous.

Saul Bellow describes self-esteem issues with a somewhat lighter touch in his playful story "A Father-To-Be" (2002). Rogin is 31, a research chemist, and on the way to dinner with Joan, his fiancée. But first, he has to pick up the groceries she requested. Joan is beautiful, in debt, and unable to find suitable employment. The definition of "suitable" is rather vague. Meanwhile, Rogin is expected to pay her bills. His thoughts turn resentful, until he reflects that everyone's life is burdened. He enters the delicatessen, imagining the cares of all the shoppers and clerks. Elated, he buys extravagant delicacies for Joan.

As I read this story, I see a dance, a *pas de deux*, between Rogin and Joan. Each has areas of entitlement. Sometimes they come together, each catering (literally and figuratively) to the other. But, at other times, the claims of one strike the other as outrageous. Rogin seems like a caretaker until we read that he is finding his mother difficult because, on Friday night, she "had neglected to cut up his meat for him, and he was hurt" (p. 507). Rogin finds equanimity as he fantasizes about the lives of the other passengers on the subway. He remembers some dreams. In one, he is carrying a woman on his head. He wonders if the dream is about his mother or Joan. In another dream, an undertaker offers to cut his hair, and he refuses. We can imagine that Rogin fears that he will pay an ultimate price for his (sexual) relationship with Joan. Rogin's gaze fixes on another man in the subway car. The man is well but not ostentatiously groomed. He wears expensive shoes that Rogin sees as warning people not to go too near, seeming to "draw about himself a circle of privilege, notifying all others to mind their own business and let him read his paper" (p. 509). The man reminds him of Joan. Would they have a son like this man, if they married? An awful thought! Would such an outcome make the preceding years of struggle seem worthwhile? "To suffer, to labor, to toil and force your way through the spikes of life . . . only to become the father of a fourth-rate man of the world like this, so flat-looking with his ordinary, clean, rosy, uninteresting, self-satisfied, fundamentally bourgeois face. What a curse to have a dull son!" (p. 509). Rogin is outraged that we are all tricked into sacrificing our lives merely to perpetuate the race. The life force in us betrays us by "trampling on our individual humanity, using us for its own ends like mere dinosaurs or bees, exploiting love heartlessly" (p. 510). Rogin's mind flashes on the face of Joan's father, with his ugly, selfish blue eyes. He exhorts himself not to be a mere instrument! He declares to himself that he won't let himself be used, that he has his own right to exist. Rogin is shadowboxing with entitlement. He struggles to feel like a special, particular person and not a mere vessel. And he resents that Joan does not seem at all encumbered by inner turmoil: "Her lack of consciousness of guilt amazed him. He did not see how it could be" (p. 512).

Rogin vows to himself to have a serious talk with Joan. Does she think he was made to carry the burdens of the whole world?

> Do you think I was born to be taken advantage of and sacrificed? Do you think I'm just a natural resource, like a coal mine, or oil well, or fishery, or the like? Remember, that I am a man is no reason that I should be loaded down. I have a soul in me no bigger or stronger than yours. (p. 512)

But all his self-righteous anger and all his resolve evaporates as soon as she holds him, trying to wash dirt out of his hair. She presses against him and "surrounds" him. The water she pours seems like it comes from within him: "it was the warm fluid of his own secret loving spirit" (p. 513). He forgets his anger at Joan, her father, and their future son and abandons himself to the feeling of being cared for.

Bellow invites us to experience the shifting sands of self-esteem deficits. One minute Rogin is the entitled, and the next he is railing at Joan's entitlement. His own tendency to expect special treatment makes him abhor similar pulls in others. He is either over-burdened, catering to someone else's selfish needs, or else he will be the one to be served. As we all tend to do, Rogin finds, in Joan, a person who can perpetually play out his issues with him.

I remember a *New Yorker* cartoon that illustrated the marriage of a grandiose narcissist and someone suffering from low self-esteem. The husband, a great and commanding figure, strutted down the street, exclaiming, "Me, me, me," while behind him his cowering, long-suffering wife cried, "Why me, why me, why me?" Thus, succinctly, we have the marriage of the grandiose person with someone all too ready to agree that she has little worth and should be grateful for any kind of attention. While, of course, these two have more in common than it may appear, in this chapter I emphasize the qualities of those consciously suffering from low self-esteem, who present themselves as feeling inferior, while I discuss overt grandiosity in the next chapter. There, I also deal with some commonalities between these two sets of human dilemmas.

The following are some aspects of the experience of people suffering from conscious low self-regard:

- Tendency to collaborate with feeling shame, or the sense of inadequacy, inferiority.
- Tendency to compare oneself unfavorably to others. Vulnerability to envy and jealousy.
- Feeling of being ordinary, commonplace, "a dime a dozen," easily replaced.
- Tendency to view interpersonal relationships in hierarchical terms.
- Vulnerability to utter humiliation. Tendency to collaborate with it.
- Being overly accommodating to others. Heightened fear of offending others. Extreme need to be accepted.
- Despising oneself. Feeling self-disgust, contempt.
- Fearing shame and humiliation. Feeling one can die of it.
- Projecting one's own negative view of oneself into the minds of others.
- Feeling puzzled about what others could value about oneself.
- Identification with others' over-valuation of themselves. Willingness to cater to grandiose people because of admiration for their love for themselves.
- Tendency toward secretly feeling spiritually above others, because of one's "humility," or better values.

It is remarkable how many of these qualities are embodied in the father in John Updike's story "The Lucid Eye in Silver Town" (1965). Marty August, Jay's father, takes him to visit Marty's rich and successful brother, Quinn, who is in New York on business. Unlike his brother, Marty has to watch every penny. When his wife proclaims that she hates the August family, Marty obligingly admits that she has every reason to, with the exception of Quinn and her son, the only ones who made anything of themselves. This makes Jay miserable, and he declares that he finds nothing more enraging than his father's tendency to easily agree with others' opinions.

Marty assesses himself as inadequate and inferior to his brother, his wife, and his son. They have drive, ambition, and intelligence. He has none of these qualities. Marty enacts his fear of offending his brother by convincing Jay to stay out of sight while Quinn talks to his business associates. Jay wants his father to feel entitled to a place at the table, literally and figuratively. But Marty feels he doesn't belong and needs to demonstrate it. Is he catering to Quinn's grandiosity, treating him like the big man of business? Is he projecting his own view of himself as worthless, assuming everyone else sees him that way? Or is he being quietly, secretly morally superior, demonstrating that he is too humble to need attention? Regardless, Marty's behavior causes his son to suffer. Jay longs to be able to look up to his father. Jay has never before visited New York, so Marty points out some of the landmarks. Jay is touched and surprised that Marty is able to address his questions about the City, where Marty had looked for work when he was younger. Jay feels a newfound respect for his father and hopes to nurture it.

But this moment is short-lived. When Jay shows off his knowledge of art, topping a comment of Quinn's, Marty returns to his usual placating and self-effacing attitude, claiming to not be able to understand the conversation.

As they head home, Marty feels the need to point out how Quinn ducked paying a bill and left it for his much poorer brother. The moment could be seen as evidence of Quinn's selfish entitlement and lack of empathy and generosity. But Marty frames this as one more demonstration of Quinn's superiority, suggesting that this is how fortunes are made and that he knew Quinn would do it.

After Marty drives the point home, declaring that this is why Quinn is so much better off than he, Jay throws a tantrum. He simply can't take his father's self-loathing and uncritical admiration for Quinn. Jay explodes and then, later, reflects that he did it because he wanted to shock his father out of regarding himself as old and tired. This is such a vivid example of a son's sorrow, pain, and compassion for his father's humiliation. The tantrum apparently was not Jay's first: On the train back home, he admits that it was a sort of shared ritual – Jay screaming, Marty nodding complacently.

Does the father realize that his son must separate from Marty's martyrdom? Is his endurance another secret demonstration of moral superiority? Does Marty take pride in Jay's entitlement to voice his anger? Does he understand that Jay's rage is a product of his love for his father and his grief for his father's permanently low self-esteem? By calling Marty a midwife, it seems to me that Updike is suggesting that Jay's protests are giving birth to his ability to find value in his family and in himself. Marty is always good at stepping aside and making way for the other person, but, perhaps, this time it serves a purpose.

Tory, in "A Red Letter Day" (1954) by Elizabeth Taylor, is another parent who suffers from a sense of insufficiency. When we meet her, she is arriving for visiting day at her son's school. Of course, Tory has no idea what to wear. She unfavorably compares herself with another arriving parent, Mrs. Hay-Hardy. Immediately upon seeing that ample lady, Tory feels inferior. Tory reflects that she is just not "a great feather bed of oblivion" (p. 447) like Mrs. Hay-Hardy. Tory's marriage ended in divorce, and, while she loves her 11-year-old son, Edward, she doesn't love only him. Tory is unsparing in her self-criticism and harsh in her judgment of their relationship: "Between Edward and me there is no premise of love, none at all—nothing taken for granted, as between most sons and mothers, but all tentative and agonized" (p. 447). She concludes that she and Edward are amateurs at being mother and son. They have no tradition to build on, and no gifts for the job: "We try too piteously to please one another, and if we do, feel frightened by the miracle of it" (pp. 447–448).

Of course, this is nothing like the rapport Tory imagines Mrs. Hay-Hardy enjoys with her sons. She is deemed important enough to warrant an appearance by the headmaster's wife, who wouldn't dream of missing an opportunity to visit with such a "profitable womb." Tory silently chastises herself as, clearly, not a born mother. Her despair heightens as the day drags on, and she and Edward try to fill the time with shopping and visiting a museum. Both want the day to go well but don't know how to make that happen. With his mother, Edward feels "unsafe, wounded and wounding, and, oppressed by responsibility" (p. 453). After some uncertainty about how to say farewell to each other, Tory and Edward part. Edward is "radiant with relief," and Tory thinks about the lonely evening ahead of her with Edward's photograph next to her bed. Each eagerly looked forward to this red-letter day, and each tried desperately to hide their despair from the other. But Edward has a life to return to, while Tory has only her catalogue of self-recriminations and failures.

In a touching first-person narrative, "My Mother" (2002), Andre Gide allows us entry into the mind of another exquisitely sensitive young man as he watches his mother cope with her unsteady self-esteem. While Mother is able to be at ease in a drawing-room, she is undone by the thought that her highly placed husband might not be proud of her.

> What my Mother had waited for in vain was not a compliment from my Father; it was just the certainty that she had managed to seem worthy of him, that he had not been disappointed in her. But what my Father thought I never could tell any more than she; and that evening I realized that every soul takes away to the grave, where they will be forever hidden, some secrets. (p. 100)

The son has a further, painful but instructive insight. Mother's low self-esteem and fear of Father's disapproval prevent her from questioning the dictates of middle-class society, despite her nature's refined sensibility. Because Mother doesn't believe in herself, she feels compelled to imitate the crowd, instead of following her own, better instincts. She remained too nervous and uncertain of herself to make her nature take the upper hand. She kept to the end her respect for other people and their opinions, always anxious to improve, but accepting the conventional view of improvement; always making efforts to do better and never realizing, because she was too modest, that the best in herself was precisely what required from [her] the least effort of will. (p. 102)

Gide recognizes that those with self-esteem deficits yearn for acceptance and may fall back on slavish imitation, bartering away their potential uniqueness in the hope that this will win them a good approval rating. Mother seems similar to Mann's adoring wife, Anna, in the story "A Gleam" (see above). Both take it for granted that their husbands have a right to evaluate their worth. Both see themselves as deserving the failing grades they will no doubt receive. To each, following the crowd seems the only option. Anna goes along with Baron Harry's public display of his flirtations, and Mother submits to the rules of social protocol. Of course, an abundant feminist literature comments on the price of such "bargains." But, as Saul Bellow makes clear (see above), a man can also suffer from inner conflict about whether to submit to the narcissistic entitlement of another, hoping that meekness will earn approval. Interestingly, Bellows' character, Rogin, clearly feels tremendous rage at having to comply with Joan's program to get her acceptance. But in Gide's story, as in Updike's, it is the more fully entitled son, on behalf of his under-entitled parent, who revolts against this deal. In Gide's story, the son vows not to follow his mother's example: "What a warning to me! How strong the twist left by her upbringing must be" (p. 101). Some rebel against being locked into the inferior role, but many take it for granted that it is their lot in life. For example, Thomas Mann's Anna can't question her position as Baron Harry's supplicant, although we might see her rage as surfacing in her dreams of Harry falling ill and requiring her care. Knowing that you are willing to sell your soul for approval/acceptance is, perhaps, the worst way to die of shame.

In his story "Death in the Woods" (1988), Sherwood Anderson describes another way to die. The old woman in his story does not suffer conscious shame, but she does, in my view, die as a result of a lifetime devoid of any sense of entitlement. She starts life as a "bound girl," an orphan/servant to a German farmer who sexually abuses her, causing his wife to resent her and treat her badly. From this terrible situation, she is "rescued" by Jake, who beats her if she fails to provide food from their meager farm. Her daughter dies and her son grows up to be a copy of his father, an abusive alcoholic. When the son brings a woman home, "the son and his woman ordered the old woman about like a servant. She didn't mind much; she was used to it. Whatever happened, she never said anything" (p. 235). Once, a butcher speaks to her in a friendly way, suggesting that her husband and son deserve to starve, given how they treat her. She doesn't understand, since she doesn't really see herself as a person with any meaning, except to feed horses, cows, pigs, dogs, and men.

Eventually, her load is, literally, too heavy, and she can't carry it in the snow any longer. She lies down and gives in to the pull of death: "The old woman died softly and quietly."

Anderson sees a kind of perfection in the woman's story. Her life was dedicated to feeding and the food on her back brought her death. In his words, "A thing so complete has its own beauty" (p. 230). It does, but it also has its own tragedy and horror. It is fascinating to me, how many of the stories of low self-esteem, as well as the stories of grandiosity, involve some kind of death. Perhaps people with both disorders are nearer dying of shame than they sometimes realize.

Although strictly speaking it is not a work of fiction, I include Kafka's "Letter to His Father" (1953) because it is such an astonishing description of what can crush a human being's self-esteem. This letter can be read as a manual explaining how to narcissistically cripple a child. It was written as a message to Kafka's father, but his mother refused to hand it to her husband, as Kafka requested her to do.

Kafka portrays his father as utterly confident, intimidating, harshly critical, self-satisfied, hot tempered, and tremendously disappointed in the young and timid Franz. Apparently, Kafka senior wanted to bring up a strong, brave, practical, secure son. But, partly because of Franz's innate temperament, but largely because of his father's treatment of him, Franz fell far short of the mark.

For the sake of brevity I will list some of the qualities inculcated in Franz by his father, from Franz's point of view:

- Franz says that he suffers from a sense of not mattering. How did this come about? As a partial explanation, Franz offers a memory from his early childhood, expressing the hope that it captures the flavor of many other moments. One night, Franz whimpered for water, and his father carried him to the pavlatche (balcony) and left him there, alone, in his nightshirt. In Franz's own words:

    Even years afterwards I suffered from the tormenting fancy that the huge man, my father, the ultimate authority, would come almost for no reason at all and take me out of bed in the night and carry me out onto the pavlatche, and that meant I was a mere nothing for him. (p. 17)

- Franz felt vastly physically inferior to his father, who was strong and broad, while Franz was skinny and weakly. Added to this was his feeling of intellectual inferiority, partly due to the father's self-confidence and absolute belief that he was always right in any argument. Confronted with his father's unwavering certainty, Franz often found himself unable to speak or think at all, which furthered his sense of ineptitude.
- Franz was especially vulnerable to being criticized in public. His father did not hesitate to humiliate him in this way.
- Franz believed that he became cold, indifferent, detached, and preoccupied with his imagination, as ways to feel self-sufficient. But he still suffered from fear, which expressed itself in constant worry about his health. He was always concerned about his digestion, hair falling out, and other anxieties. His interpretation of the meaning of these anxieties is profoundly psychologically astute:

But since there was nothing at all I was certain of, since I needed to be provided at every instant with a new confirmation of my existence, since nothing was in my very own, undoubted, sole possession, determined unequivocally only by me—in sober truth a disinherited son—naturally I became unsure even of the thing nearest to me, my own body. (pp. 89–91)

- No amount of success changed Franz's view of himself, since his view was based entirely on what his father thought of him. Any success was "strengthening for a moment, nothing more, but on the other side your weight always dragged me down much more strongly" (p. 93).
- Perhaps worst of all, was Franz's inability to believe in his own opinions. He tells his father, "Not even your mistrust of others is as great as my self-mistrust, which you have bred in me" (p. 125).

Franz exemplifies many of the characteristics (listed earlier in this chapter) of people suffering from low self-regard. He clearly accuses himself of collaborating with his father in creating his own sense of inadequacy. He is constantly comparing himself unfavorably to his father, among others. He feels tremendously vulnerable to humiliation. He assumes others will share his disgust and contempt for himself. At least on the surface, he seems to over value his father, buying into the father's grandiose self-assessment. But I sense in Franz, as in many who express low self-regard, a secret feeling of spiritual or moral superiority. Franz feels it necessary to provide a rejoinder to his letter. He outlines an argument his father might use against the son's accusations. In it, Franz suggests that his letter demonstrates his secret feeling of superiority to his disgraceful father. In accusing his father of such horrendous behavior, isn't Franz standing above his father and looking down in judgment? Who is superior, and who inferior: the selfish, self-important, punitive parent or the victimized, innocent child?

Kafka's brilliant self-analysis anticipates more current thinking, in that the same data can be seen from more than one angle, and seemingly masochistic behavior can have its sadistic side. People often repeat a script but not necessarily their original role in the script. Is the letter a verbal beating that Franz is administering to his father? While acknowledging that this letter can be seen from more than one perspective, I truly admire its clarity about some ways a child's self-esteem can be crushed, and the lifelong vulnerability, indecision, fear of humiliation, and profound insecurity that can be the lasting legacy.

The narrator in Dostoevsky's short story "The Meek Girl" (1989) sees himself as an expert in crushing a human being's self-esteem. His wife has just committed suicide. As her body lies waiting for the undertaker, her husband struggles to make sense of her death. They had met years before in his pawnbroker's shop, when poverty forced her, at age 16, to pawn her precious trinkets for food for her family. Over time, he became intrigued and decided to maneuver her into marrying him. He was conscious of his pleasure at having power over her, given her impoverished circumstances. He wanted her to grovel at his feet, and he methodically ground her down. At first, she was as meek as the story's title implies. But he went too far, depriving her of any basis for self-respect, forcing her to watch as he took advantage of other customers in his shop, endlessly reminding her that she had nothing of her own. Finally, she began to rebel and look more critically at his behavior. As their relationship grew more contentious, she visibly weakened until, icon in hand, she threw herself out the window and died. The story ends with the husband's pitiful cry as he finally realizes that he has tortured her to death: "when they come to take her away tomorrow, what will I do?" (p. 295). Here is the ultimate expression of the deadly effect of the systematic destruction of a human being's sense of self.

Treatment

How can we help someone with self-esteem deficits develop an adequate sense of worth? My clinical experience suggests the importance of the idea that human beings should get credit for having the courage to look in the mirror, no matter what we see when we do so. I feel very strongly about this, and, I am sure, this conviction expresses itself in my work with patients.

I also feel strongly that low self-regard is as much a product of interpersonal interactions in the *present* as it is a product of past experiences. Another way to say this is that people who have suffered narcissistic injuries find ways to replicate these scenarios, further damaging their self-esteem. We can understand this as a compulsion to repeat, as an effort to change the outcome, as a familiar role re-enacted because of its familiarity, as a product of insufficient entitlement, or, I am sure, in many other ways. Regardless, it is usually the *ongoing* self-esteem injuries that account for the degree of narcissistic deficit, in my opinion. This suggests that interrupting this cycle would be therapeutically beneficial. But how?

Irwin Hoffman (2009) presents an intriguing therapeutic possibility. He has developed the technique of modulating his patient's self-criticism by becoming a non-critical internalized object. In his own words, when a patient has internalized terribly critical voices, the clinician can say something like:

> Those voices that are telling you you are a loser are ignorant, selfish, stupid voices and you should tell them to shut up; just shut the fuck up! And you know what else? You and I, we are going to beat them. It may take some time but we are going to beat them and we are going to create grounds for you to thrive with a sense of pride in yourself and with a sense of joy in living that should have been your right and your experience from day one! (p. 621)

In Hoffman's battle with negative introjects, he takes on the project of interrupting the patient's ongoing self-esteem damage. Of course, his treatment of the patient is predicated on their mutual understanding of the history that created the deficit in the first place. But in this paper, Hoffman aims to alter the patient's inner dialogue by inserting his voice into it. He breaks the injurious cycle in a way that I find extremely compelling.

Many of the stories in this chapter illustrate that those who have suffered damage to their sense of self allow others, in their *current* life, to treat them badly, thus reinforcing the original injuries. Jacoby, the humiliated husband in Thomas Mann's heartbreaking story "Little Lizzy," is a great example. His acquiescence in being publicly scorned seems to invite abuse. Clearly, one's participation in allowing oneself to be humiliated can augment the utter degradation of it. Whether (in the present) the abusive criticism is coming from outside or inside, complying with it adds further insult to the injury.

Silvan Tomkins (1963) beautifully captures the agony of shame:

> If distress is the affect of suffering, shame is the affect of indignity, of defeat, of transgression and of alienation. Though terror speaks to life and death and distress makes of the world a vale of tears, yet shame strikes deepest into the heart of man. While terror and distress hurt, they are wounds inflicted from outside which penetrate the smooth surface of the ego; but shame is felt as an inner torment, a sickness of the soul. (p. 118)

Most clinical situations are not as extreme as the examples from fiction in this chapter. Most wives wouldn't dress their husbands in silly costumes and subject them to public scorn. But I have certainly witnessed the effects of more gradual, more subtle, but nevertheless thoroughly corrosive shaming. In the example that comes to mind, my patient's wife implies that she is more competent and has to handle all social contact, because he is inept. Unfortunately, this is a message that my patient all too easily accepts. He is a person who often expresses fear that his "limited intelligence" will be unmasked. This man, well into his fifties, is truly afraid he will be seen as too limited intellectually to be befriended, even though there is much evidence of his professional gifts. His history includes acute shame about the status of his family in their community. They were the poorer neighbors in an upper-middle-class environment. The patient's mother struggled to afford a home in an area that allowed him to attend fine public schools. Mother had to work in a field that could be seen as blue or as white collar, depending on your point of view.

Through this work, Mother made the acquaintance of a highly cultured public figure, who took the patient under her wing and introduced him to the finer things. He was extremely appreciative, but always felt out of his depth, worried he would unintentionally expose his ignorance.

As a middle-aged adult, the patient glowingly recalls his cultural initiation. He still feels profoundly grateful for his patron's attentions, largely undeserving, haunted by lingering yearnings to measure up somehow, to being intelligent enough for her rarified circles. So, many years later, social occasions still quickly become intelligence tests for him. Any misstep costs many points. Reviewing his performance in our session, he cringes with shame. His wife's attempts to "damage control" his "faux pas" augment his sense of ineptitude. My patient's past primed him to view himself as socially inferior and submit to his wife's "superior" social judgment. With each instance, his self-esteem sinks. So, the damage from the past facilitates further damage in the present. I sometimes find myself playing out versions of Hoffman's approach (see above) by trying to add my voice to the ones in the patient's head.

In keeping with my overall belief that our emotions exist in a system, with a change in any one of them affecting the levels of them all (Buechler, 2008), I understand shame as modulated by the other feelings that are present or absent. Another patient comes to mind, whose shame is often accompanied by rage and envy of those (like myself) that she assumes are better off. She feels herself to be at a permanent disadvantage. The race of life is rigged against her. We can look at this from many angles. In one sense, paranoia is merged with low self-esteem. Or we can focus on the combination of her profound shame, anger, and envy, and the absence of modulating curiosity. While I have often been interested in exploring what brings on her bursts of frustration, she has been less interested, especially in the early years of our work together. Having been subjected to sexual abuse and ongoing ridicule in her family, she certainly has good reason to be resentful about her faulty preparation for life. But, as in the other clinical example (above), she participates in perpetuating the cycle. She chooses to get involved with men who demean her, ignore her needs, and put her in the position of begging for attention. Shaming in the present reinforces the damage from the past.

In so many cases, profound self-esteem deficits result from inattention. This has been well documented in the literature, by writers such as Shabad (2001). The child who can't have a palpable impact on a parent is likely to suffer self-esteem deficits. For example, what happens when a child can't get a parent's *full* and *joyful* attention? What message is conveyed? I suggest that often the child swallows whole a feeling of unworthiness and unimportance. A pattern coalesces of negative judgment about one's worth, based on another's inattention.

Briefly, a patient of mine was literally abandoned for as long as a year at a time, left with relatives and other temporary caretakers by a distracted, depressed mother and a self-involved father. Even when the parents were physically present, my patient could sense that their minds were elsewhere. She frantically tried to capture her mother's focus, only to fail and withdraw into a lifelong hurt, lonely, angry sulk. This brings me to a growing concern of mine. I believe a central challenge today is the effect of technology on our ability to give our children our undivided attention. Clearly this is not an entirely new problem. Parents have had difficulty fully attending to children in previous eras. But, more and more, our focus is fractured. As our cell phones vibrate and our emails collect, as we are texted, facebooked, and twittered, we lose the ability to concentrate solely and soulfully on each other. As soon as we glance at our children, offering them our eyes and minds, something distracts us. They lose us, perhaps for the tenth time that morning. Our children themselves are similarly fractured in their ability to focus. As our attention spans shorten, how will this affect our children's sense of self-worth? Can a child feel seen, wanted, held in mind by a parent scrolling computer screens and eying a cell phone? When that child grows up, will she have a strong, centered sense of self or will she feel unable to really matter?

A child who didn't feel her presence captivated her own parents, a child who rarely elicited excited joy and rarely felt she fascinated anyone, will likely live with a hunger to know how she counts. It may be impossible or, at least, extremely difficult to truly fill that hunger. I believe that mattering becomes the subtext, and often the text, of her treatment.

To conclude, I can only suggest the vital role of the analyst's passionate engagement in this enterprise. To capture the analyst's emotional involvement, to fill her mind, to be able to break her heart, and sometimes elicit her joy, are necessary for the patient to heal from the traumatic sense of insufficiency created when children repeatedly feel that they can find no way to earn their parents' undivided attention.

References

Anderson, S. (1988). A death in the woods. In P. S. Prescott (Ed.), *The Norton book of American short stories* (pp. 220–230). New York: W. W. Norton & Company.

Bellow, S. (2002). A father-to-be. In C. Neider (Ed.), *Great short stories of the masters* (pp. 503–513). New York: Cooper Square Press.

Buechler, S. (2008). *Making a difference in patients' lives: Emotional experience in the therapeutic setting.* New York: Routledge.

Dostoevsky, F. (1989). The meek girl. In D. McDuff (Trans.), *Uncle's dream and other stories* (pp. 253–296). New York: Penguin Books.

Gide, A. (2002). My mother. In C. Neider (Ed.), *Great short stories of the masters* (pp. 99–102). New York: Cooper Square Press.

Hoffman, I. (2009). Therapeutic passion in the countertransference. *Psychoanalytic Dialogues*, 19, 617–637.

Joyce, J. (2002). Araby. In C. Neider (Ed.), *Great short stories of the masters* (pp. 199–204). New York: Cooper Square Press.

Kafka, F. (1953). *Letter to his father* (E. Kaiser & E. Wilkens, Trans.). New York: Schocken Books.

Mann, T. (1997). A gleam. In *Little Herr Friedemann and other stories* (pp. 132–143). London: Minerva.

Mann, T. (1997). Little Lizzy. In *Little Herr Friedemann and other stories* (pp. 80–85). London: Minerva.

Mann, T. (1997). The hungry. In *Little Herr Friedemann and other stories* (pp. 101–108). London: Minerva.

Shabad, P. (2001). *Despair and the return of hope.* Northvale, NJ: Jason Aronson, Inc.

Taylor, E. (1954). A red letter day. In R. P. Warren & A. Erskine (Eds.), *Short story masterpieces* (pp. 445–454). New York: Dell.

Tomkins, S. (1963). *Affect, imagery, consciousness: Vol. II, The negative affects.* New York: Springer.

Updike, J. (1965). The lucid eye in silver town. In M. Crane (Ed.), *Fifty great American short stories* (pp. 632–643). New York: Bantam Dell.

Chapter 4

Grandiose Posturing

Mrs. Delphin Slade is especially proud of being Mrs. Delphin Slade. In "Roman Fever" (1994), Edith Wharton creates the kind of narcissist many people love to hate. She is eternally jealous, scheming, entitled, grandiose, and exceedingly callous. She is particularly callous toward her best "friend," Mrs. Ansley. Their relationship has a long history, steeped in veiled competition. They are both focused outward, intent on keeping up appearances, especially after both become widows. As old skeletons make their way out of the closet, we come to understand Mrs. Slade's viciousness and how ruthlessly she pursued her "friend's" husband. But, when all the secrets are revealed, Mrs. Ansley has the last laugh. She, rather than Mrs. Slade, captured both husbands' hearts.

Mrs. Slade epitomizes many of the qualities we encounter in the grandiose narcissist:

- A lack of empathy.
- An over-estimation of one's powers, talents, or other qualities.
- Over-valuation of status, appearances, and the more superficial aspects of life.
- Tendencies toward envy, jealousy, competition, and comparison.
- Judgments of one's worth based on the reactions of others.
- Feeling of being above the rules that apply to ordinary mortals.
- Vulnerability to insult.
- Need to shine, from the start of any enterprise, which results in an inability to start from the beginning of an enterprise and see it through.
- Difficulty finding real meaning and purpose in one's life.
- Depression, particularly as aging advances, when it becomes clear that one's talents and reach have limitations.
- Absence of a "bank account" of prior experiences that indicate one does have worth, in the eyes of others and in one's own estimation. Feeling defined by every event, incident, "test."

Some of these qualities are illustrated in a fascinating story by Thomas Mann, "The Blood of the Walsungs" (1997). This story brilliantly anticipates ideas developed by Kohut generations later.

Briefly, Kohut (1984; Mitchell & Black, 1995) described experiences of sameness with another person that can ultimately contribute to healthy development. This essential likeness between oneself and another can be central to building a resilient sense of self. At first, it may contribute to grandiosity, but eventually, as it is exposed to bearable frustrations, a more realistic picture of the self is established. What is unrealistic is held up to the light of day, and the child learns to bear imperfect connections with greater resilience.

But what happens if the light of day too perfectly *confirms*, rather than disconfirms, a grandiose picture of the self and the other? To me, this is the subject of Mann's story. Siegmund and Sieglinde are twins, the son and daughter of a wealthy businessman. Herr Aarenhold, their father, has earned enough money to keep his family in grand style. In surrounding the family with luxury, no expense is spared, so that their clothing is made of the finest fabrics and their table is set with the finest linens. At 19, the twins look very much alike and go everywhere holding hands. This happy situation is disturbed by the betrothal of Sieglinde to von Beckerath, a 35-year-old, well-born government official. Von Beckerath is clearly an outsider in this family and of no interest to Sieglinde. In contrast, she gives her rapt attention to her brother Siegmund: "They held each other's narrow hands between the chairs. Sometimes their gaze sought each other's, melting together in an understanding from which everybody else was shut out. Von Beckerath sat next to Sieglinde on the other side" (p. 164).

It is one week before the wedding. Von Beckerath is having lunch with the family. The twins, along with their siblings, are exulting in their superior taste: "Their highest praise was a grudging acceptance, their criticism deft and ruthless; it snatched the weapons from one's hand, it paralyzed enthusiasm, made it a laughing stock" (p. 166). Von Beckerath is clearly out of his depth. He gets smaller and smaller in his chair, unhinged by their arrogance, while they

> fell upon a single word of his, they worried it, they tore it to bits and replaced it by another so telling and deadly that it went straight to the mark and sat in the wound with a quivering shaft. Towards the end of luncheon von Beckerath's eyes were red and he looked slightly deranged. (p. 166)

Siegmund asks permission to accompany Sieglinde to the opera. It will be the last time the twins have the opportunity to go to the opera alone. Of course, it is a production of the *Walkure*, with its story of the tortured love between another Siegmund and his Sieglinde. The two love stories echo each other like a musical theme and variation.

What I find most fascinating is the way Mann describes the grandiosity and depression in Siegmund, Sieglinde's twin. His life serves his tastes, leaving no motivation for any other goals. In Mann's words:

> Siegmund found in his heart that he had no time for a resolve, how much less then for a deed ... The preparation, the lavish equipment for what should

have been the serious business of life used up all his energy. How much mental effort had to be expended simply in making a proper toilette! (p. 169)

Although he has some talent as an artist, nothing is ever expected of him. He muses on the effect of this, wondering whether, somehow, it has dislodged his sense of reality. In a beautifully succinct sentence, Mann sums up the twins' despair: "They were like self-centered invalids who absorb themselves in trifles, as narcotics to console them for the loss of hope" (p. 170).

After the opera and a light meal, they retire to their separate rooms, but soon rejoin each other. Siegmund looks at Sieglinde and declares her just like himself. He goes on: "Everything about you is just like me—and so—what you have—with Beckerath—the experience—is for me too" (pp. 184–185). In a feverish attempt at logic, he calls what is about to happen "revenge," and the twins abandon themselves to their feelings for each other: "They loved each other with all the sweetness of the senses, each for the other's spoilt and costly well-being and delicious fragrance . . . They forgot themselves in caresses, which took the upper hand, passing over into a tumult of passion" (p. 185).

Mann is able to evoke Siegmund's sense of superiority at the same time as his vague apprehension of his ultimate worthlessness. Only the twin who bears his likeness is of real interest to him. Yet even their love has a static quality. Like Siegmund himself, it has no future. It may celebrate an ecstatic moment, but only as a diversion from an inevitably tragic reality.

Mann's story illustrates the temporary nature of the satisfaction we can gain from seeing ourselves as exactly like another. It gives us confirmation and connection. But its joys can't encompass change. Growth disrupts the magically perfect bond.

I think Mann understood the insecurity of a sense of self based on feeling superior to others. When Siegmund looks into Sieglinde's eyes, he sees his own empty beauty. Like Narcissus, drawn toward his own reflection, Siegmund is captivated by himself. In this story (unlike Kohut's narrative of a twinship that can ultimately contribute to healthy growth, as described above), there is no friction between the pair, so Siegmund has no opportunity to gradually learn how to adjust to slight frustrations. Siegmund's inner need is too perfectly met by the outer reality of Sieglinde. Siegmund has no pull toward striving, no reason to grow. Like a sailboat in still water, he drifts and stalls. Although still alive to sensation, his spirit has passed away or, perhaps, never came alive.

In another fascinating story, "The Dilettante" (1997), Mann gives us a tortured narcissist, replete with the childhood history that helped shape him. He has a mother, perpetually lost in melancholy, whose main companions are melodies. His father, on the other hand, is all action, powerful and proud. A toy theater gives the growing child his own world, where, in fantasy, he can shine every night. The father is unequivocal in his disapproval of his son's preoccupation: "You will never get anywhere in life like this" (p. 40). But his mother responds warmly. Significantly, while he plays the piano, he can never get himself to learn how to read music, which limits the development of his native abilities.

The father is the first to call his son a "dilettante." When he passes his eighteenth birthday, both parents ask him what is to be done with him. Having no idea what he wants to do, he agrees to enter the lumber business. He performs his tasks mechanically, only paying concerted attention to his story books. At this point, he is still able to feel superior to boys from poorer backgrounds, which allows him to be satisfied with his own life. When his parents die, he decides to take his inheritance and travel. There are moments of pure pleasure, especially when he is able to successfully entertain acquaintances he meets on his journeys. But travel becomes more tedious, and he decides to settle and create a contemplative life. While he enjoys setting up his new home, he feels some anxiety, "a faint consciousness of being on the defensive" (p. 47). He suffers from "the slightly depressing thought that I had now for the first time left behind the temporary and provisional and exchanged it for the definite and fixed" (p. 47).

As a clinician, I am familiar with some of the ways this fictitious moment can sound when it is described by a prospective patient in an initial therapy session. Some complain of problems with making commitments, or report others' dissatisfactions with their inability to make choices. Like Peter Pan, some seem unwilling to grow up. But, at some point, life refuses to be put on hold. A girlfriend declares that marriage must be now or never. A career opportunity makes a limited appearance. Friends begin to settle into their lives, willingly exchanging the provisional for the permanent. The narcissist becomes uneasy, as he or she realizes that any firm commitment spells limitations of some kind, but failing to commit will result in a different set of limitations. How can someone addicted to fantasy, where what is possible stretches to the furthest reaches of imagination, accept the confines of a limited role? The temporary is endlessly expansive, but the permanent can feel like a depressing, confining Procrustean bed.

Increasingly, it feels that way to our dilettante. He passes his days in leisure, often able to look down on the ordinary pursuits of those around him. But more and more frequently, he feels unhappy in his isolation. Rather than a chosen way of life, it has become a compulsion, for he can no longer introduce himself to strangers, "being insecure myself and unpleasantly aware that I could not make clear even to a drunken painter exactly who and what I was" (p. 49).

Musing, he concludes that there are two kinds of happiness, inward and outward. He needs the outward recognition, in order to find inward delight. He deeply craves being a favorite of the gods even though he knows that "the real point is what one thinks of oneself, to what one gives oneself, to what one feels strong enough to give oneself!" (p. 51). But he can't even let himself admit he is unhappy, because then he would lose all self-respect. He thinks of unhappiness as ugly and contemptible.

The dilettante's misery is complete when he meets a beautiful, wealthy young woman, who has no interest in him but shows her love to her male companion. He describes her as having high spirits born of "an inward and unconscious poise" (p. 55) in contrast to his own groundless pride. He makes another, even more painful comparison between the man she admires and himself. The chosen man has real self-respect while he feels himself to be "Shut out, unregarded, disqualified, unknown, hors ligne-declasse, pariah, a pitiable object even to myself" (p. 56). He contrives an encounter with the young woman, as a final test of whether his low opinion of himself is justified. Of course, she continues to have no interest in him. This inflicts a mortal wound:

> Since that moment it is all up with me. My last remaining shreds of happiness and self-confidence have been blown to the winds. I can do no more. Yes, I am unhappy; I freely admit it, I seem a lamentable and absurd figure even to myself. And that I cannot bear. (p. 59)

For the dilettante, at this point, the only choice is suicide. Reflecting on this, he realizes that it is not the loss of the woman that has driven him to self-destruction. It is the loss of himself: "One does not die of an unhappy love-affair. One revels in it. It is not such a bad pose. But what is destroying me is that hope has been destroyed with the destruction of all pleasure in myself" (p. 59). He sees that his "love" for the woman is really a form of vanity. He is tormented because she is a prize he cannot have. As he puts it, "Love was the mere pretext, escape, and hope of salvation for my feelings of envy, hatred, and self-contempt" (p. 60).

Looking back on his life, he recognizes a central conflict. He couldn't do without people, because their applause was vital to him. But, unable to forge a self, he was of no use to society, so he had to hide from it. In a line that, I think, presages our current understanding of the potentially powerful impact of shame (which we frequently try to differentiate from guilt), he suggests that a "bad conscience" is always, really, a "festering vanity" (p. 60). He has become a pitiable and disgusting spectacle in his own eyes. And, he concludes, others will no doubt share his low opinion of himself. As a final degradation, he predicts that he won't even be heroic enough to kill himself: "In the end I shall go on living, eating, sleeping; I shall gradually get used to the idea that I am dull, that I cut a wretched and ridiculous figure" (p. 61). This, he decides, is the dilettante's doom.

Mann has isolated one of the greatest problems for the narcissist: Self-esteem is determined by audience reaction. This creates extreme dependence which can itself feel shameful. But, even worse, no audience always applauds. The narcissist has no inner "bank account" of solid self-esteem to provide reserves in the absence of applause or in the presence of "boos." Every encounter is significant, every failure is self-defining. It is as though, with each "test" of his quality, the narcissist is meeting himself for the first time and asking the usual questions we use to get acquainted. What do you do for a living? How well have you fared, according to our society's standards of success? How much are you worth?

I have always believed that time is the narcissist's chief enemy. When we are young, investing in temporary relationships and career possibilities seems adventuresome and appropriate. But, often, there is a point when this lifestyle turns sour. I think of it as the point when traveling begins to feel like wandering. The dilettante reached that point and lost hope.

The loss of hope and its tragic consequences are movingly portrayed in Willa Cather's story "Paul's Case" (2002). Paul, the adolescent protagonist, has much in common with Siegmund and the dilettante, and some significant differences. Paul is a motherless teenager, living with his father in ordinary circumstances, obliged to go to school with peers he sees as vastly inferior to the glamorous lifestyle that animates his stolen hours. Whenever he can, he escapes into music or theater and the fairy-tale beauty of a wealthy life. Like Siegmund, he defines himself in contradistinction to commoners. The monotony of ordinary peoples' lives would be worse than living in jail. His neighbors are "sickening men, with combings of children's hair always hanging to their coats, and the smell of cooking in their clothes" (p. 236). Paul gets by on lies and frequent forays into privileged enclaves until his father and school authorities make that impossible, so he robs his employer and runs away for a brief fling with New York's upper crust. Of course, it is only a matter of time before the jig is up, his theft is discovered, and his father is searching for him. The thought of "sinking back forever into ugliness and commonness" (p. 226) is unbearable. Paul kills himself, stepping in front of a moving train, realizing too late that now he will surely miss out on a vast world of unexplored beauty.

Like Siegmund, Paul feels at home in finery and loathes the ordinary. Like the dilettante, he has no patience for the step-by-step process of gradual accomplishment. But unlike the dilettante who longs for a positive audience reaction, Paul's only desire is to be beauty's onlooker: "He was not in the least abashed or lonely. He had no special desire to meet or know any of these people; all he demanded was the right to look on and conjecture, to watch the pageant" (p. 237).

The complex relationship between insecurity and grandiosity is at the heart of Paul's case, as it was in the dilettante's. Paul has to assert that he is completely different from those around him. It is an absolute necessity, not just a matter of fact. Paul is as much a captive of this necessity as the dilettante is a prisoner of his need to escape his father's dull life. Despite his cocky bravado, Paul has always been tormented by dread: "There had always been the shadowed corner, the dark place into which he dared not look, but from which something seemed always to be watching him—and Paul had done things that were not pretty to watch, he knew" (p. 234). Unlike Siegmund, the dilettante, and Mrs. Slade, Paul is not really at home in the elevated circumstances he temporarily inhabits. He knows that the vile, dead, common world will eventually reclaim him, and, just as certainly, he knows he can't bear it.

Insecurity intertwined with grandiosity is evident in the story "Flowering Judas" (1964) by Katherine Anne Porter. Braggioni is a heavy-set, extravagantly dressed, vain Mexican revolutionary, who serenades a beautiful woman, Laura, nearly every night. Laura hates his miserable singing, but she, and everyone else, can say nothing about it. Braggioni is

> so vain of his talents, and so sensitive to slights, it would require a cruelty and vanity greater than his own to lay a finger on the vast cureless wound of his

self-esteem. It would require courage, too, for it is dangerous to offend him, and nobody has this courage. (p. 372)

Braggioni loves himself tenderly, unstintingly, and his followers "warm themselves in the reflected glow" (p. 372). Like many others, Laura owes her position and salary to him, but unfortunately for her, he is in love with her. Braggioni has an adoring wife, who waits patiently for him, but that has no impact on his courting of Laura. Laura has the tenuous task of resisting him without appearing to resist. Braggioni tries to convince Laura that they are really alike. Though Laura is much more modest, she and Braggioni do share sharp feelings of disappointment in their comrades and, in general, in life as they find it.

During the day, Laura teaches English to Indian children, goes on errands for the cause, and visits prisons, bringing food, cigarettes, and money. She questions her own motives for the work she does. She is very beautiful and pursued by many men, but her soul says "no" to all of them. Is she really as flawed, as incomplete as Braggioni?

Braggioni confesses to Laura how hurt he was in the past by a rejection. When he was 15, he tried to commit suicide because of a girl he loved, who laughed at him. He bitterly brags that "[a] thousand women have paid for that." He goes on, "One woman is really as good as another for me, in the dark. I prefer them all" (p. 381).

Braggioni seems to have no empathy for his wife, a hardworking union organizer. When she weeps, because she never knows who he is with, or when he plans to return home, he tells her: "Unless you can learn to cry when I am not here, I must go away for good" (p. 381). That day, he takes a room in a hotel. This lover of humanity is pretty harsh toward human beings!

Braggioni taunts Laura, forcing her to load his pistols. At last he goes home to his wife, and Laura loses herself in terrifying dreams of death.

Laura wonders whether or not her stoicism and devotion to the cause are a form of grandiosity, not unlike Braggioni's. While moral superiority can be a form of grandiosity, I think Laura shows an empathic responsiveness to those around her that makes her different from him. She loves the "tender round hands" of the children she teaches. She cares about the fate of the prisoners and tries to ease their boredom and fear. But it is true that she needs to be special and always finds extravagantly noble routes to distinguish herself.

In Jane Bowles' story "A Day in the Country" (1992), Senior Ramirez epitomizes the narcissist's lack of empathy, over-valuation of appearances, over-estimation of himself, and superficiality. He and his friend, Alfredo, arrange a picnic for themselves and two prostitutes, Julia and Inez. For Senior Ramirez, the "picnic" is really an opportunity to brag about his champagne, cavort with total abandon, and treat the women any way he likes. Inconveniently, Julia starts the day ill and has a severe accident due to Senior Ramirez's rash behavior. Thus, Julia is no longer any fun, which abruptly ends the picnic. She is dropped off and left alone to deal with her injuries however she can. Bowles gives us an acute analysis of where Senior Ramirez gets his zest: "Senior Ramirez's principal struggle in life was one of pride rather than of conscience; and because his successes were numerous each day, replenishing his energy and his taste for life, his strength was easily felt by those around him" (p. 6).

The need to trumpet that she is unusual, unique, and different from everyone around her is a driving force in Zoe, the protagonist in Lorrie Moore's story "You're Ugly, Too" (1999). Like so many of the characters considered in this chapter, Zoe is a subtle amalgam of grandiosity and insecurity. She teaches American History in a nondescript Midwestern college. Her eccentricities include skipping into class singing "Getting to Know You." She sees her students as complacent, sharing their parents' middle-class consumerism. Zoe never fails to find a way to distance herself from them. She feels different and incomparably superior. They have been purchased, but not Zoe. On a double date, when the other woman indulges herself in bragging about her feats of memory, Zoe remarks that she knew a dog that could do the same thing. Needless to say, there is no second date.

From childhood on, Zoe needed to emphasize her uniqueness. Even in the first grade, she refused to join a club, the Elf Girls, because she wouldn't wear the same dress as everyone else. But there are other times that Zoe doesn't feel she is better than everyone else. In fact, some days, she doesn't have any sense of who she is. She looks at herself in the mirror and sees a woman without any particularity. Seeing this unidentifiable image, Zoe wonders how her students and colleagues are able to recognize her.

As I have already noted, time is the enemy of the narcissist. When Zoe begins to show her age, she declares herself too old for fun. This happens just as her younger sister, Evan, announces that she is marrying her rich boyfriend. Noticing a hair growing on her chin, Zoe leaves a party, goes to the bathroom, and bloodies herself yanking out the hair. She can't stand what the hair seems to her to announce.

Zoe's despair highlights how depressed the narcissist eventually feels. Her "humor" revolves around the meaninglessness of what others take seriously. The punch line of her funny stories often involves a suicide. She can make fun of the pretensions of others, but she doesn't see how her own contempt and pride cut her off emotionally, rendering her life empty and devoid of purpose.

Entitlement is portrayed as even more sinister in Mary E. Wilkens Freeman's story "Luella Miller" (1988). With astonishing clarity, this tale illuminates the deadly effect on others of the title character's extreme self-centeredness. Lydia, now in her eighties, is reminiscing about Luella, who was a neighbor. In her youth, Luella was a willowy blonde beauty with extraordinary grace. She was hired as a teacher, although she lacked credentials and aptitude for that profession. But Luella was able to get others to do the work of teaching for her, along with her housework and everything else that needed doing. Unaccountably, people were willing to sacrifice their own welfare for hers. But, mysteriously, those who served Luella kept rapidly fading and dying, no matter how robust they were before they made her acquaintance. One after the other, her husband, sister-in-law, and various friends lost their lives caring for Luella's daily needs. Her comfort mattered most to those who served her, just as it evidently mattered above all else to Luella herself.

No one ever understands Luella's impact. It is as though she sucks all the air out of a room. Soon after her sister-in-law, Lily, comes to stay with Luella: "her rosy color faded and her pretty curves became wan hollows. White shadows began to show in the black rings of her hair, and the light died out of her eyes" (p. 128). And yet, Lily continues to serve Luella willingly and devotedly. Lydia, a neighbor and the story's narrator, loses all patience with Luella's unblinking sense that she has a right to be served. Without fully understanding it, Lydia knows that Luella is lethal, and angrily confronts her: "You kill everybody that is fool enough to care anythin' about you and do for you" (p. 133).

As often happens in the narcissist's personal life and treatment, some people find their entitlement unbearable and become enraged at them for it, while others are willing to subordinate themselves and prioritize the narcissist's needs over their own. This story makes concrete the death of the self of the narcissist's caretaker. In reality, the servant is more likely to languish, becoming more self-effacing and, ultimately, more depressed. The spirit dies, if not the body.

A deadly depression surrounds and, eventually, envelops the narcissist. Those around him (including his therapist) often become depleted, in one sense or another. And, eventually, the narcissist himself loses heart. Chapter 3 focused on those who initially present with self-esteem deficits. In this chapter, characters introduce themselves as grandiose, entitled, and above the crowd. In reality, these are two sides of the same coin. The grandiose have hidden self-esteem deficits, and the overly entitled are harboring the seeds of deflated depression. As in literature, when prospective patients present one of these aspects, it is only a matter of time before the other side surfaces.

Treatment

The philosopher Seneca once said we spend our whole lives preparing to die. Far from a morbid statement, I see this as expressing the truth that all human beings spend our whole lives overcoming our narcissistic self-involvement. We have to make a significant enough investment in the lives of others and in ongoing life so that the loss of our own, personal lives is bearable to us. How can we help our patients overcome their excessive narcissism? The analyst must be a person who is unusually aware of his or her *own* self-esteem issues. In moments that have the potential to shame one or both participants in a treatment session, we make choices that reflect what most matters to us. Should I make an interpretation that is likely to shame my patient if it is also likely to enlighten? Should I share a countertransference reaction that will probably bring me moments of shame? While (fortunately) there is no way to prescribe how to deal with these moments, I suggest that (especially when we know we are dealing with a grandiose patient) it can be very useful to keep track of *fluctuations* in our own self-regard. This focus alone may alert us to opportunities to work on the patient's self-esteem as well as our own.

Shame's role in the treatment of narcissism, and, more generally, in all human experience, has been the subject of many articles and books, particularly since Kohut's (1971) and Helen Block Lewis's (1971) groundbreaking contributions. For an excellent overview of the roles of shame and pride in the treatment of narcissism, I recommend the work of Lansky and Morrison (1997); more recently, Andrew P. Morrison (2008), Donna M. Orange (2008), and I (Buechler, 2008) compared our views on the role of the analyst's shame in treatment.

The shame-prone person can be extremely challenging to treat. Generally, I feel that a therapeutic stalemate can often result if the patient is preoccupied with how he looks while the analyst hopes for him to value the quality of his experiences in life more than his image. The patient may opt for no life at all, rather than embracing a life that is limited but possible. As I have already mentioned, aging can become a nightmare for someone with self-esteem issues. Losing his grip on the few gratifications he uses to distract himself, the spiritually bankrupt narcissist succumbs to depression. He has gone as far as his native professional talents can take him. He can't invest too much in relationships or find meaning in a political cause or religious faith. In the future, he sees the gradual loss of all that he has attained. Aging renders no spiritual benefits, deepening attachments, or significant investments in the next generation. Only professional catastrophe lies ahead, as he anticipates being eclipsed by younger colleagues. Often, his sense of purpose is limited to a desire to hold on to what he has for as long as he can.

As I see it, the narcissistic aspect of each of us is a principal obstacle to living fully. It motivates focusing on our standing in the world, rather than our experiencing life. Eventually, it becomes a source of conflict in treatment, since analysis inherently values *all* insight that is genuine, but narcissism opposes shame-inducing insights while accepting gratifying insights. Thus, while the analyst believes that a session is valuable if it contributes to the store of truths about the patient, for the narcissist the goal is to feel good about himself *now*. The truth may or may not accomplish this goal.

If treatment is ongoing, what frequently occurs is that both participants see more clearly how the patient's life is stalled. As was true for Mann's dilettante, the narcissistic patient has not been able to move forward in crystallizing a life because that would define him as imperfect. He may have collected the outward trappings of a life: a career, a partner, possessions, and so on. But in some deep recess, he does not believe this is his real life. While he may deeply regret missed opportunities and deeply envy others who are more successful, he does not really seem to believe that his life counts. It is as though this life is a kind of antechamber, a waiting room that will soon open onto his glorious, real life.

Patients who won't recognize what they have and have not done with their lives can't self-reflect much in treatment. This puts *analysts* in the painful position of failing at their job. They may lose track of its purpose and feel ashamed that that they are fraudulently posing as analysts, while really accomplishing little. In short, this work brings out the analyst's potential for narcissistic difficulties.

Of course, analysts, like everyone else, have individual reactions to the experience of failure. Some try to cover it up. In treatment, this might result in analyst and patient engaging in years of busywork, or becoming adept at distracting themselves, and each other, from the fact that the patient's life is going by. Some of us are angered by the feeling of failure and need to blame someone. It is easy to use the analytic literature and language to pin the blame on the patient. This may temporarily help the analyst avoid a shameful sense of inadequacy. But, over time, nothing can bring back lost opportunities, and eventually, both patient and analyst must face the patient's unlived life.

One way to describe the strain of treating narcissism is to refer back to one of the first to try: Echo, in the myth of Narcissus, in Ovid's (1955) *Metamorphosis*. You may recall that in this poetic story the beautiful boy, Narcissus, falls in love with his own image. This spells his doom, for he is then fated to be lost, gazing at his reflection in the water. Echo loves and wants to save Narcissus, but because she can only repeat her lover's words, she does not have the power to pull him away from gazing at himself. To me, this story illustrates what can happen as we try to save the narcissist from himself. If we fall in line with him too much, we lose our own center, which is the source of our strength.

I believe that in the treatment of narcissism, the analyst must do much more than merely echo. We sometimes have to struggle out loud with our conflicts about what to prioritize. It often seems to me, when analysts credit self-disclosure as having helped a patient, what helped was not the disclosure itself, but the values embodied in the act of choosing to disclose. The analyst is saying, in effect, "I am willing to give you information you could use to shame me. I am willing to do whatever it takes to reach you." The analyst is behaviorally expressing valuing the treatment more than her own pride and, more generally, life more than image. I view the treatment of empathic failures similarly. What I believe the patient often derives from this work has mainly to do with how the analyst relates to his own self-esteem. I see the value of work on empathic failures as deriving from their providing an opportunity for the analyst to fail, acknowledge the shortcoming, react without undue shame, guilt, or denial, and move on. Paradoxically, there is much narcissistic gratification to be gained from honest self-confrontation. That is, if we are willing to brave the narcissistic injuries inherent in seeing ourselves clearly we can develop self-respect for having integrity. It takes courage to face one's shortcomings. The analyst must help the patient learn to respect herself for facing herself.

One challenge for the narcissist's analyst is to communicate a strong sense of purpose. The treatment and, more generally, life itself is inherently important. Nothing in the culture's dismissive attitudes toward analysis, or in the neutrality and abstinence requirements of the traditional role, or in the postmodern turn away from singular truths, negates the need for the analyst to maintain a passionate, steadfast expression of therapeutic purpose.

Without inspiration from the analyst's sense of purpose, the grandiose patient will not feel sufficiently called upon to deal with the crucial issue of time. As already mentioned above, time is narcissism's enemy, since it pressures us to accept reality's limitations. But unless life has purpose, how does the passage of time matter? Unless it is important to have a life, what difference does it make if narcissists let their only chance at life go by? Without purpose, it doesn't matter if life is squandered in the hope that some day a truly impressive role will come along. The narcissist's analyst must capitalize on the pressure of time, but that can only happen if life has purpose.

In the treatment of narcissism, we encounter our deepest priorities as human beings. What really matters? When am I willing to look foolish, rather than miss a therapeutic opportunity? Each of us has to come to our own conclusion about what we will fight for. Somehow we must embrace the paradoxes essential to our role. We need the humility born of recognizing our limitations, but also passion born of fierce conviction. I must know that I can only see subjectively, yet I must believe in my vision with all my heart.

I have often imagined a first session with Mann's dilettante. He comes to treatment just as he is beginning to lose his grip. He wants to reinstate his old sense of superiority. I quickly begin to want him to examine how he is living his life, so he can challenge assumptions. He insists on feeling better about himself before he leaves my office. I worry that this first session will also be our last. Of course, there is no way to guarantee that it won't. But I think the treatment has a better chance if I am very aware of fluctuations in my own sense of self-esteem as the session progresses. That may alert me to moments when I am trying to *make* the dilettante face himself out of my own narcissistic needs. Do I feel I lose face (in my own eyes) if he doesn't face himself? Is that obscuring my clinical judgment, my empathy, and my capacity for kindness?

References

Bowles, J. (1992). A day in the country. In R. Ford (Ed.), *The Granta book of the American short story* (pp. 1–11). London: Granta Books.

Buechler, S. (2008). The legacies of shaming psychoanalytic candidates. *Contemporary Psychoanalysis*, *44*, 56–65.

Cather, W. (2002). Paul's case. In A. H. Bond (Ed.), *Tales of psychology: Short stories to make you wise* (pp. 220–244). St. Paul: Paragon House.

Freeman, M. E. W. (1988). Luella Miller. In P. S. Prescott (Ed.), *The Norton book of American short stories* (pp. 125–136). New York: W. W. Norton & Company.

Kohut, H. (1971). *The analysis of the self*. New York: International Universities Press.

Kohut, H. (1984). *How does analysis cure?* Chicago, IL: University of Chicago Press.

Lansky, M., & Morrison, A. (Eds.) (1997). *The widening scope of shame*. Hillsdale, NJ: Analytic Press.

Lewis, H. B. (1971). *Shame and guilt in neurosis*. New York: International Universities Press.

Mann, T. (1997). The blood of the Walsungs. In *Little Herr Friedemann and other stories* (pp. 159–186). London: Minerva.

Mann, T. (1997). The dilettante. In *Little Herr Friedemann and other stories* (pp. 36–62). London: Minerva.
Mitchell, S. A., & Black, M. J. (1995). *Freud and beyond: A history of modern psychoanalytic thought*. New York: Basic Books.
Moore, L. (1999). You're ugly, too. In J. Updike & K. Kenison (Eds.), *The best American short stories of the century* (pp. 652–670). New York: Houghton Mifflin Company.
Morrison, A. (2008). The analyst's shame. *Contemporary Psychoanalysis*, 44, 65–83.
Orange, D. M. (2008). Whose shame is it anyway? Lifeworlds of humiliation and systems of restoration. *Contemporary Psychoanalysis*, 44, 83–101.
Ovid (Publius Ovidius Naso). (1955). *Metamorphosis* (M. M. Innes, Trans.). New York: Penguin Books.
Porter, K. A. (1964). Flowering Judas. In R. P. Warren & A. Erskine (Eds.), *Short story masterpieces* (pp. 371–385). New York: Dell.
Wharton, E. (1994). Roman fever. In A. W. Lidz (Ed.), *Major American short stories* (pp. 377–389). New York: Oxford University Press.

Chapter 5

Hysterical Bargaining

I wonder whether Seymour Freedgood, the author of the story "Grandma and the Hindu Monk" (1965), ever studied Freud. His story so beautifully illustrates hysterical conversions when the body speaks for the psyche.

Grandma, the titular head of a Jewish family, comes to stay at their summer house on an island off Long Island. The house is overrun with college students, teenagers, and assorted family friends. Grandma, whose sight and memory are failing, is immersed in the Old Testament. She believes in strict adherence to the rules of the faith as she understands them. By her standards, even Hasidim fall short, since they don't seem to value Moses' laws as much as they love singing and dancing in praise of God. Her mind dwells in the period when the Jews had to flee Egypt and beware of strangers who might want to steal from them or do them harm. Seymour, her eldest grandson, has learned how to assuage her worries. He answers her ritual questions (what time is it? where is Seymour?) with well-practiced, soothing replies.

All is well until Seymour invites a Hindu monk he met at college to stay at the family's home for the summer. He knows that his siblings and parents will have no trouble with this visitor's presence, but he is apprehensive about Grandma. His fears turn out to be justified. Seymour tries to prepare her, referring to the monk as a "Hindu rabbi." This reassures her, but only temporarily. Seymour tries to understand his grandmother's anxiety in the context of her worldview. Grandma interprets every current event according to archetypes from the Old Testament. Her eyes search for danger, which she anticipates from any stranger. She needs frequent reassurances that the family "caravan" is secure. When Grandma comes upon the monk praying in a fervent, passionate way and seemingly actually hovering over his bed, she is terrified and faints. She soon lapses into a virtual coma, delirious and unable to move her legs. Their doctor, clearly anxious that Grandma will be permanently bedridden, mumbles that it is all in her mind. Interpreting that Grandma doesn't *want* to be able to get up, the doctor suggests that they call in a psychiatrist. But the monk, in consultation with a pious friend of the family, has another approach. The monk is going to go into Grandma's room and try to penetrate her consciousness. The doctor is violently opposed to this idea, but the monk gets his way. The monk declares that he can show Grandma the virtues of enthusiasm and song, rather than doctrine and ritual. He then suggests that helping Grandma is a matter of convincing her that she has done nothing blasphemous by allowing a mystic into her home. Grandma needs to understand that salvation can come from within, from the heart and via emotional engagement, rather than interpretation of written rules. How will this help Grandma? The monk explains that she will stop fighting herself and come to realize that her own negative thoughts and feelings are keeping her paralyzed. As she accepts this, she will find she is able to move again, and even dance if she wants to. And, indeed, it works. The monk plays inspired music, which seems to incorporate nature itself in its purity, freshness, and celebration. Seymour's brother urges Grandma to stand, and she does, finally welcoming the monk into their home.

This story echoes an early theory about conversion hysteria. Freud (1895) advanced the idea that the symptoms result from conflicts between our unacceptable wishes and our superego. An event occurs that brings this conflict to a head. We are unable (Breuer, 1895) or unwilling (Freud, 1895) to remember the event, so our feelings about it split off from our memory of it. This forces us to "convert" the memory into a physical symptom. Treatment requires us to peel time back, recollect the memory, and reconnect it with the feelings that belong to it.

The monk in Freedgood's story intuitively understands Grandma's conflict between her need for emotional expression and the strict religious doctrines by which she lives. The traumatic event (seeing a Hindu monk in her home) brings this conflict to the point of a crisis. We can suppose that the only way Grandma can preserve her beliefs is to paralyze herself in order to avoid temptation. If she can't move, she certainly can't dance or even know she might long for it. The monk forces her to confront her wishes by, in effect, making them irresistible. She hears the joy and the piety in his music. It is as though she looks into his soul and her own and realizes that he loves God as well as she does. Welcoming the monk into her home, she also welcomes passion into her heart.

Post-Freudian analysts formulated another theory, which centered on the person's style of relating with others. Basically, the idea, put forth by Lionells (1995) among others, is that "this pattern of relinquishing personal power and abilities in the interest of preserving some particular pattern in relationships is the essential paradigm for understanding hysterical pathology from an Interpersonal perspective" (p. 492). The person (usually a woman) agrees to the "hysterical bargain." She barters away her chances to develop herself fully as a person in exchange for being taken care of. After some period of time, since she has not fully developed her abilities, she feels as though she can't get her needs met on her own, so, even though the relationship may have lost its allure, she feels stuck living within her part of the bargain. Hysterics may appear to others to be willful, but actually, they have subjugated their will to the other person (most often a man) and then have to try to maneuver him into getting them what they need. I think of Lucille Ball on the old television show *I Love Lucy*. She knew what she wanted but didn't feel she could achieve it on her own, so she had to create absurd schemes to get her husband to supply whatever she needed. I think that part of the show's comic appeal was that the audience knew that underneath her scatterbrained persona, she was a very smart woman. The actress was able to indicate that, all the while playing the role of the ditzy flake. It was as though Lucy and the audience winked at each other and laughed at Ricky, who didn't seem to be in on the joke.

A tragic, rather than comic, picture of the hysterical bargain was captured by Cynthia Marshall Rich, in her chilling story "My Sister's Marriage" (1966). This tale is told from the point of view of Sarah Ann. As the story unfolds, we learn that Sarah Ann and her older sister, Olive, were extremely close as children. When their mother died, they shared the work of taking care of their father, a doctor. From her first words, Sarah Ann tries to influence the reader to see the events from her point of view and not from Olive's, though she doubts she will be persuasive enough to accomplish this.

When Olive meets a young man and begins to fall in love, she feels she has to hide her romance from her father but confides in her sister. While Sarah Ann does her best to portray their father's responses as loving, the reader gradually understands that this father wants to have total control over his daughters, never to share them with anyone. His "love" is really a form of possession. Sarah Ann willingly embraces the bargain he presents. She will give up having any separate interests to be taken care of by her father for the rest of her life. She makes it clear that, while she misses her sister when Olive leaves home to marry, she is happy to have her father all to herself. She is very much her father's daughter in several senses. She has learned from a master how to be ruthlessly manipulative and possessive.

Another terrible outcome of the hysterical bargain was portrayed by Charlotte Perkins Gilman in her story "The Yellow Wallpaper" (1994). I have already discussed this story in chapter 2 on paranoia, but I include it here as well, because I think initially the main character enters into an hysterical bargain, only to deteriorate later into a frankly paranoid psychotic state. With unmistakable irony, Gilman paints the picture of a doctor's wife who can't get well, because her "treatment" keeps her from doing anything meaningful. Consciously, she seems to buy her husband's appraisal of her problems. Her anger at her situation is "unreasonable." Her "fancies" are her problems. She needs to see herself as he sees her in order to maintain their equilibrium. She can't allow herself to understand the price she is paying. But her hungers won't be quieted. She wants to write and talk to stimulating people. But her physician husband, John, and her physician brother convince her that her constitution is too delicate for these activities. They tell her that she needs rest and must stay in a large room, which used to be a playroom, papered with hideous yellow, peeling wallpaper. She hates the room and especially the wallpaper. But John insists that it is where he can keep an eye on her, and her objections are unreasonable. She tells herself that John is taking such good care of her, directing her every movement. By contrast, she reasons, she fails in so many of her duties as his partner. So, at least, she ought to be obedient. John tells her that she can will away her fancies, check her irrational feelings, and be happy. But sometimes she can't tame her fantasies and bouts of anger. Secretly, she still writes and hides the evidence. She admits to herself that it tires her but wonders whether what tires her most is that she has to keep it a secret.

The wife (who is not given a name!) tells John that she is failing in this room and begs to go away. John tells her she *is* better but doesn't know it. When she protests, John tells her she can be as sick as she wants, implying that her problems result from her willfulness. She settles for getting John to promise that he won't go away.

Gradually, she sees the wallpaper becoming bars with a woman trapped inside. Step by step, she becomes more frightened of John and more certain that the wallpaper aims to kill her. She is determined to uncover the plot. She decides that part of the wallpaper's poisonous power is in its smell. Then she "discovers" the paper moving. She sees the "woman" behind its bars trying to escape: "But nobody could climb through that pattern—it strangles so. I think that is why it has so many heads" (p. 297). Soon she sees the woman creeping around during the day, and she begins to creep around, too. "The woman" trying to escape and the wife merge in the wife's mind. By this point she is clearly paranoid, although it is also clear that she has moments of stunning insight. About John, she says that he asks all kinds of questions, pretending to be loving and kind, but now she can see through him.

At last, they are leaving the house, but the wife is determined to free "the woman" before they leave by pulling down the wallpaper. Frantically, she tears at the paper. She locks the door so John can't get in and throws the key away. When he finds it and enters the room, she is crawling around. Gleefully, she tells John that she has gotten out of the paper and he can't put her back. John faints, and she has to creep around him, as (at last) she explores the area near the wall without any fear of the wallpaper.

The power of this story is magnified by a footnote. At one point in the story, John threatens to send his wife to Dr. S. Weir Mitchell. In reality, Dr. Mitchell (1829–1914) was a Philadelphia neurologist, who specialized in rest cures for female "hysterics" (he wrote a book on the subject). In reality, the author of the short story, Charlotte Perkins Gilman, was treated by Dr. Mitchell, who forbade her from engaging in all activities, including writing. Gilman found him to be a hostile presence, according to this footnote. So we can assume that this story is autobiographical, at least to some extent. Certainly, this is a sad commentary on an era in which many women felt they had to choose between full self-development and personal security. This story illustrates how one state of mind can give way to another, much more dysfunctional process (for further discussion of the main character's increasingly paranoid thinking, see chapter 2).

Fiction is replete with women who have made hysterical bargains. Take, for example, Elisa Allen, the wife of a ranch owner and the protagonist in John Steinbeck's story, "The Chrysanthemums" (1952). Elisa is 35 and brims with energy. Her husband, Henry, makes a big sale and offers to take her into town for dinner and a movie. Off he goes to finish his chores. Soon, there appears a wagon advertising the owner's ability to sharpen all kinds of tools. Stopping for directions, he tells Elisa about his nomadic life. They talk about her flower bed, and he asks her for some seeds, not for himself but (ostensibly) for a lady down the road. Elisa grows excited as she prepares a pot and soil for the seeds. She tries to describe the joy she feels planting. Her fingers are one with the plant and know what to do to make it grow. This reminds the man of some nights in his wagon, looking up at the stars. Elisa's voice grows husky as she admits to the similarity of their common experiences. She goes on to describe ecstatic moments when, looking at the stars, she rises up and feels their keen and far-reaching connection to her. After this intimate moment, Elisa seems to recollect who and where she is and is ashamed of herself. But she gives the man some work to do and continues to talk to him. When she tells him he has a nice life, he says it is no life for a woman. She replies belligerently that he doesn't know what she is capable of. When he drives off, she feels the need to scrub herself thoroughly in the bathroom. She dresses up and waits for Henry. He compliments her, telling her that she looks nice, strong, and happy, and, for once, she challenges him. Does he really know just how strong she is? But then, on the road, she spots the chrysanthemums and knows that the man in the wagon carelessly threw them there, having lied to her about taking them to a lady down the road, just for the pot and some work to do. Deliberately turning away from her feelings, she asks Henry if she can have wine with dinner and toys with agreeing to go to a prize fight. Maybe they could both go, even though she is a woman. But the brave moment passes, and she tells him that she wouldn't want to go to a fight. Turning away from him and raising her coat collar to hide her tears, she accepts that having the wine will be enough.

Elisa is hungry for vibrant life, but her role allows her scant expression of these feelings. She can grow beautiful flowers, and she can look up at the stars, but sharp sexual and aggressive urges are not allowed. For a few moments, she tries on a different life, tangy and free. But she is met with the message that she is out of her league. She may boast of her strength, but men are really in control. They can play with her. She had better know her place and be satisfied with the treats she is offered. When her defiant spirit dies, she can't even dare to show her tears.

In her story "The Other Two" (1952), Edith Wharton spells out one woman's bargain with great subtlety and psychological acumen. The "deal" between the husband and wife is the protagonist in this story, in my view. Waythorn (whose first name is never mentioned) is newly married to Alice, who has been married twice before. While Waythorn is aware of Alice's first marriage to the relatively lower-class Haskett, with whom she had a daughter, as well as her second marriage to the erratic Varick, these facts attain deeper meaning as the story progresses. From before their marriage took place, Waythorn and Alice have forged a bargain that is never expressed in words, but rather, in discreet gestures, sentences left unfinished, and the other small details that make them supremely comfortable with each other. Waythorn values Alice as a tonic to his staid, blunted emotionality: "His own life had been a gray one, from temperament rather than circumstance, and he had been drawn to her by the unperturbed gaiety which kept her fresh and elastic at an age when most women's activities are growing either slack or febrile" (p. 202). For her part, as we come to understand, Waythorn provides Alice with the social standing and security she has longed for all her life. It would be accurate (if uncharitable and unromantic) to say that, in Alice, Waythorn has bought an endless supply of Prozac, and, with each marriage, Alice has traded up, financially and socially. But what price has each paid, and what happens if the terms of their transaction become unmistakably clear?

A series of circumstances brings this to pass. By the time the story starts, Waythorn has already recognized the worth of his purchase, but now he is being forced to see its full price. "How light and slender she was, and how each gesture flowed into the next! Waythorn felt himself yielding again to the joy of possessing. They were his, those white hands with their flitting motions, his the light haze of hair, the lips and eyes" (pp. 208–209). As Waythorn gets to know his wife's two previous husbands, he realizes that no one has ever possessed Alice, including Alice herself: "Her pliancy was beginning to sicken him. Had she really no will of her own—no theory about her relation to these men?" (p. 217). Waythorn further reflects that Alice

> was "as easy as an old shoe"—a shoe that too many feet had worn. Her elasticity was the result of tension in too many different directions. Alice Hasket—Alice Varick—Alice Waythorn—she had been each in turn, and had left hanging to each name a little of her privacy, a little of her personality, a little of the inmost self where the unknown god abides. (pp. 217–218)

At first, Waythorn can't bear to be clear about the terms of their relationship but, gradually, he embraces it again: "If he paid for each day's comfort with the small change of his illusions, he grew daily to value the comfort more and set less store upon the coin" (p. 218). After all, he benefits enormously from Alice's artifice. Waythorn comes to believe that, after all, it is a good bargain for him. Even if he doesn't truly own Alice, he has a woman who knows how to make a man happy. How does she do this? It is, Waythorn decides, an art "made up, like all others, of concessions, eliminations, and embellishments; of lights judiciously thrown and shadows skillfully softened. His wife knew exactly how to manage the lights" (p. 219).

I see Waythorn as having decided that Alice is a performance artist, playing the role of Mrs. Waythorn with consummate skill. The fact that she has bartered away any real sense of herself doesn't matter. What counts is her effect on him. Neither Alice nor Waythorn cares, ultimately, that Alice is so busy adapting herself to each man that she loses track of any abiding integrity. At one point in the story, Alice has no trouble lying to save (Waythorn's and her own) face. Waythorn isn't any more troubled by this than that she made a mistake in how she read his feelings about her first husband. For both Alice and Waythorn, Alice's value lies in her ability to read and smooth out the lines on a man's face. Alice is a success at her art because she has no self, so she can be whoever her current husband needs her to be. In M. Masud Khan's (1975) thinking, the hysteric's sense of self is blank or absent. Marylou Lionells (1995), an analyst who has written extensively about hysterical bargains, explains that "hysterics assume there is an unacknowledged bargain in which the authority permits covert gratification of fantasies as long as they remain admiring and appreciative" (p. 509).

Of course, the cultural context affects the roles people tend to play in relationships of all kinds. The "heyday" of the hysterical bargain may have passed. But unarticulated promises still operate as the ties that bind, in some couples more than others. Perhaps nowhere else are culture and character so inextricably intertwined. Some cultures and eras make certain bargains more common. Our parental role models and the messages we get from the media, among other influences, affect how we feel about a person forfeiting full self-development so as to be taken care of. But, at least to some extent, the readiness to make this exchange reflects a particular style of relating interpersonally and, more generally, of bearing the helplessness of the human condition.

The old-fashioned, gendered version of the bargain is portrayed in a unique way in a story by Dorothy Parker, entitled "A Telephone Call" (1956). The editors call this story an "interior monologue." In it, a woman begs God for her boyfriend to call her on the telephone. Apparently, she has not been "good," meaning she has not been pleasing to him. She has expressed sadness, which won't do. She promises God that, if only her boyfriend would call, she will once again be the sweet person she was when they first met, the person he grew to love. Explaining the situation to God, she describes how women have to behave in order to keep men interested. The woman can't ever imply that the man made her sad. Then the man would see her as possessive and leave her. She concludes that they will always have to be cautiously nice but not quite honest and open with each other in order for things to work out. In the last pages, she becomes more and more pathetically desperate. She would promise anything, if only her boyfriend would call. But she seems to know that she has overstepped her limits and broken their bargain, and she will never be forgiven for that.

In "Labor Day Dinner" (1991), Alice Munro gives us a portrait of a more contemporaneous couple. Some aspects of the old bargain are retained. Roberta, at 43, feels she owes her partner, George, an apology for letting her body grow older. At the same time, she is furious about feeling that way. Her eyes tell the story succinctly, as she weeps "in spurts" and wears dark glasses to cover up her pain. George's judgments are unrelenting. Although Roberta works hard to keep the house clean, cook, put up preserves, and care for her teenage daughters, George sees her as having no intention to do "serious work" (for money). From his point of view, Roberta has a persistent wish to be admired and courted, which is something he despises. Roberta knows that George's attitude is damaging her but condemns her own responses as "hysterical," using the word to reject her own "unjustified" affective intensity. Munro captures the hysteric's choked-off rage, claustrophobia, and profound sense of having betrayed herself to preserve a relationship. Before meeting George, Roberta illustrated books, but now she hasn't got the time or the psychic space to do this kind of work. Her sacrifice seems to lower her further in George's eyes. And now her body, her one potentially admirable asset, is aging and losing its appeal. Roberta reflects on her current state, using the term "hysterical" derisively to mean overly emotional. In the "murderous" silence between them, Roberta feels herself curling up like a jaundiced leaf. But then she criticizes the image as "hysterical" and exaggerated:

> Also hysterical is the notion of screaming and opening the door and throwing herself on the gravel. She ought to make an effort not to be hysterical, not to exaggerate. But surely it is hatred—what else can it be?—that George is steadily manufacturing and wordlessly pouring out at her, and surely it is a deadly gas. (p. 136)

When Roberta dresses to go out, George criticizes her outfit, telling her that her armpits are flabby and she shouldn't reveal them. She blames herself, since she ought to have foreseen that George, six years her junior, would develop disgust for her body. She takes his hatred as just punishment. But for what? "For vanity. Hardly even for that. Just for having those pleasing surfaces once, and letting them speak for you; just for allowing an arrangement of hair and shoulders and breasts to have its effect" (p. 137). Maybe her crime is having laid herself open to humiliation, by not realizing in time that her body has lost its allure.

Roberta's 17-year-old daughter, Angela, watches her mother become someone who doesn't ask for anything. Angela writes in her journal that she has seen her mother change "from a person I deeply respected into a person on the verge of being a nervous wreck. If this is love I want no part of it. He wants to enslave her and us all and she walks a tightrope trying to keep him from getting mad" (p. 147).

But then, things turn around in a way that I think earlier writers would not have conceived. Roberta rescues herself by realizing that her life with George has its pleasures and pains, and she could genuinely bear being with him or being without him. At the end of the story, George and Roberta come perilously close to dying in a car accident. At first, all they can feel is the strangeness of the moment. Life is so precarious. A few inches one way or the other can make the difference between living and dying. A moment can erase everything. We fight internally and with others, insisting that we matter, demanding to be taken seriously, and yearning to be loved. We defend ourselves from feeling our utter dependence with our contempt, indifference, and pride. While we are alive, we clamor for justice, no matter how rarely we have encountered it. We each make our bargains, hysterical or otherwise, trying to find a way to bear the human condition. And then, in a flash, it is all over, and the score becomes official, however fairly or unfairly we have been treated.

Treatment

> [H]ysterics may be said to be the greatest liars to no purpose in the whole range of human personalities . . .
>
> Sullivan (1956, p. 209)

> In fact, if we give it (hysteria) its rightful identification as the sworn enemy of our capacity to be fully human, we may give ourselves a crucial advantage in the struggle we must constantly engage in to transcend it.
>
> Farber (1966, p. 117)

Despite the significant role hysteria plays in the history of psychoanalysis, some analysts sound contemptuous and disrespectful when they write about these patients. Having co-taught a course on hysteria (with Marylou Lionells) for a number of years, I have thought a great deal about why this is so. I think it is important to focus on this question, because clinicians may not be fully aware of these attitudes, but they can play a significant role in their work. Here, I mention a few of my own ideas about why patients who relate in this style have sometimes evoked such intense, negative reactions.

- The sheer intensity of some of the hysteric's emotional expressions can elicit anxiety in the clinician. We may then resent, blame, and verbally label hysterics for what they "make us" feel.
- We get confused about what is and what is not willed by the patient. To what degree is hysterical emotionality a carefully orchestrated performance, aimed to have a specific interpersonal effect? Some clinicians feel differently about patients if they seem to be "getting away with" being manipulative.
- The hysteric doesn't allow the clinician to stay in familiar (verbal) territory, since much of the patient's communication is via the body. If we are not comfortable in this sensual/sexual/physical nonverbal territory we may label the hysteric vulgar or superficial.
- The way the patient relates to autonomy and power may not garner our respect. Some patients try to play out the usual "hysterical bargain" (see above) *with us*. It is as though the patient asks, "If I seem to give up all power, and cede it to you, will you take care of me?" Clinicians can have difficulty remaining empathic with someone willing to barter away so much.
- At first the patient may appear to be particularly well-suited to participate in an analytically oriented treatment. That initial impression of dedication to the work, eagerness to please, and access to feelings can make it hard to bear what often follows. The patient, who seemed so impressionable, turns out to be fairly impenetrable. A battle of wills awaits us. Their attitude of extreme "compliance" (part of the hysterical bargain) is exactly what the patient noncompliantly refuses to surrender.
- The sheer contradiction in the patient's self-presentation can be baffling. Here is a person highly in touch with emotions yet not necessarily self-aware. He or she seems to cede power in a bargain to be taken care of yet is powerfully willful.
- The patient's dependency can evoke our anxiety and/or contempt. Often, the patient wants treatment as a supplement to their interpersonal life, rather than as a bridge to making that life more satisfying. Thus, from the start, clinician and patient may have different goals.

- The deals the patient tries to establish are hard to make explicit. This can put us in an uncomfortable position, feeling coerced but unable to be clear enough about it to express it in words.
- The literalness and concreteness of some of the patient's conversion reactions pose a treatment challenge. A disgusted patient who presents symptoms of nausea may be unaware of the connection or, perhaps, unaware of the existence of disgust. This can evoke a complicated response in the clinician. First of all, the symptom is so real, so raw, that it can feel as though the patient is forcing us to have an unpleasant sensation. But at the same time, we may feel alone with our sense of what the experience means. Some patients are adamant that we understand their physical discomfort as a purely medical issue. Any psychological interpretations of its meaning can be met with angry resistance. We can be accused of insensitivity and a lack of sympathy for their suffering.

I am suggesting that, partially as a result of these issues, patients who present with hysteria can evoke a punitive response in clinicians. Feeling forced, manipulated, anxious, seduced, and teased, we can harshly judge them (as Sullivan and Farber did, along with many others). Some of us react by withdrawing or withholding the affective responses the patient yearns for. When the patient begs for warmth, we are unusually cold. We condemn them for their "neediness" and give less than usual. We are too willing to bypass careful inquiry into what the patient is feeling. We punish patients for our own discomfort with them by losing our best analytic selves. We are at our worst partly, I suspect, out of revenge. It is as though we are so disappointed in the patient that we act as though they don't deserve our best. At times, we become caricatures of the withholding analyst.

It is a tremendous challenge to respond effectively to this material. I think we need to be especially aware of every interpersonal compromise, every "deal," every bargain, as soon as we can sense it is in the air. We have to refuse to make deals silently, insisting on voicing them, examining them together, and reflecting on their meaning. Sometimes we have to be willing to "set off" intense emotions in the patient. For example, a woman gets extremely angry and tearful if I point out the part she played in a conflict with her husband. She may not be intentionally discouraging me from bringing up this topic, but I may *feel* manipulated. It is as though she were offering me a bargain: Don't bring up painful topics, and the session can be pleasant and calm. For me, this can be a "lose/lose" situation. If I bring up her part in the bargain, I am in for a stormy and problematic session. But if I don't, I am likely to feel like I let both of us down. I view maintaining my own sense of integrity as a crucial ingredient in this work.

But it is equally important to remain aware of pulls in ourselves to force something on the patient. I also think we need to pay special attention to our own bodies. Are *we* converting psychological tensions into physical symptoms? If so, why now?

I think it vital to keep in close touch with what I am feeling and, most especially, any impulse in me to "rid" myself of my more intense emotions. Is something making this feel necessary to me? Why?

Generally, I am in favor of voicing what Bollas (1987) calls the "unthought known." That is, I feel and think out loud even before I have fully understood the experience. This seems especially important in working with patients presenting with hysterical relatedness. This may be the only way to gain access to much that is going on between us.

The Hindu monk in Seymour Freedgood's story ("Grandma and the Hindu Monk"), discussed in the first pages of this chapter, seems to have had a profound understanding of how to deal with hysteria. Previously, I conjectured about the causes of Grandma's conversion symptoms. Here, I focus on the monk's "therapeutic" stance. As recounted above, in this story, Seymour, the grandson, invites a Hindu monk to the family's summer home. Grandma's mind seems to be ensconced in a vague period of history, somewhere between Exodus and her own early childhood. Seymour is aware that the appearance of a Hindu monk may evoke a troubled and troubling reaction from his grandmother. But he doesn't expect that she will faint, lapse into a coma, and be unable to use her legs. The doctor orders that everyone, and most especially the Hindu, must stay away from Grandma. He suggests that Grandma's swollen legs are refusing to heal and that Grandma might benefit from talking to a psychiatrist. But, ignoring the family's protest, the monk insists on talking to Grandma privately, claiming that joy and celebration are more important to belief than strict adherence to doctrine. It is this message that he believes will cure the terrified old woman. He reaches Grandma by understanding her conflict between her lively bodily wishes and her extreme piety. She is healed by being able to integrate the intense feeling in her body with her heart's devotion to God. It is very meaningful to me that the monk really practices what he preaches. His *actions* are as passionate as his words. He simply won't be dissuaded from trying to reach Grandma through his fervent beliefs. Family members try to stop him from entering her room, and the doctor forbids it, but he charges ahead. And when he finally reaches Grandma's bedside, what does he do? He dances, joyfully playing his cymbals and drums, and he prays. Grandma, radiant and now standing up, welcomes the Hindu into her home and heart.

What heals Grandma? Is it the idea that passionate movement and pious devotion can co-exist? That seems to me to be what the author thinks. But I suggest that, while that is part of what cures Grandma, it wouldn't have been as effective if the monk's actions weren't consonant with his message. The monk doesn't just advocate for song, he *sings*. He doesn't just talk about prayer, he prays. He embodies his message. He lives it out loud. This is the great challenge of clinical work. How can we live our messages palpably enough to heal ourselves and others? It isn't enough to help the patient gain insight into his or her proclivity toward making hysterical bargains. Regretting the freedom they have bartered away in search of care and security won't cure anyone by itself. These insights are important and are usually necessary to the treatment process. But, much of the time, I (along with many other analysts) would say they are necessary but not sufficient.

Particularly in the work with someone presenting with hysteria, the clinician has to relate in a way that makes bargains conscious to both participants. Whatever "deals" are being struck, eventually they must be acknowledged. I am not saying that we can avoid making deals or even that we should try. But, for example, when my patient (unconsciously) offers me an easy session if I avoid certain topics, I need to be capable of knowing it. That means to me that even if I accede to her wishes, my acquiescence can't be so automatic that I don't know that I am agreeing with something. The monk in this story really believes that dance is a form of prayer, no less sacred than any other. Similarly, we have to believe that it is possible to have a secure relationship without giving up one's autonomy. We have to believe that hysterical bargains truncate life *unnecessarily*. We have to have faith in something richer, something more alive.

References

Bollas, C. (1987). *The shadow of the object*. New York: Columbia University Press.
Farber, L. (1966). *The ways of the will*. New York: Basic Books.
Freedgood, S. (1965). In M. Crane (Ed.), *Fifty great American short stories* (pp. 596–621). New York: Bantam Dell.
Freud, S., & J. Breuer (1895). *Studies on hysteria*. In J. Strachey (Ed. & Trans.), *The standard edition of the complete psychological works of Sigmund Freud* (Vol. 23, pp. 139–207). London: Hogarth Press.
Gilman, C. P.(1994). The yellow wallpaper. In A. W. Lidz (Ed.), *Major American short stories* (pp. 286–300). New York: Oxford University Press.
Khan, M. R. (1975). Grudge and the hysteric. *International Journal of Psychotherapy*, 4, 349–357.
Lionells, M. (1995). Hysteria. In M. Lionells, J. Fiscalini, C. H. Mann, & D. B, Stern (Eds.), *Handbook of interpersonal psychoanalysis* (pp. 491–515). Hillsdale, NJ: Analytic Press.
Munro, A. (1991). Labor Day dinner. In *The moons of Jupiter* (pp. 134–159). New York: Vintage.
Parker, D. (1966). A telephone call. In J. Moffett & K. R. McElheny (Eds.), *Points of view: An anthology of short stories* (pp. 13–20). New York: New American Library.
Rich, C. M. (1966). My sister's marriage. In J. Moffett & K. R. McElheny (Eds.), *Points of view: An anthology of short stories* (pp. 200–213). New York: New American Library.
Steinbeck, J. (1952). The chrysanthemums. In M. Crane (Ed.), *Fifty great short stories* (pp. 337–347). New York: Bantam Dell.
Sullivan, H. S. (1956). *Clinical studies in psychiatry*. New York: W. W. Norton
Wharton, E. (1952). The other two. In M. Crane (Ed.). *Fifty great short stories* (pp. 201–221). New York: Bantam Dell.

Chapter 6

Obsessive Controlling

The battle lines are drawn quickly in Flannery O'Connor's short story "Everything That Rises Must Converge" (2002). We are introduced to Julian as he escorts his mother to her weight reduction class at the Y. Julian is the resentful, unemployed son of a self-righteous, bigoted, absurdly vain woman. Given all she has done and, presumably, will have to continue to do for this ill-equipped, nasty progeny, mother feels that taking her to class once a week is the least he can do. And that seems to be the only point on which they agree.

From the first, Julian sees this outing as a series of obstacles to the devoutly desired outcome of getting away from his mother at the end of the journey. At first, he tries to check his temper as she natters away. Mother's conversation tends to veer toward racial slurs against blacks, who, in her view, don't belong in the same universe with fine ladies like herself. Julian is outraged and humiliated by her public display of prejudice on the bus. As she enters, scanning the bus for blacks and finding none, she announces, "I see we have the bus to ourselves" (p. 543). From that point on, there is all-out war between Julian and his mother. She will take any opportunity to "bond" with "her kind" and make it clear that she is above the lower classes and people of color; he will take advantage of any chance to mock her pretensions. When a black man sits down, Julian leaves his mother's side to sit next to him: "Having got the advantage, he wanted desperately to keep it and carry it through. He would have liked to teach her a lesson that would last a while, but there seemed no way to continue the point" (p. 546). Julian wants to drive his point into her like a stake through her heart.

For a few moments, Julian retreats into fantasies of "the ultimate horror": bringing a black woman home to meet Mother. At last, the winning move. There would be nothing she could do. But real life gives him a more immediate win. A black woman enters the bus wearing the same hat as Mother. Julian grins, thinking, "Your punishment exactly fits your pettiness. This should teach you a permanent lesson" (p. 549).

That is Julian's fervent desire: to teach his mother a permanent lesson. To penetrate her pretentious façade. To get through to her. Eventually, he gets his wish in a way he could not have predicted. His mother tries to give a black child a penny, but the child's mother throws it back in her face and takes a swing at her. Mother collapses on the sidewalk. Driving the point home, Julian declares, with triumphant satisfaction, "You got exactly what you deserved." Julian draws out the lesson: "That was the whole colored race which will no longer take your condescending pennies . . . You aren't who you think you are" (p. 552). Mother silently changes course, taking the street toward home instead of the one that heads toward the Y. Suddenly, she falls to the pavement. Julian tries to get help, but there is no answer to his cries. In the saddest possible way, Julian has won the battle and lost the war. He certainly has penetrated her, and she is permanently changed.

Julian and his mother have each put making their point ahead of everything else. Each absolutely must convince the other. They batter each other with their "points." Neither really understands how much is at stake in their fierce fight. Julian knows he is enraged and utterly determined to win. What he doesn't know is that he is willing and able to kill her. What she doesn't know is that if she loses their war, she will lose her whole life. Like all obsessive battles, the hate is in the ferocity of it. It is a passion that goes way beyond the content. It is pure, absolute willfulness; the utter, ruthless determination to drive a point home at all costs.

Obsessive rigidity can be funny at times. We tend to laugh at the tyrant who insists on our following his rituals to the letter because we know he is in the grip of those rules himself. He is ludicrous as well as pathetic. For example, Samuel Beckett's (1955) character Molloy savors sucking stones by the sea. But, for Molloy, it is absolutely essential to be sure to keep only one stone in each of his pockets. He must have a foolproof rule to prevent the horror of sucking the same stone twice in a row. He decides on a plan. Each time he sucks a stone, he will move every stone to the next pocket in a clockwise direction. But I am sure you can guess that this does not completely satisfy him. He can't remove all doubt that he has erred and sucked the same stone twice in a row. Molloy is hoisted by his own petard. Trying to control life, he is utterly controlled by his own scheme. Like someone caught in the trap he tries to set for another, he makes himself ridiculous and pitiful.

Some similar qualities (such as perfectionism, rigidity, and attention to minutia) play important roles in Ring Lardner's story "Liberty Hall" (1954). But in "Liberty Hall," the use of obsessive language, another very significant factor, is amply illustrated. When someone uses obsessive language, they are trying to control the listener's response through a careful choice of words (see Sullivan, 1956, for an extensive discussion). For example, if I say I am upset with you when I am really angry, I am trying to communicate my feelings without taking undue chances on provoking your wrath. Obsessive language communicates adequately, in that the listener usually understands the gist of it. But it also fails to fully and clearly communicate, most often in the realm of the emotions.

In "Liberty Hall," Ben Drake has become famous writing scores to musicals. His long-suffering wife is often occupied with shielding him from unwanted attention. He can be especially testy when visiting other couples and has developed schemes for making a fast but, hopefully, innocuous exit. At a performance, an especially ardent fan, Mrs. Thayer, assails Mrs. Drake, insisting that the couples get together. Mrs. Drake attempts various avoidant maneuvers, all to no avail. The Drakes simply must pay the Thayers a visit and stay for a week. Mrs. Thayer lures them with the promise of absolute freedom, solitude, and relaxation.

How little this promise means is abundantly clear from the moment the Drakes arrive. Mrs. Thayer has definite ideas about the seating arrangement in the limousine as well as just how Ben should take his welcoming coffee, which cigarettes he should smoke, what he should read, and other details. Like his wife, Mr. Thayer has some pretty clear notions about exactly how Ben should "relax." Offering Ben a cocktail, he asks if he would prefer a gin cocktail or a Bacardi. Ben says he doesn't like Bacardi at all. But Mr. Thayer replies that he wagers Ben will like the kind *he* has, and proceeds to explain how special this bottle is. Mr. Thayer pours a Bacardi cocktail for Ben. Succumbing to the pressure to accept it, Ben takes a sip and puts it down.

This is a perfect microcosm of an obsessive war, with words as the primary métier. Mr. Thayer seems to be offering Ben a choice, but he is really maneuvering to show Ben how privileged he is. Of course, Ben feels controlled and resents it but chooses not to make a scene. He submits but quietly asserts himself by not really drinking the Bacardi, silently signaling that he is not impressed. He seems to comply but avoids acceding to Mr. Thayer's request for admiration.

The words Mr. Thayer chooses seem innocuous, but they are really controlling and, in a sense, bullying. In effect, he is communicating that it doesn't matter what Ben wants. He will take whatever he is given, and he will like it. Without words, Ben outmaneuvers him, but, of course, there are no real winners here. The next day, the Drakes leave for home, using one of their well-practiced escape hatches (Ben's office "urgently" needs his presence at once, or a whole production will fail). The obsessive battle draws to a close, with everyone annoyed at each other and unhappy with themselves, since each was unable to get their needs met.

In a sense, words are the protagonists in I. B. Singer's great short story "Gimpel the Fool" (2006). I think of Gimpel as a fool in the same sense that Dostoevsky's protagonist (*The Idiot*, 1935) is an idiot. That is, Gimpel is very far from being a fool, but he may be seen as foolish.

By his own admission, Gimpel is easy to take in, and others take advantage of that. He believes nonsense people tell him in order to make fun of him. Here is where rationalization, an obsessive defense, plays a role. Gimpel convinces himself to let it pass. Is he really afraid of confrontation and selling himself on the story that it would not be wise to confront his torturers? By silently bearing their taunts, is he really morally superior to them? Gimpel goes to the rabbi, who tells him, "You are not a fool. They are the fools. For he who causes his neighbor to feel shame loses Paradise himself" (p. 746).

Townspeople convince Gimpel to marry Elka, a foul-mouthed, hard-bargaining woman, already burdened by a limp and an illegitimate son. Elka is Gimpel's opposite. She is tough, direct, and not ashamed to be overtly selfish.

Thus, when their first child is born a few months after the wedding, Gimpel has enough sense to wonder about the child's paternity. Elka swears the child is Gimpel's and just a few months premature. In Gimpel's own words, when he continued to question the situation, Elka and others "argued me dumb" (p. 749), so he "decided" to believe this story and many others. But is he really the fool for this? He forgets his sorrows and falls deeply in love with Elka and the baby. Confronted by Elka's abuse, Gimpel explains, "I'm the type that bears it and says nothing. What is one to do? Shoulders are from God, and burdens too" (p. 749).

As we might expect, Elka goes too far, taking another man into their bed. Gimpel discovers them together, and vows, "Enough of being a donkey, I said to myself. Gimpel isn't going to be a sucker all his life. There's a limit even to the foolishness of a fool like Gimpel" (p. 750). When Gimpel reports his discovery to the rabbi, he is ordered to leave Elka. Missing her profoundly, Gimpel retracts the story, returns to Elka, and resolves that he would "always believe what I was told. What's the good of *not* believing? Today it is your wife you don't believe; tomorrow it's God Himself you won't take stock in" (p. 751).

Thus, Gimpel convinces himself to swallow every tall tale Elka tells. He avoids confrontation, avoids scandal at all costs, and looks away from Elka's improprieties. He feels confirmed when the rabbi asserts, "Belief in itself is beneficial. It is written that a good man lives by his faith" (p. 753). On her death bed, Elka confesses that none of their children are his. Briefly, Gimpel is moved to wreak revenge but quickly changes his mind. In a dream, he sees Elka, who is suffering in Hell for her sins. Gimpel decides to leave his home, go into the world, and tell stories to children. He lives for his dreams, where he is comforted by Elka. He asks himself why it should matter whether or not something really happened. What difference does it make? Every "story" certainly "happened" in his mind and, perhaps, in his dreams. We are all headed toward death, whatever we believe while we live. The next world, the only one that really counts, will be "without complication, without ridicule, without deception. God be praised; there even Gimpel cannot be deceived" (p. 755).

Gimpel finds words that sanctify his compliance. In my language, he goes along to get along. He talks himself into believing that he is above caring how he is treated. He allows himself to be mocked and fashions justifications for ignoring it. Is that wise or foolish? I would agree with the author, I. B. Singer, who, when interviewed, referred to Gimpel as a thinking man, a man of character, who suffered greatly.

Gimpel confronts himself with a question that I think plagues most people with an obsessive tendency to use words skillfully to avoid confrontation: Is this cowardice, masochism, weakness? Or is it wisdom, moral fiber, strength? Perhaps we each have to judge this for ourselves. But, in instances when Gimpel makes a conscious choice, I see merit in his argument. Ultimately, he accepts his situation because accepting it makes his own life better. He is not "complying" out of meekness or stupidity. He is making the choice that benefits his own life. Often truth *is* a matter of perspective. Perhaps Elka was faithful in some senses and not in others. Maybe what happens in a dream is just as real as what happens in a villager's version of daytime events. Maybe words, inherently slippery, are constructive when they help us bear life with dignity and self-respect. And, maybe, Gimpel's inner strength is more real, more solid, than the gossip spread by fools.

Bartleby, in Melville's great story "Bartleby the Scrivener" (1994), also suffers from frustrations that are typical in obsessive conflicts. He can't *want* to do what he knows he *should* do. As schoolchildren (and beyond), we have probably all navigated the conflict between what we should do and what we want to do. Our homework assignment stares us in the face, as we fantasize playing freely. Or we know we should shut the lights and go to sleep, but we want to watch one more television show, or play one more video game, or read one more page. Or when we get on the scale we vow to diet until, confronted by a piece of cheesecake, we give in to the temptation we know we "should" withstand.

But Bartleby takes the conflict further than most of us would. When asked by his employer to do some work, he responds, "I would prefer not to" (p. 142). His employer, a lawyer, is astonished, speechless. Recovering, he asks Bartleby the reason for his refusal. Bartleby merely repeats, "I would prefer not to." The lawyer tries to reason with him, explaining why Bartleby should be willing to do the work. But Bartleby doesn't budge. The employer checks with his other employees. Has he the right to ask this of Bartleby? Is there any way to understand the scribe's refusal? All three confirm their boss's viewpoint on the matter. Thus begins a series of verbal duels between Bartleby and his exasperated employer. Gradually, the battle takes on greater meaning until the lawyer comes to feel that his own manhood is at stake, "For I consider that one, for the time, is sort of unmanned when he tranquilly permits his hired clerk to dictate to him" (p. 148).

At first, it seems that Bartleby is deranged. Why is he willing to lose his life rather than do his job? But then, is the lawyer any less irrational? Why does he let this stubborn, recalcitrant man take over his office, his mind, his heart and soul? What gives his interactions with Bartleby so much power over his view of his own worth?

Bartleby reminds me of Cordelia, Lear's youngest daughter in Shakespeare's play (*King Lear*, 1972). Both are foolishly tied to a concrete version of the truth, to their own detriment. Cordelia refuses to flatter her father, despite knowing his craving for it. She insists on telling him that she honors him according to their bond, no more nor less. It is the truth, but a chilling truth, that temporarily estranges father and daughter. Although the stories are different in almost every way, Bartleby has one thing in common with Cordelia: He clings to a concrete version of his "truth." He really would rather not copy legal documents. He will not yield to pressure to comply. Like Cordelia, Bartleby will not go along to get along, as most of the rest of us do, at some points in our lives.

Like Melville's Ahab (in *Moby-Dick, or the Whale*, 2000), Bartleby is single-minded. His quest is to pursue a life absolutely consonant with his real feelings or, in today's language, his "true self." By contrast, his employer is much more conflicted and confused. Once he gets immersed in Bartleby's fortunes, he is unable to steer a clear course. He wobbles between trying to negotiate a compromise and issuing firm edicts. When Bartleby begins to refuse orders, the lawyer admits that if anyone else had conducted themselves in this manner, he would have dismissed them but "there was something about Bartleby that not only strangely disarmed me, but, in a wonderful manner, touched and disconcerted me. I began to reason with him" (p. 143).

While reasoning with Bartleby goes nowhere, the lawyer decides to be lenient, in order to be able to think well of himself: "Here I can cheaply purchase a delicious self-approval" (p. 145). Now the lawyer is hooked. Somehow, he has come to question his own reactions to Bartleby, aiming to be reasonable in the face of Bartleby's irrational behavior. Thoughts of Bartleby's sad, empty life become unbearable.

As is often true in these obsessive battles, each person feels it is absolutely necessary to win at all cost. Over the course of this sad story, the price to each of the combatants climbs precipitously. The lawyer sinks into mortified melancholy, and Bartleby boxes himself into narrower and narrower self-imposed restrictions. The employer assumes various attitudes, trying to find a way he can resolve the situation. He decides to be charitable, to pity Bartleby and try to take care of him. But he soon grows weary of this approach, as colleagues chide him for allowing a clerk to openly defy him. Finding the situation unbearable, he resolves to rid himself of Bartleby, who has become an "intolerable incubus" (p. 159). However, the lawyer can't bear who he would seem like to himself if he threw Bartleby out. He reflects, "You will not thrust him, the poor, pale, passive mortal—you will not thrust such a helpless creature out of your door? you will not dishonor yourself by such cruelty? No, I will not, I cannot do that" (p. 160).

Thus, Bartleby's enemy (the lawyer's pride) is also his chief ally. The employer is wounded in his vanity by Bartleby's affronts, but it is also the employer's sense of self that will not allow him to kick Bartleby out. The lawyer's own potential to be obsessive has been recruited. Now he tries to find the perfect words to outmaneuver Bartleby. Declaring the "air" in the office unwholesome, the lawyer quits the office himself, leaving Bartleby behind. Of course, it does not end there. Bartleby continues to haunt the office, even when he is turned out by the next proprietor. The employer decides to give reasoning with Bartleby one last try. He offers Bartleby an array of job possibilities, all of which Bartleby refuses. In a moment of kindness, he invites Bartleby to his own home, but Bartleby turns him down. At last, the lawyer feels he has done what he could. He is determined to be free of thoughts of Bartleby. He wanders around, unable to attend to his own business and, of course, unable to forget Bartleby. When he returns to his new office, he finds a note telling him that Bartleby has been imprisoned as a vagrant. Going to visit Bartleby in prison, the lawyer pays someone to upgrade Bartleby's dinner, only to be told, "I prefer not to dine to-day" (p. 165). The next time the lawyer visits, he finds Bartleby lying on the ground, dead.

Melville has marvelously captured the contagious nature of obsessive conflicts. It is almost impossible to avoid getting embroiled in them. Somehow, even when we try to steer clear of them, we get pulled in. And once the game is on, winning can seem like a matter of life or death. In Melville's story, Bartleby seems to be the greater loser, although there are no winners. The lawyer is left alive but filled with heartache.

None of the hallmarks of obsessive battles have escaped Melville's attention. There is the (sometimes fierce) power struggle, the passive aggressive resistance to being told what to do, the hurt pride and feelings of castrated impotence, and, at least for the lawyer, the self-imposed restraint out of fear of becoming cruel. There is a marvelously detailed description of the indecisiveness engendered in the lawyer. If he gives in to Bartleby, is he "enabling" the scrivener; that is, protecting Bartleby from the consequences of his action (or, rather, inaction)? Is that compassionate or weak? Is the lawyer rationalizing to avoid facing his own inability to assertively confront? Or is this the expression of compassion for Bartleby's terrible handicap? Can we ever know when we are cowards, capitulating to the obsessive's unreasonable demands, or humanitarians, recognizing, and honoring, a grievous form of human suffering? At moments, Bartleby seems to be a victim of a kind of paralysis, while at other times he seems to be his boss's torturer. His behavior has the effect of torturing the lawyer, but is that its motive? Rarely can any of us escape the obsessive unscathed. That requires supreme self-knowledge and self-confidence. One would have to be completely sure that any compromise was out of strength and a firm stand was truly in the service of life.

A strikingly similar power struggle is at the center of W. Somerset Maugham's story, "The Outstation" (1954). Mr. Warburton is the Resident in charge of a foreign district that is part of Great Britain's empire. Cooper is his badly needed but equally distrusted assistant. Cooper's first moments under Warburton's command are hardly auspicious. Unlike his commander, who always dresses impeccably for dinner, tolerating no reminders that bankruptcy has forced him to leave his beloved England, Cooper is casually clad. This is a grave error. Mr. Warburton expects everything to be done "properly," which is another way to say that everything has to be done his way. He is relatively kind and courteous but demands absolute obedience.

Cooper has the impulse to make fun of Warburton's imperious ways. He feels seen as inferior to Warburton, not only because of the differences in their roles, but also because Warburton associates himself with people of the highest status, whereas Cooper comes from a much poorer background and less prestigious schools. Each looks for opportunities to show the other up and finds them. Cooper comes to think of Warburton as a snob, who loves to look down on men such as him. Cooper had not lived long in England before coming to work for Warburton, and harbors an intense dislike of the English:

> He resented the public-school boy since he always feared that he was going to patronize him. He was so much afraid of others putting on airs with him that, in order as it were to get in first, he put on such airs as to make every one think him insufferably conceited. (p. 289)

As Maugham perceptively suggests, Cooper is full of contradictions: "A sensitive man himself he was strangely insensitive to the feelings of others" (p. 290).

Warburton fulfills every one of Cooper's fears, showing him up in front of the other men: "It bitterly amused Mr. Warburton to observe that this man, who looked upon himself as every man's equal, should look upon so many men as his own inferiors" (p. 291). Finally, they clash in public, when Cooper dares to open Warburton's newspapers, spoiling the order in which Warburton expects to find them. Forlorn, his treasure spoiled, Warburton "folded up the papers as neatly as he could, placed a wrapper round each and numbered it. But it was a melancholy task" (p. 293). A line in the sand has been crossed. For Warburton, ruining the order of his newspapers is an unthinkable crime. Vowing vengeance, he swears, "I shall never forgive him . . . Never" (p. 293).

Meanwhile, Cooper, for his part, has the "ill-bred man's inability to express regret" (p. 294) toward Warburton but also toward the men who serve him. The men refuse to work under Cooper, unless they are ordered to do so by Warburton. This is intensely shaming to Cooper: "He swallowed his humiliation, but the impatient contempt he had felt for Mr. Warburton's idiosyncrasies changed into a sullen hatred" (p. 294). Thus, we see how obsessive perfectionism and narcissistic needs lead both men into intense struggles for control. As the battle rages between them, with the men in their service as pawns, they fight out of wounded pride. As in the case of Bartleby and the lawyer (above), we could profitably focus on the narcissistic aspect of the conflict. But, at the heart of each tale, there is a fierce power struggle that takes over and grips the characters. It is as though only one of each pair can survive.

Warburton schemes to get his nemesis fired by reporting Cooper's mistakes. In the author's words, "Hatred will often make a man clear-sighted" (p. 297). Warburton reports ways Cooper is misusing his power. Cooper accuses Warburton: "You disliked me from the first moment I came here. You've done everything you could to make the place impossible for me because I wouldn't flatter you" (p. 298). And, a bit later, Cooper really aims for the jugular: "You snob. You damned snob. You thought me a cad because I hadn't gone to Eton. Oh, they told me in K. S. what to expect. Why, don't you know that you are the laughing stock of the whole country?" (p. 298). They come close to a physical row, and, when Cooper finally leaves the room, Warburton reflects that the younger man could beat him in a fight: "Tears of mortification ran down his red, fat face. He sat there for a couple of hours, smoking cigarette after cigarette, and he wished he were dead" (p. 300). At the same time, Cooper is flinging himself on his own bed and crying. Later that night, Cooper is found dead, having been murdered by one of the men under him. When he first sees Cooper dead, Warburton is startled, not because he is shocked but "because he felt in himself a sudden glow of exultation. A great burden had been lifted from his shoulders" (pp. 306–307).

For me, the last paragraph of the story is the most chilling:

> Mr. Warburton took his Times and neatly slit the wrapper. He loved to unfold the heavy, rustling pages. The morning, so fresh and cool, was delicious, and for a moment his eyes wandered out over his garden with a friendly glance. A great weight had been lifted from his mind. (p. 308)

Cooper, who was after all a human being, had become a weight, an obstacle in the way of his peace, his rituals, his authority, and his pride. That was *all* Cooper was. His elimination has no more meaning than that. He became a *thing* where, once, he was a person. Cooper is hardly a sympathetic character, but the degree of hatred he evokes in Warburton is shocking. Once again, we are shown that it can be extremely dangerous to get in the way of someone fixed on his rituals and prideful fictions.

Is anyone more infuriating than a perfectionistic obsessive? Is anyone more absurd? And yet, he often evokes our affection along with our contempt and scorn. I wonder if that is because he is so easy to caricature. Take, for example, Clarence Day's hilarious portrait of his father in "Father Wakes Up the Village" (1952). Clarence Sr., a successful businessman, expects his ice to be delivered perfectly in a solid block. Nothing else will do. Period. Of course, his way to consume liquid is the only "correct" way to do so, so his way has to be strictly followed. Mother thinks Father "fussy," but Father sees himself as merely "civilized."

All is well until calamity strikes, and, one day, the iceman doesn't come. This is immediately recognized as a crisis by the entire family. Two sons are dispatched to an official at the ice company to let him know that something must be done *immediately*. Arriving home after a hard day at the office, Father is apprised of the dire situation. He says that he will take the iceman's damned head off if he doesn't deliver immediately. To make absolutely sure to avoid catastrophe, Father orders an extra refrigerator filled with ice to be delivered to his home immediately as well.

To be sure, an abundance of ice arrives in time for Father's dinner, and much to his delight, his usual routine of dinner, coffee and cognac is restored: a rare moment of utter tranquility in the life of a perfectionist. Father uses the occasion as a teaching moment for his sons, declaring that whatever they find to do, they should do their damnedest. He certainly follows his own rule.

In this story, I hear the son's exasperation matched by his affection and even admiration for his father. Father is one of a kind. He is always, unquestionably, himself. The genuine article. He can be predicted and easily caricatured. There is something to be admired in his absolute insistence on things being done the "right" way. It is very hard to live with (especially for Mrs. Day) but also very hard to forget. Such a father creates countless memories in the people around him. They are forever bonded by their mutual remembrance of "the time Father did …" Perhaps, along with aggravation at how hard he makes the lives of others and resentment at how little he seems to care about that, people love him because he brings them together. Those immediately around Father know that they are in the same boat, whether or not they choose to be. They have all known moments of rebellion against Father's rules, followed quickly by the realization that life is much easier if they will only give Father *exactly* what he wants.

But being perfectionistic can lead to tragedy as well as comedy. In his story "Brooksmith" (1952), Henry James provides an example of this. Brooksmith is the butler of an extremely sociable, well-loved gentleman named Mr. Oliver Offord, a retired diplomat, who excels at creating a comfortable social atmosphere for his well-heeled friends. His greatest asset in this endeavor is his butler, who makes sure every social occasion at the Offord residence goes off without a hitch. Brooksmith is described as a "spare, brisk little person, in his cloistered white face and extraordinarily polished hair, which told of responsibility" and "looked as if it were kept up to the same high standard as the plate" (p. 57). Brooksmith is an artist, in that he creates the ideal salon and keeps it going so long as his master's health holds out. He devotes his life to controlling every detail, so that guests are even more comfortable than they themselves could realize, until health problems overwhelm Mr. Offord. As the old gentleman puts it, "c'est la fin de tout" (p. 59). It certainly is the end of everything for Brooksmith. Brooksmith's dilemma is how much to try to "carry on" the salon despite Mr. Offord's illness and inability to fully participate. He decides to allow himself to substitute for his master because he is "saturated with the religion of habit" (p. 60). He even allows himself to follow his own inclination to be more discriminating about who could attend since, in Brooksmith's mind, his master has gotten too lax on this subject of late. As Mr. Offord fades into death, the question uppermost in some friends' minds is: What will become of Brooksmith?

While Offord and Brooksmith are emblematic of a particular time and place, the dilemma is much more widespread than that might suggest. What happens to the obsessive perfectionist as times and fashions change? Aging often brings forced retirements of one kind or another. If we spend our lives sacrificing to a god of perfection, we may well wake up one day and find ourselves replaced by someone younger and less exacting. It isn't only cowboys in America's Wild West that outlived the era that supported their way of life. Many who occupy tamer professions end their careers with some of the same feelings of obsolescence. Our sell-by date has passed. I think perfectionists are more likely to suffer this fate because they so fervently advocate for their sensibility, in their actions if not in words. Clarence Day declares that there is only one right way to deliver ice to his doorstep; he knows what it is, and it is the way it has always been delivered in the past. For him, the "proper" delivery of ice and his own ego are one and the same. Delivering the ice in any "imperfect" way is equivalent to negating Clarence Day. There is no room for fashion's inevitable changes.

I find the end of Brooksmith's life extremely sad. When Offord dies, Brooksmith explains that "it's just the loss of something that was everything" (p. 64). Brooksmith is unable to adjust to serving in anyone else's home because, as James puts it, he had been in Arcadia. Brooksmith tries to work as a waiter but can't bear serving anywhere that is less perfect than Mr. Offord's home. He sinks into poorer and poorer circumstances. Finally he "disappears," perhaps having killed himself. His friend concludes, "now I trust that, with characteristic deliberation, he is changing the plates of the immortal gods" (p. 70). Such can be the fate of the perfectionist. Almost by definition, he is unable to absorb the shocks we all encounter as our world changes. If our ties to our "perfect" ways are sacred to us, we may associate our very selves with them and feel personally cancelled, negated, outmoded as the rest of the world moves on.

Treatment

When I discuss the treatment of obsessive disorders, I frequently read a passage from Samuel Beckett's "Molloy" (1955), which I mentioned in the beginning of this chapter. I ask candidates to note their feelings as they listen to this man, driven to desperate lengths to make sure that the stones in his pockets are distributed "correctly," so as to *guarantee* that he never sucks the same stone twice in a row. It is an almost absurd series of steps describing the movement of stones from left to right, from coat pocket to trouser pocket, and from hand to mouth, all for the sake of balance, of both the contents of his pockets and the contents of his mind.

We find ourselves laughing at him but, at the same time, feeling uneasy and annoyed. Such a fuss, as though getting it perfectly right matters so much! We are exasperated by the infinite details, the exquisite (self-) torture, and our own impatience as we long for him to be satisfied. And yet, our hearts break a little for him, for he is a slave to his self-imposed necessities. We also recognize a bit of ourselves in him. We obey our own routines and (implicitly) imbue them with magic. Why does anything have to be just so?

What I like to call obsessive territory is a land of doubt where magic reigns. Reality is shaped by words and controlled by rules. Punishments are nebulous and severe, but get everything just right and you are in line for a world of peace and security. Except that that magical safe realm never materializes.

For the sake of clarity, I briefly summarize some of the hallmarks of obsessive living, as I understand it. Most were already illustrated by the short stories in the preceding section of this chapter.

- Obsessive language is indirect enough to keep out of severe trouble (most of the time) but clear enough to sound communicative. I like to describe it as at a 45-degree angle away from a direct, simple statement. It is close to accurate, but in its attempt to avoid any possible conflict, it has to obfuscate. For example, the person who is angry with me says she is "upset," because she is afraid that if she uses the word *angry* I might respond with my own anger. Most likely she is not aware of substituting the word *upset* for the word *angry*. It is a smooth process, well-practiced by the time she first enters my office.
- Obsessive living is an effort to control important events, largely by keeping tight control over small details. Perhaps I desperately want to control whether or not I stay alive today. I can't be entirely sure of doing so, but I can make sure I follow rules I have magically invested with the power to keep me safe. For example, I can consume exactly 1500 calories, and 12 vitamin pills, one each hour, and so on. In Sullivan's (1956) language, concern about certain details substitutes for control over more major issues. I like to call this the "look over there" syndrome. Just as a magician distracts the audience so they don't notice how the trick works, obsessive defenses focus us away from a part of reality and toward another part that seems within our control.
- The effort at control leads to perfectionism, procrastination, and difficulty with decisions and commitments. Often, it also leads to intellectualization

- (a translation of the alive and unpredictable into something regimented and safely studied).
- An underlying issue is a conflict between what the person should do versus what he or she wants to do. The person feels something like "I should do my homework, but I really want to play games." As soon as someone obsessive starts leaning in one of these two directions, the other beckons. For example, in treatment, if the discussion starts to favor one side, what follows is an airtight argument for the other side.
- Ironically, the obsessive often creates exactly what he or she is trying to avoid. Desperately wanting to be liked, he may try so hard that others get exasperated, instead of pleased.
- As is true for others in varying degrees, the obsessive person wants to live a better, freer life, but is not willing to really change how he lives. In other words, he wants the outcome to change without giving up his defensive style. Years ago, a patient came to see me because he wanted to feel less tired, but he was by no means willing to change his 16-hour-a-day work schedule!

When treating obsessive patients, analysts sometimes fall back on their own obsessive devices. They may get caught up in creating intellectualized theories about the patient, instead of engaging in a more alive (but less predictable and controlled) interchange. Both participants may get involved in conjecturing about the patient's "real" feelings and motives, spending years perfecting theories about the patient, while real life goes by.

Just as theory building can be contagious in treatment, so is obsessive, indirect language. As Sullivan noted (1954), it can be hard to *monitor* the patient's anxiety level without becoming overly careful to avoid raising it. Noticing when the patient's anxiety increases is central to Sullivan's approach, but this can easily morph into obsessively watching our every word and censoring anything that might provoke conflict.

Even if we have not participated in a treatment characterized by frequent power struggles between an obsessive patient and an obsessive analyst, we have all heard about them. For example, the analyst can become highly controlling, in an effort to *get* the patient to be less obsessive. We can try to wrestle the patient's defenses to the ground, so to speak, but in the process we become obsessive ourselves. Fundamentally, it can be harder to analyze the patient's tendency toward power struggles if we contribute to it in the session (although it can be done retrospectively).

We sometimes interpret the patient's underlying hostility in a hostile way. We may miss the patient's vulnerability because we are so caught up in our own exasperation with him. In a sense, this absence of sensitivity to the patient's anxiety is itself hostile. In addition, sometimes we become aggressive in the *manner* of our interpretation, trying to pin patients down and force them to see "the truth." This is a common countertransferential response, one that can take subtle enough forms to escape our awareness. If the patient fears conflict, we may unwittingly reinforce that fear with our countertransferential acting out. But we may not immediately recognize this, especially if the frightened patient seems to improve in a desperate attempt to placate us.

Fear of our own sadism and aggression can lead us to confuse patients, as they may have been mystified in their early life. We may imply that what we are doing is for the patient's own good when it is really acting out our hostility. Of course, analysts are not alone in using excessive zeal to cover up their true motives. In his comic masterpiece *Hard Times* (1958), Dickens provides us with a particularly vivid example. Thomas Gradgrind, a school teacher, is utterly determined to blast his young charges' minds with knowledge.

> Indeed, as he eagerly sparkled at them from the cellarage before mentioned, he seemed a kind of cannon loaded to the muzzle with facts, and prepared to blow them clean out of the regions of childhood at one discharge. He seemed a galvanizing apparatus, too, charged with a grim mechanical substitute for the tender young imaginations that were to be stormed away. (p. 5)

Dickens' language could hardly be more explicit. They are to be forcibly penetrated, for their own good, of course. Children are sometimes easier victims of mystification than adults. They may accept our assertion that we are acting in their interest, rather than listen to what they feel, which may be a more accurate measure of how they are being treated.

Aside from excessive zeal, power struggles, intellectual theory building, and linguistic obfuscation, the treatment of obsessive patients has a few other inherent dangers. Seen by the patient as withholding, we may actually fulfill this description. For example, if we feel the patient is trying to "force" us to make his decisions for him, we may respond by being unusually reluctant to voice opinions of any kind.

Finally, the sheer difficulty of our role (combined with our own character issues) may promote excessive doubting in us. We may become indecisive or overly equivocal, perhaps in an effort to compensate for authoritarian impulses. For example, the patient may ask for help in understanding the goals of the treatment, but we may be unable to participate, having become lost in an exaggerated effort to entertain multiple perspectives. Although, intuitively, we sense how this person could live more fully, we become unable to use these glimmers. Having gotten completely absorbed in obsessively collecting all possible perspectives, we lose track of any clear direction.

In short, there are all kinds of ways to be obsessive with an obsessive patient. To conclude this chapter, I name some aspects of how we can work with these issues, from my point of view.

1 *I favor a very direct, sparing use of words.* I try to "call a spade a spade" as succinctly as possible. If I find myself getting lost in intellectualized theories, extensive explanations, excessive details, indirect expressions of hostility, or overly wordy interpretations, the first thing I try to do is stop talking. It may

help simply to interrupt the process. A quick review of what just happened may clarify some triggers of my own obsessive defensiveness and how it reflects the process between me and the patient.

2 *Alive curiosity, playfulness, and humor are especially important in this work.* If I feel the process is deadening, I ask why. Do I feel coerced? When the patient poses a question, do I feel I have a choice about responding, or do I feel constrained to answer? How might each of us be contributing to the narrowing of available options for our responses to each other? For example, sometimes a non sequitur is useful, since it implicitly asserts the freedom one person can retain with another. Humor is often another saving grace. It can allow us to make a point while remaining any ally.

3 *I try to "graze" on the material, moving from a focus on what is going on between us, to an aspect of the patient's recent dreams, to something from the person's history, to a feeling I had before they came in, and so on.* Obsessive people are often terribly concerned with functioning well, starting *now*. We have to respect this concern, without getting stuck trying to *make* it happen. A fixation on symptoms is one way this plays out, where we get overly determined to "cure" the patient of his symptoms immediately. We may then get sidetracked in arguments and fail to recognize that we are locked in a protracted power struggle, enacting our own potential for obsessive interactions.

4 *If our own sense of competence is at stake in how the patient responds to our interpretations, we are likely to become obsessively tight and controlling.*

5 *It is often helpful to follow Sullivan (1956) in emphasizing the interpersonal function a behavior is serving.* For example, if a person's confusion is tabling decisions, maybe (unconsciously) he is not wanting to make decisions!

6 *I try to notice when patients are getting caught up in figuring out the "right" path.* I like to say that many choices are not between the right decision and the wrong one, but between vanilla and chocolate. They are different choices that lead to different experiences.

7 *In this, as in all my other clinical work, I am trying to focus just beyond what the patient already consciously knows.* Obviously, to express what is consciously known doesn't add much. But to suggest something completely outside the patient's awareness will not be resonant. Something in between these extremes may nudge the patient toward greater self-understanding.

8 *Particularly with obsessive patients, I ask what else could be true besides what is already known.* Sometimes, someone who uses obsessive defenses can't see that behavior can have multiple motivations, and events can have many explanations that are true, even if they contradict one another.

9 *In this, as in all treatments, I try to be mindful of the intensities of feelings in each of us.* I am curious about what evokes changes in intensity as the session progresses. In addition, I watch to see whether our anxiety, shame, guilt, sadness, loneliness, and other feelings are remaining at tolerable levels. Sullivan (1954) emphasized monitoring fluctuations in the patient's anxiety, but I think it can be useful to keep track of changes in all emotional levels in both participants.

10 *I have found that, sometimes, a focus on obsessive language very early in treatment helps the work become more meaningful.* Obsessive language obfuscates the material. If the patient and I quickly understand the anxiety triggering this defense, it may become less necessary to the patient. Of course, the danger of this approach is that it may backfire. The patient may feel shamed by having obsessive language pointed out and may become more, rather than less, indirect. I think it is often a matter of developing enough trust that the patient knows you are not trying to humiliate him but, rather, that you feel this approach is vital to the work.

11 *I try to foster a collaborative atmosphere, where it feels as though each of us is "putting into the pot" whatever may be useful.* It doesn't matter who thought of something first. Of course, the alliance is always crucial in treatment, but I think it is especially important in obsessive territory. We may have to live through battles for control, be able to experience them, and look for their meanings without getting permanently stuck. But if we have a good enough partnership, we can survive the inevitable difficulties.

12 *Like all clinical work, treatment of obsessive patients does not occur only in the analyst's office.* Once the patient is a true collaborator, once you have helped her spot her own obsessive techniques, she can observe herself using them and self-reflect about the anxiety, or shame, or guilt, or sadness she is trying to avoid. As we know, Sullivan (1954) developed the notion of the analyst as participant-observer, but I think it is equally important for the patient to become a participant-observer. With obsessive material this can reduce the shame of self-recognition to tolerable levels. But, more generally, I believe that much of the treatment goes on outside our offices. Life itself powerfully motivates and facilitates lasting change. That is, for all of us, what happens to us in our significant relationships outside treatment, as well as within treatment, moves us and may motivate our efforts to try out new ways of being in the world. I have known many patients who have been willing to exert tremendous efforts to grow so as to become better parents. In treatment, we provide help overcoming the patient's obstacles to learning from new interpersonal experience, but then, for treatment to be most effective, this work needs to continue outside the sessions.

13 *To say this in another way, I believe that people generally have adequate resources to cope with much of life, if they are free to use them.* This defines our role. We facilitate the patient's ability to use his or her potential to learn from life experience. Obsessive patients are wasting energy, trying to be safe in inherently unsuccessful ways. Once this coping pattern loosens its hold, other changes are possible.

14 *I think we have to accept that, frequently, the middle phase of the treatment of obsessive patients brings some profound feelings of loss.* The patient is saddened by recognizing that life has been wasted in useless battles, obfuscations, avoidances, procrastinations, and so on. This feeling seems to me to be unavoidable.

Elsewhere (Buechler, 2008), I have discussed the ways the analyst can serve as a contrast, catalyst, and relational challenge to facilitate the patient's growth. I will not repeat this material here, except to say that many interpersonal risks are first taken in sessions. Patients experiment with us, daring to be more direct, trying out new behavior. Hopefully the patient sees that emotional intensity, conflict, and, even anxiety need not be so assiduously avoided. Once they are able to let go of obsessive functioning, most patients value the experience of encountering life more directly. Less fearfully, their interpersonal scope widens. There are greater opportunities for curiosity, joy, love, and other rich moments. Life with fewer obsessive detours is keener. It is too good to miss.

References

Beckett, S. (1955). *The unnamable: Part of trilogy including Molloy and Malone dies*. New York: Alfred A. Knopf.
Buechler, S. (2008). *Making a difference in patients' lives: Emotional experience in the therapeutic setting*. New York: Routledge.
Day, C. (1952). Father wakes up the village. In M. Crane (Ed.), *Fifty great short stories* (pp. 315–321). New York: Bantam Dell.
Dickens, C. (1958). *Hard times*. New York: Harper & Row.
Dostoevsky, F. (1935). *The idiot* (C. Garnett, Trans.). New York: The Modern Library.
James, H. (1952). Brooksmith. In M. Crane (Ed.), *Fifty great short stories* (pp. 53–70). New York: Bantam Dell.
Lardner, R. (1954). Liberty hall. In R. P. Warren & A. Erskine (Eds.), *Short story masterpieces* (pp. 225–237). New York: Dell.
Maugham, W. S. (1954). The outstation. In R. P. Warren & A. Erskine (Eds.), *Short story masterpieces* (pp. 275–308). New York: Dell.
Melville, H. (1994). Bartleby the scrivener. In A. W. Lidz (Ed.), *Major American short stories* (pp. 135–167). New York: Oxford University Press.
Melville, H. (2000). *Moby-Dick, or the whale*. New York: The Modern Library.
O'Connor, F. (2002). Everything that rises must converge. In C. Neider (Ed.), *Great short stories of the masters* (pp. 538–553). New York: Cooper Square Press.
Shakespeare, W. (1972). *King Lear*. In *The Arden edition of the works of William Shakespeare* (pp. 1–206). London: Methuen.
Singer, I. B. (2006). Gimpel the fool. In D. Gioia & R. S. Gwynn (Eds.), *The art of the short story* (pp. 744–756). New York: Pearson Longman.
Sullivan, H. S. (1954). *The psychiatric interview*. New York: W. W. Norton.
Sullivan, H. S. (1956). *Clinical studies in psychiatry*. New York: W. W. Norton.

Chapter 7

Anguished Grieving

From my perspective, James Agee's *A Death in the Family* (2009) remains one of the most poignant stories ever written. This autobiographical work won the Pulitzer Prize for literature. Grief and shock war for ascendance as Mary suffers the sudden loss of her beloved husband. At first, Mary is numb from the paralyzing dislocation of the news of his fatal accident. But gradually, Mary begins to understand how life would never be the same:

> Mary meanwhile rocked quietly backward and forward, and from side to side, groaning, quietly, from the depths of her body, not like a human creature but a fatally hurt animal ... And as she rocked and groaned, the realization gradually lost its fullest, most impaling concentration: there took shape, from its utter darkness, like the slow emergence of the countryside into first daylight, all those separate realizations which could be resolved into images, emotions, thought, words obligations. (p. 280)

Each realization of what it will mean to live the rest of her life without him stabs her, penetrates the numbness, until grief overcomes shock. Nowhere in literature have I found a more affecting portrait of grief's passages. Our initial refusal to recognize its enormity postpones but does not diminish our suffering. And then we begin to apprehend how the loss will affect our mornings, our Sundays, our New Years. Gradually, we are battered into resignation. Eventually, we give in to sorrow.

I believe that portrayals of grief in fiction are far more vivid than anything in our analytic literature. When Lear (Shakespeare, 1972) repeats the word *never* he expresses, in that one word, the unbearable shock of forever losing the daughter he so deeply loved.

With Katherine Anne Porter's story "Theft" (1952), we see that the loss of trust can be as searing as the loss of a person. When a woman's purse is taken

> she felt she had been robbed of an enormous number of valuable things, whether material or intangible: things lost or broken by her own fault, things she had forgotten or left in houses when she moved: books borrowed from her and not returned, journeys she had planned and had not made, words she had

waited to hear spoken to her and had not heard, and the words she had meant to answer with; bitter alternatives and intolerable substitutes worse than nothing, and yet inescapable: the long patient suffering of dying friendships and the dark inexplicable death of love—all that she had had and all that she had missed, were lost together, and were twice lost in this landslide of remembered losses. (pp. 227–228)

Our losses can conspire to form a landslide that carries us down to depths of abject sorrow. We grieve for the lives we have had and lost and for the lives we have never known.

So many poets and prose writers have depicted grief. Perhaps W. H. Auden (2010) best expressed the mundane backdrop that so often highlights how profoundly alone we can feel when we are swept up in sorrow.

> About suffering they were never wrong,
> The Old Masters: how well they understood
> Its human position: how it takes place
> While someone else is eating, or opening a
> Window or just walking dully along. (p. 3)

Can grief be treated? Should it be? Should we aim to diminish it, or are we more helpful if we aim to accompany it? What can exacerbate and/or prolong grief, so that it takes on a life of its own? And, perhaps the most difficult question, how does it differ from depression?

Only one way of discerning the difference between grief (however prolonged) and depression makes sense to me. Since grief can extend over a lifetime, I cannot use duration as a way to differentiate them (for a cogent discussion of this issue, see *The Loss of Sadness*, A. V. Horwitz and J. C Wakefield, 2007). But I think that those who are depressed tend to see themselves in a negative light, while those dealing with grief, however painful, are less likely to do so. Emotion theory (Izard, 1972) sees depression as a complex emotion with sadness at its core but with other emotions complicating it. In some ways, this is similar to Freud's (1917) distinction between mourning and melancholia, but *Freud emphasized ambivalence* as the emotion that can turn grief into depression. As I have suggested previously (Buechler, 2000, 2008) I think *shame*, *guilt*, and *regret* can transform sorrow into depression. In this state, the sufferer bears two types of impoverishment. The interpersonal world is lonelier, with the lost person gone. And the ashamed, guilty, or regretful self is also poorer. When intense shame, guilt, or regret accompany sorrow, the person doesn't have the resources to cope with the loss. Bearing grief is a heavy burden. It requires an emotional self-care that may be impossible to extend to oneself in states of severe shame, guilt, or regret.

This chapter and the next will highlight the difference between grief, which is relatively uncomplicated by an impoverished sense of self, and depression, which has lowered self-esteem at its core.

"In the Gloaming" (1999), by Alice Elliott Dark, is a story poised on the brink between grief and depression. Janet is caring for her son Laird, who is dying at the age of 33, presumably from an HIV-related illness. Martin, Janet's husband and Laird's father, absents himself from his family as much as possible, which has been his approach to life in general, but is more notable as Laird's life ebbs away. Every evening as night is falling, Janet and Laird enter into conversations that are an extraordinary departure from their previous discussions. Now they really talk about their lives, their loves, their yearnings. They talk as they have never talked before. Janet comes to cherish the gloaming and this new intimacy with her son. Always prone to deny the unbearable, she is unable to face how little time is left to them. At times, their frank discussions evoke Janet's self-reproaches and feelings of guilt and inadequacy. She confesses to Laird that her children are the only extraordinary things about her. She feels guilty about her impact on him when she worries about Laird, and he subsequently has a bad night, feeling she somehow caused it with her thoughts. She struggles not to cry in front of him, telling herself there will be plenty of time to cry. She has impulses to flee but fights them off. She defends her husband, Martin, to Laird but feels dishonest. She has startling, unhinging revelations. For example, "Suddenly she realized: Laird had been the love of her life" (p. 697). Janet feels responsible for the very atmosphere, apologizing for the landscape when it is gray, as though the fading light is, somehow, her fault. She also blames herself for her own pain: "She had allowed herself to imagine a future. That had been her mistake" (p. 699). Later, she reflects that she had tried never to ask for too much, but perhaps she had done so after all.

Janet sees herself as inadequate and blameworthy in so many ways. But at the end of the story, when Laird dies, she is able to get angry at *life*, crying, "A child shouldn't die before his parents" (p. 704). Like Lear, Janet is trying to comprehend that her child will never be alive again. It is unthinkable. And yet, it is true. She was his mother but unable to protect him.

Shortly after this moment, the story ends. I imagine Janet's endless grief, and I wonder if it will be laced with so much guilt and shame that it takes the form of depression. Whether or not this occurs, Janet has to find a way to bear that she and Laird will never share another sunset.

A mother and her dying son are also the protagonists of David Leavitt's gripping story "Gravity" (1992). Theo, who is in the last stages of death from AIDS, has to be injected four times a day to try to prevent blindness. His mother, Sylvia, takes care of him with a matter-of-fact competence. She seems to be "coping" well, but is she? Most of the time she is calm, except for one time when she wants to shop more, but Theo needs to go home. Sudden sorrow breaks through Sylvia's usual demeanor, as she squeezes her eyes closed so tightly she fractures the shadow on their lids.

Theo is concerned about the impact that taking care of him is having on his mother, since her characteristic reticence might prevent her from expressing it. When Sylvia takes Theo shopping and suddenly throws a heavy crystal bowl toward him, the fragile Theo can barely keep it from dropping to the floor in shards. Why does she do this? Theo's ability to catch the bowl momentarily heartens Sylvia who, perhaps, feels for an instant that she and Theo have prevailed and gravity has lost.

The story is aptly titled. Theo is gravely ill and approaching the grave. But, for this moment, he triumphs over gravity, snatching a small victory from the jaws of defeat. Perhaps in this gesture Sylvia makes them a winning team, one more time.

Kate Chopin's "The Story of an Hour" (2009) was originally written in 1894, but I think it can still shock and challenge us today. Mrs. Mallard hears from a friend that her husband, Brently Mallard, has died in a railway accident. She doesn't seem to suffer from shock or disbelief. She weeps at once, instantly taking it in, and then insists on being alone. Even though she loves him, a pervasive feeling of freedom steals over her. Everyone believes she is isolating out of overwhelming sorrow, but that is not the case. But then, quite suddenly, Brently appears. The news of his death had been inaccurate. It is at that point that Mrs. Mallard's heart gives out and she dies, according to the doctors, "of joy that kills" (p. 123).

Is this story merely a demonstration of how women who are oppressed by male domination yearn to be free? I don't think so. Like other feelings, I think relief and joy can accompany sorrow and shape it. Mrs. Mallard did not hate her husband. Far from it. During the hours she thought Brently dead, "She knew that she would weep again when she saw the kind, tender hands folded in death; the face that had never looked save with love upon her, fixed and gray and dead" (p. 122). But that is not all she knew. She *also* saw "a long procession of years to come that would belong to her absolutely. And she opened and spread her arms out to them in welcome" (p. 122).

Kate Chopin's story expresses the truth that seemingly contradictory emotions can nevertheless exist side by side. While the doctors think she died of sudden joy at seeing that her husband was still alive, the reader knows that actually she was overwhelmed by the pain of losing her dream of freedom. In short, when Brently appears, very much alive, his wife dies of sorrow, not joy, even though she sincerely loves him. Perhaps she feels she can't go back to the less complicated vision of their relationship that she held before this false alarm. In any event, at each step, conventional, one-dimensional thinking leads to a misunderstanding of what Mrs. Mallard is really feeling.

Despite this ending, I don't see Mrs. Mallard as ashamed, guilty, or regretful. I think she likes herself well enough and accepts her ambivalent feelings toward Brently. An introduction to the story suggests that it is autobiographical in theme. Chopin was widowed at age 32. In her diary, Chopin admits that after her husband died, she had her period of most significant growth as a person. But she goes on to say that she would have given up this growth in a "spirit of perfect acquiescence" (p. 120) if her husband had lived.

Terence Rattigan's play "In Praise of Love" (1985) charts the struggle of a husband and wife to limit grief's toll. There are four characters: Lydia; her husband, Sebastian; their son, Joey; and their friend, Mark. As the story unfolds, we learn that Lydia is dying of a progressive disorder somehow related to her starvation as a child during World War II. Sebastian, a literary critic whose temperament suits his profession perfectly, seems completely lost in his books and detached from her. Their favorite sport is bickering over cultural fine points. But, as we gradually discover, behind the scenes Sebastian and Lydia are desperately trying to protect each other from the grief of Lydia's impending death. Sebastian is creating elaborate ruses to hide from Lydia that her illness has reached a terminal stage. At the same time, he laments to Mark that over their many years together he has failed to fully cherish her, and soon it will be too late. Meanwhile, Lydia is scheming to bring Joey and Sebastian closer so they will have each other when she is gone. She even tries to set up a future romantic entanglement for Sebastian, without his knowing about her part in it. At the end of the play, Lydia hides her tears and quietly disappears, leaving Sebastian and Joey to their game of chess.

Sebastian and Lydia do have deep regrets along with their sorrows, but surely, there can hardly be a greater expression of love than the protective maneuvers with which they try to soften each other's grief. Sebastian does all he can to give Lydia the gentlest death possible, and Lydia thinks only of what might cushion the blow for him and Joey. We are left to speculate about the success of their efforts to shield each other, but I think it is clear that each will know they gave it their all.

Conventional thinking about "normal" grieving and culturally based assumptions lead to misunderstandings in Bharati Mukherjee's story "The Management of Grief" (1992). Shaila, an Indian wife and mother, is living in Canada with her husband, Vikram, and their two sons. Vikram and the boys are returning from a trip to India when the plane is bombed and splits in two. They were 30 minutes from Heathrow airport. Shaila and other "relatives" are taken to Ireland to identify photographs of the victims. Judith, a social worker, contacts Shaila, hoping to enlist her help in getting the relatives to cooperate with authorities. Shaila asks how she was chosen. It is because she is a "pillar," having taken the news calmly. Shaila answers that each person must grieve in their own way, but Judith insists that Shaila is the strongest of the survivors because she is coping so well. Shaila answers that, by the standards of some of the other survivors, she is behaving oddly and badly. Furthermore, she wishes she could express her grief through more drastic acts, even suicide. Shaira insists that the others will not see her as a model, and she does not view herself that way either. She feels like a freak, but her "terrible calm" will not go away.

In Ireland, the relatives receive information about what happened on the premise that information helps people grieve. The plane broke in two. Unconsciousness was instantaneous. It happened just after breakfast. Later, someone tells her about the sharks.

A neighbor, Kusum, who has lost her husband and daughter, tries to drown in the sea off Ireland's coast, which is as close as she can get to them. Shaila stops her, telling her that it isn't yet their time to die. Shaila herself has not eaten or brushed her teeth in the four days since the crash. Kusum questions her own reactions, telling herself that she is selfish to grieve, since, according to her religion, her husband and daughter are in a better place. Shaila starts to enter the water, too, but is stopped by another hopeful relative, who is living on the possibility that some might have been able to swim to safety. Shaila begins to hope, too. This trip celebrated her older son's 14th birthday. Shaila thrusts toys in the water for her sons and a poem for her husband. In the poem, she finally tells him how much she loves him. She has never actually said it before, since she was not brought up to be so forthright about her feelings. But, she decides, now is the time to express them.

Officials show her the photograph of a boy, expecting her to recognize it as her older son, but she insists it is not him. She cries, and they think she is sorrowful because his body has not been found, but actually her tears are tears of joy, because she believes he is still alive.

Shaila goes home to her mother in India and stays for several months. Her grandmother understands the losses in religious terms, unlike her parents. Six months into her journey, she has a transporting experience in a temple. Her husband descends and takes her hands in his. He tells her she is beautiful and asks what she is doing. She asks him what she should be doing, and he tells her to go on with her life, to finish what they started. She decides to leave India, although she does not understand her husband's message.

Meanwhile, other relatives have coped in different ways, some remarrying, some becoming more devout and joining ashrams. Judith, the social worker, explains that acceptance is a goal in grieving. Acceptance means you make plans for moving ahead with your life and speak of the victims in the past tense. The stages to pass through are rejection, depression, acceptance, and reconstruction. Judith has compiled a list of the stages each relative has achieved. There is so much that Judith misunderstands and so much that Shaila can't tell her. For one thing, she can't explain that her family still surrounds her, from which she derives comfort and even joy.

But Shaila puzzles over her husband's message. She tries to understand the meaning of her life now and exactly what it is that she started with Vikram and must finish on her own. Then she hears her husband tell her that her time is come, and she must be brave. At the end of the story, still not clear where she is going, she just starts walking.

Although Shaila is suicidal at one point and floundering, I don't see her as depressed but, rather, as struggling to bear the unbearable. How does someone "cope well" with losing her husband and sons? What is a "normal" reaction? How much do cultural and religious teachings affect the definition of "healthy" sorrow? Is it normal to hear your loved one speak to you after he is dead? Is it normal for some people, given their religious backgrounds, but not for others? More generally, can one person ever really understand the grief of another, or the best "management of grief"?

The absurdity of Judith's graph of grief reactions reminds me of Joan Didion's fury at a psychiatrist with a similar template for measuring sorrow. In "The Year of Magical Thinking" (2005), which is autobiographical, Didion recounts her husband's death and her state of mind during and after her enormous loss. Didion makes abundantly clear what she thinks of the grieving process as it is sometimes described in the psychiatric literature and elsewhere. She quotes one psychiatrist as advocating a stepwise treatment for "pathological" mourners. First, the clinician reviews how the death occurred, then, if the treatment is going well, the patient expresses anger at the dead person. What follows should be some sort of emotional reliving that helps the mourner understand their true impulses toward the deceased. Finally, "Using our understanding of the psychodynamics involved in the patient's need to keep the lost one alive, we can then explain and interpret the relationship that had existed between the patient and the one who died" (p. 55).

By turns, Didion is incredulous and outraged. How could this psychiatrist presume he has superior knowledge of her love for her husband and the meaning of losing him? How absurd it is to assume there are unvarying stages of grief, emotions in a predictable order! While Didion does not spell this out, we can imagine that she is reacting to the implicit notion that grief has a "normal" duration, and if it is taking too long, there must have been something wrong with the relationship when the deceased was alive. As Didion so eloquently phrases it, "Grief turns out to be a place none of us know until we reach it" (p. 188). For example, no one, including Didion, would have predicted that, after John died, she would be unable to give away his shoes, because somewhere in the recesses of her mind, she imagines he might still need them some day. This "magical thinking" hardly fits Didion's characteristic style. Generally, she is a blunt, journalistic author who aims straight for the unvarnished truth. But, as she illustrates, the land of grief has its own customs and personal variations, borne of ungovernable necessities.

I don't believe Joan Didion is psychotic because she keeps her husband's shoes or for any other reason. Nor would I say, from this evidence, that she is depressed, although I can't be certain of this without more information. Sadness is a natural response to loss and should not be confused with depression. In the psychiatric literature, as already noted above, the aptly titled book *The Loss of Sadness: How Psychiatry Transformed Normal Sorrow into Depressive Disorder* (Horwitz & Wakefield, 2007) makes this point repeatedly. The authors' belief is that by concentrating on "symptoms," such as the duration of grief, we tend to pathologize intense but normal sorrow. Sadness is a normal reaction to obvious losses in love, work, and other arenas, as well as less obvious losses, such as of a belief or a dream. For a time, clinicians ascribed to the notion that grief has a normal sequence of stages, from protest through eventual acceptance, but I think that way of thinking is less popular, although it still exists, perhaps in less formulaic terms.

John Bayley (1999a, 1999b) has provided eloquent reflections about his experience of caring for his wife, the philosopher and fiction author Iris Murdoch, during her protracted decline and death from Alzheimer's disease. Like Didion, Bayley challenges conventional descriptions of "normal" mourning. After Iris dies, John (1999a) tells us that he sleeps quietly with Iris beside him. But, one morning, after spilling his tea, "I wanted to tell Iris about it, but when I got upstairs I found that she was not there and I couldn't tell her" (p. 43). John is no more psychotic than Joan Didion. He "knows" Iris is dead, but that has no bearing on whether or not he can feel her presence and talk to her. It seems likely that John will keep Iris with him for as long as he lives. Does that "duration" mean that he is depressed? Since he will fail to "move on," from one "stage" to another, is his mourning pathological? Hardly.

In "A Silver Dish" (1981), Saul Bellow gives us a marvelous illustration of Freud's concept of the working through process in normal grief. Rather than going through a series of predetermined stages, we mourn a bit differently each time something in our lives reminds us of our loss. Woody Selbst is a substantial, capable, 60-year-old man, whose ailing father, Morris, has just died. On each of the subsequent days, he writes himself a note about his father. But on Sunday, as the church bells ring, he is suddenly profoundly shaken by the enormity of his loss. Thinking himself a pragmatic, healthy, worldly man, he can't understand how he could be so easily overcome by such emotion. I think Bellow is showing us how Woody is doing the work of mourning, one day at a time. The Sunday church bells remind Woody of the father he knew on Sundays, and he mourns the loss of that father as they toll. Saturday he mourned a slightly different loss. Thus, mourning is not exactly the same from one day to the next or from one person to the next, and its variations cannot be predicted or outlined by a theory of stages. Its qualities are shaped by the history of the relationship between the mourner and the person who died.

Interestingly, Morris was far from an ideal father, and their relationship was rife with struggles, and yet Woody deeply misses him. Morris was a cheat, a gambler, a liar, and a thief. In a flashback, Woody remembers a time during his adolescence when Morris involved him in the theft of a silver dish. Woody was appalled and tried to stop Morris, which led to a physical altercation. Although Woody abhors Morris's behavior, he also recognizes that he and Morris have a great deal in common. Whether or not he likes it, to some extent he has been shaped by his street-smart dad. What Morris has (and others in his family lack) is aliveness, a physicality, an appreciation of the excitement of risk, an ability to live by his wits and to be guided by impulse. Morris can be egregiously selfish, and in some way, although it isn't rational, Woody loves him for it.

As Morris's death approaches, the old man wants it over with and tries to pull out the intravenous needles that are keeping him alive. Woody climbs into his hospital bed and holds on to his father, who is trembling. Woody tries to prevent Morris from dying, but, once again, the old man has his way. Woody feels his father's body grow cold despite his best efforts, and he is left to conclude that it was impossible to overcome his father's incredible strength of will.

There is love, admiration, exasperation, and exquisite pain in that conclusion. Woody will always mourn for Morris, who was distinctively, engagingly, utterly, himself.

Alice Munro's story "Bardon Bus" (1991) describes some strengths we can develop in the process of grieving. Interestingly, a character in the story suggests women have an advantage over men, in being forced to live in the world of loss and death. Men can continue to attract younger women as they age, but it is not as easy for women, so they are forced to confront mortality. This puts women ahead of the game, so to speak, since "you won't get any happiness by playing tricks on life. It's only by natural renunciation and by accepting deprivation, that we prepare for death and therefore that we get any happiness" (p. 122).

The story is written in the first person. The main character is a middle-aged woman who is given no name. She describes fragments of her relationship with "X" and its aftermath. Both researchers, they are temporarily working in Australia. X is married, while the woman is divorced. From the start, they know the affair will last only until each has to return home.

At home, at first, she treasures her memories of her time with X. She welcomes them, delights in them. But, at some point, that changes. She wants to escape them but cannot: "They had become a plague. All they did was stir up desire, and longing, and hopelessness, a trio of miserable caged wildcats that had been installed in me without my permission, or at least without my understanding how long they would live and how vicious they would be" (p. 123). She needs help, but feels that the only person who could really help her is X. Then, she has a beautiful dream of embracing him, with their souls mingling. Shortly after this dream, she feels she has started to let go of X. Here is how she describes her experience of letting go: "A lick of pain, furtive, darting up where you don't expect it. Then a lightness. The lightness is something to think about. It isn't just relief. There's a queer kind of pleasure in it, not a self-wounding or malicious pleasure, nothing personal at all" (p. 127).

To my way of thinking, this is a superb description of one difference between grief and depression. However extraordinarily painful grief is, for however long it lasts, it is not primarily self-punishing. Something in us knows it is part of life for everyone. That doesn't diminish the pain. But, in a sense, it isn't personal. Loss is part of the deal we all have to make with life.

This brings me to the idea that, in grief, a saving grace may be the feeling of connection with other sufferers. This is the subject of Raymond Carver's poignant story "A Small, Good Thing" (2002). Ann and Howard are planning their son Scotty's birthday party. On the way to school the day of the party, Scotty is hit by a car. Most of the story takes place in the hospital, where the desperate parents wait in vain for their son to come out of a coma. For a while, the doctors hold out hope. Only the nurses seem to be able to believe Scotty will really die. And then, he does.

Ann and Howard get a series of harassing calls from the baker, demanding that they pick up and pay for the birthday cake they had ordered. Ann wants to confront him, so they drive to the bakery, although it is very late at night. Ann tells the baker that her son is dead. She admits that he couldn't be expected to know that, but then she spits out, "Bakers can't know everything—can they, Mr. Baker? But he's dead. He's dead, you bastard!" (p. 24). Her sorrow overtakes her anger and she collapses, shaking, sobbing that it isn't fair.

The baker asks them to sit down, apologizes, and tries to explain that his lonely life has left him socially unfit. He doesn't have children, friends, lovers. He makes cakes so others can celebrate. He has forgotten how to act like a human being. He asks their forgiveness. All he knows how to do is bake. He serves them rolls: "'You probably need to eat something,' the baker said. 'I hope you'll eat some of my rolls. You have to eat and keep going. Eating is a small good thing in a time like this' he said" (p. 25). At first they can't eat, but, gradually, they do. They take in his offering, recognizing that grief has distorted them all in different ways. It would be just as absurd not to eat the rolls as it is to have them. So why not share a small, good thing.

On a similar subject, the play "Rabbit Hole" (Lindsay-Abaire, 2006) explores each parent's reaction when their young son is killed in a bicycle accident. The father wants to get rid of his toys, perhaps have another child, and move on. The mother holds on tight to every memory, every sensation, everything left to her. Is one grief healthier than the other?

My contention is that we cannot discern normal grief from depression by looking at the pain's duration, since normal grief can last a lifetime. Nor can we expect it to follow any particular program or sequence of feelings. As I elaborate in the next chapter, when I try to distinguish prolonged grief from depression, I focus on the way the person feels toward themselves. Like depression, grief can include a sense of self-diminishment, since we will never again be exactly who we were to the deceased. That is, if my cousin Jim really enjoyed my humor in a very particular way, when he dies, I probably will never be exactly that kind of clown with someone else. In a way, I lose that self along with my loss of Jim. But I am unlikely to hate myself for it or feel that I am stupid and inadequate, as I might in a state of depression. My grief might even engender genuine compassion for myself. I have lost my best audience. I am poorer but not worthless. I might be inclined to scan for whatever reliably brings me comfort, unlike the depressed, who tend to refuse to look. Another way to say this is that in grief I am a better, kinder, more loving parent toward myself than I am in depression. This difference is certainly one of degree and often very difficult to discern. The depressive's attack on himself or herself may take many forms, from cutting remarks to cutting their flesh, from verbal annihilation to suicidal threats, gestures, and attempts. However we understand the many causes of such behavior, it is not merely a response to the sadness that, inevitably, punctuates every life.

Amy Tan's marvelous story "The Joy Luck Club" (1992) depicts a variety of losses and attempts to cope with them. The narrator is Jing-mei, or June, a young woman whose mother died two months ago. Her father invites her to take her mother's place at the next meeting of the Joy Luck Club, a group of women who play mahjong together at each other's houses. Jing-mei feels unequal to the task of replacing her mother in any sense, but she comes to the meeting because her father wishes it.

As the story progresses, we get a clearer sense of why Jing-mei's mother created the club. Many years before Jing-mei's birth, Mother and her first husband and two infants moved to Kweilin, a beautiful town in China, because they hoped it would be safe from an impending Japanese attack. Her husband, an officer, then went off to the northwest town of Chungking. But Kweilin does not prove safe. As Japanese bombers arrive, the mother tries to walk to Chungking with a bit of food, clothing, and a baby under each arm. Gradually, along the road, she sheds everything, including the two babies, as her overburdened hands lose all their power to function. On that road, along with her two little children and everything else, she also loses all hope. It is after that horror that the mother has the idea of the Joy Luck Club, because she needed motivation to simply keep moving. My understanding is that the unbearable memories so threaten the mother's emotional balance that she feels it is necessary to *add* something good to her life in order to be able to go on living.

So, the Joy Luck Club is born. It is a gathering of four women who periodically gossip, eat, and play mahjong into the early morning hours, forgetting their sorrows. The mother explains that it is not about denying the grief and pain they all experienced, but rather to try to prevent the continuance of the unbearable trauma and longing for a past that is now gone.

Mother goes on to ask how long anyone could stare at arms and legs hanging from telephone wires and other gruesome sights permanently stored in her mind's eye. She and her friends decide to start the Joy Luck Club and pretend each week is the beginning of a new year. They will feast, laugh, play games, tell happy stories, and try to forget the horrors they have suffered.

Mother has a theory about what causes emotional problems. Each of us is made up of five elements, like fire, wood, and water. A disproportionate amount of any one of them causes trouble. For example, too much fire would make someone have a bad temper. Mother is a keen observer, with a ready "diagnosis" of other people's imbalances.

When her mother dies, Jing-mei feels they never really understood one another. She always sensed her mother's disappointment in her. Jing-mei never gave her mother something tangible to brag about. She wasn't a genius at anything, like some of the other daughters were. And Jing-mei realizes she could never really comprehend the tortures her mother endured. This gap in understanding makes them strangers forever. And yet, there are some hopes and beliefs Jing-mei does inherit from her mother. She sees that her mother's friends long for her to pass on some of her mother's truths. Here we encounter another kind of loss. The older women are frightened that Jing-mei and others her age won't appreciate their mothers' wisdom, in part because it is spoken in Chinese and not English. Hope won't pass from one generation to the next. The daughters will dismiss "joy luck" as not a word and, therefore, meaningless. So Jing-mei promises to pass the stories on. I think of the intricate balances we all need. There has to be sufficient joy to bear our sorrows. We need enough of a sense of continuity as well as progress. Family members are intimate and forever strangers. We have to respect the legacies handed down to us by preserving and destroying them. Every generation bears the loss of its world and its way of experiencing joy and luck.

Treatment

A year after the March 11, 2011, earthquake, tsunami, and nuclear meltdown in Japan, a writer for the *New York Times* reflects on the effects of the disasters. Citing published accounts, Iyer (2012) concludes that many Japanese people are able to see that "life means a joyful participation in a world of sorrows" (p. 6). The happy moments don't erase the losses, nor do the losses prevent us from knowing happiness. Both ideas can be held in mind at the same time.

I don't think of working with grief as "treating" it but, rather, as accompanying it and working with the patient on their other feelings so that the grief is bearable. Sadness is an inevitable human response to loss. However protracted, it is "normal." It seems to me to be an error to try to shorten it. As I discuss in the following chapter, I feel very differently about depression, which certainly should be treated. But pain is integral to being human, as Lee Stringer (2001) movingly expresses:

> One grows older and more knowing over time; life's more facile charms grow dim; the soul yearns, seeking more than could ever be had on this earth, more than could ever be wrought out of three dimensions and five senses. We, all of us, suffer some from the limits of living within the flesh. Our walk through this world is never entirely without pain. (pp. 112–113)

Elsewhere (Buechler, 2010), I suggest that, for each of us (non-clinicians as well as clinicians), our attitude toward suffering probably correlates with our posture toward intense emotionality in general. I have addressed attitudes about emotional intensity extensively (Buechler, 2004, 2008), so I will not repeat the bulk of this material. Briefly, I believe that each clinician has a rough idea of fitting expressions of sadness, rage, anxiety, and other feelings. However unformulated these notions may be, I think they have tremendous impact on our behavior in sessions. We may not have reflected much on how we arrived at our particular profile of appropriate emotionality. My own understanding is that it is generally influenced by our individual character style as well as our training analyst(s), supervisors, teachers, patients, and personal relationships. For example, life experience, professional training, and personal characteristics have rendered some of us more comfortable than others when we are in the presence of intense rage in ourselves and/or another person. These differences impact our focus on the material in a rage-filled session. Similarly, for each of us, our formulated and unformulated attitudes about strong feelings in general, and intense sadness in particular, will impact our attitudes as we accompany grieving patients.

In the 2010 paper, I explore how clinicians' attitudes about pain affect our stance toward the patient's defenses. In the first stance I discuss, the clinician (perhaps without having fully formulated it) sees suffering as best eradicated. From this vantage point, the patient's defenses could seem (at least temporarily) like allies. An adherent of this point of view might argue that, since most of us have accepted the notion of dissociation as an aspect of *normal* functioning

(Bromberg, 1998), we could say the same for denial, repression, splitting, projection, and the other defenses. Since defenses help us delimit suffering, shouldn't we *avoid* disrupting them (at least, early in treatment)?

We work far differently if we hold the second attitude I discuss, and see patients' *problems* as stemming from how they try to *avoid* conscious awareness of suffering, rather than the suffering itself. From this vantage point, defenses, such as splitting, dissociation, repression, and denial, are to be *overcome* so that painful memories can be put back into their affective context. In Freud's time, it was thought that this *remembering itself could cure*. Today, while we still ask patients to remember, we believe that some of the therapeutic action depends on their becoming more able to "stand in the spaces" (Bromberg, 1998) between their dissociated states. In other words, if I believe that grief is part of life, I focus on how patients defend against knowing about their grief, partially so that they can experience it with more immediacy, but also so they will no longer need the defensive process. This stance suggests to patients that bringing all of their self-states together will not harm them but, rather, will set them free. Whereas full self-awareness felt dangerous in the past, it will be curative now. It will spare the energy that has kept self-states apart, saving it for more constructive purposes. It will foster the joy of integrity or appreciation of one's wholeness. It will facilitate awareness of lifelong interpersonal patterns. In our presence, we tell patients, it is safe and desirable to remember, once more, with feeling.

A third attitude some clinicians (and non-clinicians) hold is that suffering is the royal road to enlightenment. Health requires *a full embrace* of it. Of course, this attitude has permeated some religious stances, but it plays a role in some forms of treatment as well. For those who see suffering as the path toward enlightenment, humanistic wisdom, or personal identity, defenses are *neither* friend nor foe. They are simply not the point. Unlike their colleagues in the first two groups, these analysts are neither loath to interpret defense nor eager. Their focus is elsewhere. They are looking for hurt, not for *what blocks* awareness of pain, but for *the humanizing function of the pain itself*.

At times, I have leaned toward each of these three attitudes, but the third is my most frequent stance. It is beautifully illustrated (see discussion above) by Raymond Carver's story "A Small Good Thing" (2002). Sadness can bring human beings together in mutual appreciation of the inevitability of suffering. Our specific sorrows help to define us as particular people, but they also draw us into the common fold.

Very early in my career, I treated a member of a political group whose ideology is especially personally repugnant to me. At first, I wondered if I could work with him. A better understanding of his suffering helped me enormously. Basically, I was able to feel some compassion along with many other countertransferential responses. Without this connection, I don't think I could have sustained a working relationship with him.

I see the clinician's attempt to accompany sorrow as an effort to have an impact on the patient's overall balance of emotions. Our feelings form a system

(Buechler, 2004; Izard, 1972) with alteration in any emotion impacting all the others. So, for example, if I become more curious, that will affect my level of anger, sadness, joy, and so on. In treatment, I think we are very frequently decreasing the patient's loneliness, which has an effect on the whole emotional balance. Grief shared is not entirely the same as totally solitary grief. It still hurts. But other feelings are present along with the pain. That may make it bearable.

I have (Buechler, 2008) considered treatment to be a laboratory for strengthening both participants' capacities to bear grief. I think of loss as an ongoing experience in therapy, as in the rest of life. For example, after a moment of inattention or a misunderstanding, my patient and I feel a tiny rupture. Perhaps it is a minor and fleeting experience. But it may still recruit our feelings about the limitations in our relationship and, more generally, in our connections with others. We have a momentary hope of being understood, and then something disrupts it and it is gone. We feel the first buds of real mutual appreciation just as the session ends, and we wonder if it will be there next time. These microcosms coalesce around more major, concrete loss experiences. For example, in the termination phase, we may grieve for all our unsatisfied hopes, all our lost opportunities, and all the times we lacked the courage to say what needed to be said. The clinician and/or the patient may seem to be "overreacting" to the ending of their work, but perhaps that is because we don't understand all the strands that contribute to their sorrow. In treatment, we (both) have a chance to become better acquainted with what I would call our personal signature style of grief. Each of us brings a lifetime of experience with loss to every new sorrow, just as we bring our history of joyous moments to each new joy. Understanding ourselves, and being understood by another, includes becoming fully acquainted with this signature style of grieving. My grief may have a major anxiety component, because of my loss experiences, whereas yours may be filled with anger at life's unfairness. I believe in helping people better comprehend who they tend to be, when they are feeling shame, guilt, sorrow, joy, love, loneliness, and other basic human emotions.

My own belief about working with grief, specifically, is that I am striving to help the patient grieve without becoming clinically depressed. That is, I am trying to help this person feel sorrow relatively uncomplicated by excessive shame, guilt, or any other powerful, self-critical feeling. I see this stance as similar in spirit to Sullivan's thinking. My understanding of Sullivan (1953, 1956) is that he believed that human beings can find ways to cope if we are not overly encumbered by "parataxic distortions" of our interpersonal experiences. Thus, in this thinking, treatment helps the patient access natural capacities to deal with life. Similarly, I think human beings can bear sorrow if it is *just* sorrow. It is when it is accompanied by severe shame, guilt, or other debilitating feelings that it becomes paralyzing depression (see next chapter). For example, in a state of shame we don't have the resources we need to cope with significant loss. In the absence of potentially healing feelings, and with the presence of emotions that deplete the sense of self, we can't keep our emotional *balance*. It is then that we "fall" into depression.

References

Agee, J. (2009). *A death in the family*. New York: Penguin Books.
Auden, W. H. (2010). Musee des beaux arts. In K. Young (Ed.), *The art of losing: Poems of grief and healing* (p. 3). New York: Bloomsbury.
Bayley, J. (1999a). Last jokes. *The New Yorker*. August 2, pp. 38–43.
Bayley, J. (1999b). *Elegy for Iris*. New York: W. W. Norton & Company.
Bellow, S. (1981). A silver dish. In N. Sullivan (Ed.), *The treasury of American short stories* (pp. 421–444). Garden City: Doubleday & Company.
Bromberg, P. (1998). *Standing in the spaces*. Hillsdale, NJ: Analytic Press.
Buechler, S. (2000). Necessary and unnecessary losses: The analyst's mourning. *Contemporary Psychoanalysis*, 36, 77–90.
Buechler, S. (2004) *Clinical values: Emotions that guide psychoanalytic treatment*. Hillsdale, NJ: Analytic Press.
Buechler, S. (2008). *Making a difference in patients' lives: Emotional experience in the therapeutic setting*. New York: Routledge.
Buechler, S. (2010). No pain, no gain? Suffering and the analysis of defense. *Contemporary psychoanalysis*, 46, 334–355.
Carver R. (2002). A small, good thing. In A. H. Bond (Ed.), *Tales of psychology: Short stories to make you wise* (pp. 1–28). St. Paul: Paragon House.
Chopin, K. (2008). The story of an hour. In J. Kelly (Ed.), *Seagull reader stories* (pp. 120–123). New York: W. W. Norton & Company.
Dark, A. E. (1999). In the gloaming. In J. Updike & K. Kenison (Eds.), *The best American short stories of the century* (pp. 688–704). New York: Houghton Mifflin Company.
Didion, J. (2005). *The year of magical thinking*. New York: Alfred A. Knopf.
Freud, S. (1917). Mourning and melancholia. In J. Strachey (Ed. & Trans.), *The standard edition of the complete psychological works of Sigmund Freud* (Vol. 14, pp. 237–258). London: Hogarth Press.
Horwitz, A. V., & Wakefield, J. C. (2007). *The loss of sadness*. New York: Oxford University Press.
Iyer, P. (2012). One year later, a new resilient Kyoto. *New York Times*, Travel section. March 25, p. 6.
Izard, C. E. (1972). *Patterns of emotion: New analysis of anxiety and depression*. New York: Academic Press.
Leavitt, D. (1992). Gravity. In J. C. Oates (Ed.), *The Oxford book of American short stories* (pp. 741–745). New York: Oxford University Press.
Lindsay-Abaire, D. (2006). *Rabbit hole*. Broadway production.
Mukherjee, B. (1992). The management of grief. In J. C. Oates (Ed.), *The Oxford book of American short stories* (pp. 697–713). New York: Oxford University Press.
Munro, A. (1991). Bardon bus. In *The moons of Jupiter* (pp. 110–129). New York: Vintage.
Porter, K. A. (1952). Theft. In M. Crane (Ed.), *Fifty great short stories* (pp. 222–229). New York: Bantam Dell.
Rattigan, T. (1985). *In praise of love*. In *Terence Rattigan plays: Two* (pp. 171–257). London: Methuen Drama.
Shakespeare, W. (1972). *King Lear*. In *The Arden edition of the works of William Shakespeare* (pp. 1–206). London: Methuen Drama.
Stringer, L. (2001). Fading to gray. In N. Casey (Ed.), *Unholy ghost: Writers on depression* (pp. 105–114). New York: HarperCollins.
Sullivan, H. S. (1953). *The interpersonal theory of psychiatry*. New York: W. W. Norton.
Sullivan, H. S. (1956). *Clinical studies in psychiatry*. New York: W. W. Norton.
Tan, A. (1992). The joy luck club. In Richard Ford (Ed.), *The Granta book of the American short story* (pp. 599–619). London: Granta Books.

Chapter 8

Depressive Self-Harming

How Does Depression Differ From Grief?

"All through life that piece of crepe had hung between him and the world; it had separated him from cheerful brotherhood and woman's love, and kept him in that saddest of all prisons, his own heart, and still it lay upon his face, as if to deepen the gloom of his darksome chamber, and shade him from the sunshine of eternity" (p. 498). Thus did Nathaniel Hawthorne describe the protagonist in his story "The Minister's Black Veil" (1952). This chapter explores the terrain of that prison of the heart. Many authors have charted it. It is the asylum of Dickens' (1986) Miss Havisham, the world inhabited by those, like William Styron (1992), for whom the darkness has become visible.

Depression is both like and unlike grief, as Freud (1917) and countless others have suggested. As with grief something has been lost. But, I suggest, in depression the loss is more fully interior. One has lost one's own light. While an exterior loss may have contributed, the depressed person mourns him or herself. This death in the midst of life transfixes us, like specimens caught in amber. Depression's paralysis makes movement monumentally, impossibly effortful. The experience of depression has been beautifully captured by Lesley Dorman (2001):

> Depression is a place that teems with nightmarish activity. It is a one-industry town, a psychic megalopolis devoted to a single twenty-four-hour-we-never-close product. You work misery as a teeth-grinding muscle-straining job (is that why it's so physically exhausting?), proving your shameful failures to yourself over and over again. Depression says you can get blood from a stone, and so that's what you do. (p. 236)

Inhabitants of this "one industry town" seem to cling to their citizenship. Should we try to entice them to travel? Should we signal to them that their suspension of life is probably temporary, as Styron (2001) advises?

> A tough job, this calling "Chin up" from the safety of the shore to the drowning person is tantamount to insult, but it has been shown over and over again that

> if the encouragement is dogged enough—and the support equally committed and passionate—the endangered one can nearly always be saved. (p. 122)

Or is it better to heed depression as a meaningful signal that something that is wrong?

> [W]hat we call depression isn't really a disorder at all but, like physical pain, an alarm of sorts, alerting us that something is undoubtedly wrong; that perhaps it is time to stop, take a time-out, take as long as it takes, and attend to the unaddressed business of filling our souls. (Stringer, 2001, pp. 112–113)

As friends, family, or therapists of people who are depressed, should we try to persuade the sufferer that life can be better or that the pain will pass, or should we aim to alleviate the loneliness by sharing in it?

In the previous chapter, I suggested that, while grief can last as long as depression, in grief the sense of self-worth is less likely to be profoundly diminished. I believe that, while the grieving person and the depressed person have both suffered some form of loss, the lowered self-esteem often present in depression complicates self care. Freud (1917) wrote of the depressed individual's ambivalence toward the *object* and *lack* of shame. I suggest that depression often includes a great deal of shame, and a central aspect is ambivalence toward the *self*. Even when the person did feel ambivalent about someone they lost, I believe that it is their *shame, guilt,* or *regret about having ambivalence* that most powerfully predisposes them to depression.

In other words, I agree with Freud that depression is more complicated than sadness and not merely a response to loss. But Freud privileged anger and ambivalence toward the object as the most likely causes of this complication. He specifically stated (1917) that shame was *not* involved in depression's pain. Of depressed people, he said:

> They are not ashamed and do not hide themselves, since every derogatory that they say about themselves is at bottom said about someone else. Moreover, they are far from evincing toward those around them the attitude of humility and submissiveness that would alone befit such worthless people. (p. 248)

But my clinical experience tells me that the *actions* as well as the *words* of those who are depressed often suggest derogatory feelings toward *themselves*. For example, in *Darkness Visible* (1992), William Styron chronicled his own descent into depression. He remarks on depression's similarities with sadness, as well as its differences. One similarity is that both involve significant losses: "Loss in all of its manifestations is the touchstone of depression—in the progress of the disease and, most likely, in its origin" (p. 56). But, a bit later, Styron highlights that the depressed person has lost a sense of self-worth along with whatever other losses have occurred: "The loss of self-esteem is a celebrated symptom, and my own sense of self had all but disappeared, along with any self-reliance" (p. 56). Since he couldn't rely on himself, Styron became extremely dependent on his wife. He wrote: "There is an acute fear of abandonment. Being alone in the house, even for a moment, caused me exquisite panic and trepidation" (pp. 56–57).

William Styron's wife, Rose, and his daughter, Polly, took notes on their experiences of him during his worst depressions. Remarkably, some of these outpourings have been published by Rose Styron, in a book chapter entitled "Strands." For example, after visiting her father, Polly wrote this synopsis: "For the next hour, he raved about his miserable past and his sins and the waste of his life and how, when they published the scandal of his life, we should try not to hate him. 'You'll hate me. You'll hate me,' he said in a whisper" (pp. 133–134).

In the same edited volume, Nancy Mairs ("On Living Behind Bars"), another sufferer of depression, wrote of herself, at college, as "nearly paralyzed by dread of my inadequacy" (p. 186). Later, she blames her lack of success, as a writer and as a person, on her "self-repugnance." These two pieces are not fiction, but they give what I think is an accurate account of the self-hate that often distinguishes the depressed from the profoundly sad. Of course, it can be posited that the hate is really meant for the internalized object, but in practice, it still manifests in the patient in the form of shame, guilt, or regret.

Sometimes fiction tells the story of depression in a character's self-destructive actions as well as self-deprecating behavior. Sherman Alexie's story "What You Pawn I Will Redeem" (2008) recounts an incredible tale of the suicidal adventures of Jackson Jackson (sometimes called Jackson Squared), a Spokane Indian boy. Homeless, he wanders the streets, spending every cent he can muster on liquor. A divorced college dropout, he feels that he is only successful at being homeless. As if to spell out how society's prejudice defines him, he expects the reader to write him off as worthless, given that homeless Indians are a common sight in Seattle and are treated with resentful dismissal. And, a bit later, he makes sure the reader understands how profoundly society's messages have sunk in, offering up himself as proof of the detrimental effects of colonialism on Native Americans. Jackson has succumbed, has become willing to be written off as worthless. But, then, in a burst of hope, fueled by unexpected kindnesses, he tries to reclaim some positive identity.

Drinking partners drift in and out of his life. At one point, having located his grandmother's powwow regalia in a pawnshop, he is determined to buy it back. Of course, he doesn't have the money. He tries selling newspapers but promptly drinks most of the money he earns and gets into a fight with a bartender that leaves him injured, exhausted, broke, and sleeping off his bender on the street. A good-natured police officer asks him why he seems bent on self-destruction. Jackson tells him that he has been killing himself ever since his grandmother's death. He thinks about why she died, wondering if the theft of her powwow regalia brought on her cancer and, alternately, if buying it back would then bring her back to life.

Jackson keeps trying, but he can't hold on to money. The police officer hands him some money to give him a chance to straighten out. He finds the pawnshop, whose owner tells him the regalia will cost him a thousand dollars. He has managed to hold on to five dollars. Perhaps out of guilt, or goodness, or both, the owner lets him have the regalia for five dollars. He promptly dons the regalia and proceeds to dance – perhaps with his grandmother – in the street, as cars, pedestrians, and even the city itself stops to watch. We aren't told what happens next. Maybe he goes on dancing, or maybe he goes on another drinking spree and loses the regalia. There is such a mixture of self-loathing and a peculiar, sweet tenderness in this man! It is hard to say what he will do. People have shown him that the world is bad and steals an old woman's prized possession, her identity. But other people have bet on Jackson, tried to help him, and shown him that the world is also good. In his depression, Jackson has been unable to muster enough love for himself to take adequate care of himself. He has always failed himself. Can some strangers' acts of kindness and Jackson's genuine love for his grandmother change this? Wrapped in her, can he begin to believe in Jackson Squared?

Elsewhere (Buechler, 2008), I have written of a form of depression that accompanies a sense of the loss of the person one "should" have been. Especially as a result of trauma, such as sexual abuse, the person mourns for the freer, more trusting, more vibrant self that could have existed if abuse hadn't stolen it away. Here, I suggest that the loss of the unharmed self often creates a depressive form of sorrow rather than an uncomplicated feeling of loss. It is easy to see how rage at the perpetrator could be the emotion that, along with sorrow, results in depression in this situation, as Freud posited. But I think shame, guilt, and regret, at not having *prevented* the abuse can be important factors. In fact, it can feel as though the victim's character is the *cause* of the abuse. For example, in Joyce Carol Oates' chilling story "Where Are You Going, Where Have You Been?" (1999), Connie is 15 and all too fixated on her appearance, at least according to her perpetually critical mother. This sharply contrasts with the praise heaped on Connie's older sister, June, who seems to do everything right. When the rest of her family goes to a barbecue that Connie is too disdainful to attend, she is visited by two much older men, who invite her to go for a ride in their car. After some preliminary banter, one of the men, Arnold, makes it clear to Connie that if she doesn't willingly go with him, he will set fire to her house and force her out of it. When she doesn't respond to that, he threatens to kill her family. Arnold easily wears Connie down, telling her things she had probably half-believed even before he said them. He succeeds in getting her to go with him willingly, convincing her that she can do no better than to be sweet and pretty and submissive, not her own person but theirs.

Connie touches her heart and feels it is not hers, just like the rest of her body. None of it is hers any more. Connie lets herself be drawn into Arnold's car, leaving everything familiar behind.

I imagine that Joyce Carol Oates saw Connie as an apt victim for a predator like Arnold. At first he tries to win her over with compliments on her looks, "cool" clothing, and just right music. He gives her the sense that he "knows" her and that she is the type of girl who should be with him. He preys on her own sense of being flimsy, superficial, a girl whose heart and body lack substance so they don't matter to anyone. As things progress, Arnold adds threats to the enticements, implying that, since she is worthless and her family members are good people, she ought to sacrifice herself. Arnold has "played" Connie perfectly. He has used her own suspicions about herself to lure her. Leaving with Arnold is suicidal in the way that adolescents often express self-destructive impulses. Out of secret beliefs that those who are critical of them are right, they give in to actions that risk harm or even death.

Another story, "Teenage Wasteland" (2002) by Anne Tyler, mines similar territory. Donny, like Connie, is 15, unsure of himself, and on the cusp of more trouble than he understands. We meet him through the eyes of his bedraggled mother, Daisy. As the story opens, Daisy is just beginning to worry. The principal has called her in to tell her that Donny is noisy, lazy, unresponsive, and disruptive in class. At first, Daisy becomes more involved, checking Donny's homework. But the problems just escalate, as Donny ups the ante, cutting class, smoking, drinking, and helping to break into another boy's locker.

Interestingly, like Oates' character, Connie, Donny also falls under the spell of someone seemingly "cool." His parents engage a tutor, Cal, who persuades them to ease their restrictions. Cal argues that their lack of faith in Donny harms his already beleaguered self-esteem. This profoundly affects Daisy:

> She saw Donny suddenly from a whole new angle: his pathetically poor posture, that slouch so forlorn that his shoulders seem about to meet his chin . . . oh, wasn't it awful being young? She'd had a miserable adolescence herself and had always sworn no child of hers would ever be that unhappy. (p. 259)

In what seems to me a nearly uncanny resemblance, Donny falls under Cal's spell, just as Connie submitted to Arnold. While Cal may not be a predator, he uses his coolness and his acute sense of Donny's vulnerabilities to gain absolute control over him. Eventually, Donny is expelled from school. Donny is enrolled in a new school, where, at first, he plods with his head down: "There was something exhausted and defeated about him" (p. 264). But Donny can't keep this up for long and runs away. As the story ends, we glimpse Donny's death through Daisy's eyes:

> As she falls asleep, she occasionally glimpses something in the corner of her vision. It's something fleet and round, a ball—a basketball. It flies up, it sinks through the hoop, descends, lands in a yard littered with last year's leaves and striped with bars of sunlight as white as bones, bleached and parched and cleanly picked. (p. 265)

Donny has disappeared into a teenage wasteland. Donny and Connie have entered a world where teenagers are wasted, in more than one meaning of the word. A particularly adolescent form of depression, a rebellious sob, has claimed their lives.

While in adolescence depression often has an unruly quality, adult depression frequently looks and feels like a physical paralysis. This is highlighted in Alice Munro's story "Dulse" (1991). Lydia, a poet, is nearing the end of her vacation from her day job as an editor. She is also facing a much more traumatic ending. Duncan, with whom she has been living, will no longer even answer her phone calls. Lydia is devastated. She walks along a street, knowing she needs to get to a bank, buy food, and get to the subway. She feels like she can't organize these tasks, or carry them out.

> She had to remember directions, and the order in which to do things: to open her checkbook, to move forward when it was her turn in line, to choose one kind of bread over another, to drop a token in the slot. These seem to be the most difficult things she had ever done. (p. 41)

Lydia finally gets home and just sits. Eventually, she gets into bed.

> She didn't feel at all like committing suicide. She couldn't have managed the implements, or aids, she couldn't even have thought which to use. It amazed her to think that she had chosen the loaf of bread and cheese, which were now lying on the floor in the hall. How had she imagined she was going to chew and swallow them? (p. 42)

Along with losing Duncan, Lydia has lost her belief in herself and, I would say, her love for herself: "She asks herself what gave him his power. She knows who did. But she asks what, and when—when did the transfer take place, when was the abdication of all pride and sense?" (p. 50). To my ears, in the phrase "the abdication of all pride and sense" Lydia lacerates herself. She stands accused of being a fool, of having betrayed herself. She has been her own worst enemy. She should have been with someone less complicated than Duncan, someone who could love her and make a home with her. With excruciating self-hate, Lydia imagines what Duncan will say about her: "Morose, messy, unsatisfactory Lydia. The unsatisfactory poet" (p. 52). Despite how tyrannical Duncan is, Lydia blames herself for failing to please him (though she also blames herself for having chosen him). Her doctor asks her how she knows she loves Duncan: "Because I suffer so when he's fed up with me. I want to be wiped off the earth. It's true. I want to hide. I go out on the streets and every face I look at seems to despise me for my failure" (p. 54). Clearly, these words express self-loathing and extreme shame.

Here are all the components of profound depression. In addition to losing Duncan, Lydia has lost her sense of being worthwhile. She can no longer even like herself, let alone love herself. She can't *care for* herself, in many senses. Duncan is unbearably cold in response to her last attempt to reach him. He writes to her in care of her employer, informing her that he will pack her things and send them to her. It is as though he deems her unworthy of even a moment of his attention and, worst of all, she agrees with his assessment.

Two Views of Depression

Elsewhere (Buechler, 1995), I have described two somewhat different views of the nature of depression. One pivots on its understanding of depressed people as suffering from an exaggerated form of *grief*, while the other focuses more on *anger* and anger-related behaviors. As I elaborate below, these two conceptions of depression lead to different prescriptions for its treatment.

Arieti was an important proponent of the first point of view, that depression is a kind of grief gone awry. In their significant book *Severe and Mild Depression* (1978), Arieti and Bemporad see depression as a sorrow that the person can't resolve. "Resolution" of sorrow requires changes in the way the mourner thinks about his or her loss. These shifts often take time. But when, for whatever reason, they don't occur, they may "turn into a more intense, unhappy feeling called depression. This feeling often replaces all other feelings except those, like guilt and self-depreciation, which are associated with sorrow" (p. 126). My own emphasis on the shame, guilt, and regret that can play a role in depression is consonant with this view.

The second approach, advocated by Bonime (1982), among others, highlights anger. What he called the "practice of depression" has anger at its core, but also includes despair, anxiety, manipulativeness, aversion to influence, and an unwillingness to enhance others.

As I see it, an emphasis on sadness, as opposed to an emphasis on anger, leads to a different focus in the treatment and a different conception of its goals. Are we primarily trying to help the patient access grief and find better ways to live with it? Or should our approach emphasize changing a hostile and maladaptive lifestyle?

Treatment of Depression

I see some differences in attitudes about the treatment of depression as reflecting these two contrasting views of its nature. Briefly, some (e.g., Solomon, 2008) imagine the treatment of depression as a process of helping the sufferer bear his or her losses. Clinicians can see themselves as decreasing patients' loneliness by accompanying them in their sorrow. Through an emotional connection, we help make the pain bearable. This would be similar to the work with grief (described in chapter 7), but, in my view, it would often need to emphasize the patient's feelings of inadequacy and unworthiness. Basically, our role would be to help the patient become better at self-care during a time when life hurts. We could understand this process in different ways. If, like Ferenczi (1929), we see human beings as needing someone to value and protect them (usually the mother) so that they may develop the ability to cherish and nurture themselves, the clinician might be understood as standing in for the mother when the parents have not fulfilled this function. In a sense, this view sees it as essential that each of us is welcomed into life. The absence of this kind of parenting leaves the individual more vulnerable, so that, when significant losses occur, depression is more likely.

In a different approach, O'Leary (2008) emphasizes helping the patient exert active effort to overcome a depressive lifestyle: "The core of the approach I recommend helps a depressed person to get moving again by encouraging and supporting personal agency, or proactivity. This requires collaboratively setting goals in several areas that appear to be related to personal well-being" (p. 548). To some extent, this view is related to Bonime's theory of the practice of depression, although it does not posit that the patient is manipulative. But, in both, depression is an unhealthy way of living life. In order to feel better, the person needs to live better. The clinician facilitates this change, partly by encouraging it or even suggesting modifications in the patient's daily routines, such as adding an exercise regimen. This view, like Bonime's, is predicated on a vision of depression as a product of choices or, at least, as affected by altering one's choices.

Do we see depressed people as primarily suffering from terrible pain, inflicted by their lives, or as living in unhealthy, maladaptive ways? Can we help them suffer better, or suffer less, or, perhaps, feel other feelings that change their overall emotional balance? This last approach has been the thrust of my own work. Since I see our emotions as existing in a system (Buechler, 2004, 2008), a change in any feeling affects them all. Thus, if I feel more curious, or angrier, or less guilty, or more anxious, it will have an impact on my depression. Whatever we help a person feel will modulate the overall balance. For me, this way of thinking, stemming from emotion theory (Izard, 1977), is very useful clinically. In a session, it allows me to focus on *any* emotion either participant is feeling. I don't have to be stuck focusing on the patient's depression, as can happen in treatment. I can focus on any feeling or its absence. For example, the absence of curiosity can play an important role in depression, from my point of view. The shame that I see as so central in many depressions can be a product of a virtually endless variety of emotional factors. In some cases, the person has never felt meaningful to anyone else or to themselves. Regardless of how much we see this as contributing to a vulnerability to depression, this clearly needs to change for depression to diminish. But, in treatment, there is no one route to follow. I (Buechler, in press) think treatment's goals and process have to be invented with each patient. Unlike some previous generations, today's clinician can't feel secure in the knowledge of what has to happen for change to occur. Early classical analysts thought they knew the sources of the neuroses and an effective, uniform therapeutic approach, but current clinicians are the products of challenges to these notions.

So, the participants in a treatment have to discover what needs to change, and how to change it, in order for a particular person's depression to lift. These goals and methods won't be the same across all patients. That is, your depression and mine could have somewhat different textures. Perhaps, in mine, guilt is prominent, whereas, in yours, it is less in evidence. I think we each have a kind of "signature depression," just as we each have a particular way of experiencing anxiety (although there are also some commonalities; for further discussion of this, see Buechler, 2008). But I believe that, frequently, the patient's basic feelings about his or her own adequacy, worth, meaningfulness, and potential impact have to change in order for a depressive emotional balance to shift in treatment.

I can imagine both Solomon's and O'Leary's approaches as modulating patients' negative feelings about themselves. When we encourage self-nurturing of whatever kind, we are implicitly suggesting that the person is *worth caring about and caring for*. Perhaps it is this *implicit* message that is responsible for at least some of the therapeutic effect.

Elsewhere (Buechler, 1999), I have suggested that depression poses a particular challenge for the more classical, neutral, abstinent analyst. Briefly, neutrality means that the clinician should not be invested in any particular outcome of the patient's conflicts. For example, the clinician should not be biased toward favoring the patient's superego-driven behavior. But I don't think we can maintain that stance and encourage self-nurturance as described above. In my previous work, I tried to define a "passionate neutrality" that would retain some of neutrality's therapeutic advantages but still leave the clinician free to encourage health.

> To summarize, a neutrality I could embrace would have to leave me free to encourage the patient's active efforts to fight depression. It would have to allow me to present enough of a new relational challenge to foster hope. It would have to include a valuing of urgency about not wasting time. And it would have to leave me free to describe the patient's impact on me, so that I can help him understand the differences between his intentions and his effect. (p. 225)

Of course, clinically, I see a somewhat different mix of feelings in each depressed patient. In some, the idea of their depression as mainly a form of grief gone awry seems plausible, while in others a way of living that expresses self-hate seems most prominent. Regardless, it seems to me that something about how the person feels about themselves needs to shift in order for depression to lift. I think the change often begins in the *clinician*. That is, we may have to see the patient differently in order for them to become better able to care for themselves. In a poignant passage about her reactions to her sister's depression, Nel Casey (2001) captures an obstacle that I think is common in clinicians' responses: "There are always private suspicions in the presence of the depressed. Is this person just spiritually weaker? Am I stronger? Couldn't it be worse? . . . I wondered if Maud was clinging to her sadness, stubbornly digging her heels in on a life that had become unwieldy and disappointing" (pp. 277–278). Like others in the depressed person's life, we often feel impatient and alternate between exhorting the patient to "pull up their socks" and sympathizing with their pain. As noted above, conceptualizations of depression range from seeing it as a painful state that is *not* within the sufferer's control, to seeing it as largely a product of choices. I think this difference accounts for some of the more heated clashes between clinicians about appropriate treatment modalities. I dealt with this issue in greater detail in a paper (Buechler, 2010) on clinicians' attitudes about psychic pain and how they affect treatment technique.

I suggest that in order to help someone suffering from depression, we may first have to come to a view of them that will allow us to help them with their shame. Again, there is no one-size-fits-all treatment approach. But, since I see self-worth as key to lifting depression, it follows that the clinician needs to be capable of facilitating this growth. Regardless of whether we see a particular patient's depression as mainly a form of grief or mainly a form of self-directed anger, as outside their control or as a product of choices they could make differently, we need a profound, absolute conviction in their inherent worth as human beings.

How might this play out with some of the characters in the stories summarized in the first section of this chapter? It is hard for me to conceive of most of them coming into treatment at all. How would I try to help Lydia, Alice Munro's character, suffering from her loss of Duncan and, in a sense, from her loss of herself? Could I value her in some way that helps her feel she matters? Could I help her forgive herself for choosing and losing Duncan? Together, could we elicit her caring about herself, and caring for herself, in new ways? Could I help her empathize with her own mad sorrow and sad rage, as well as her shame, her guilt at letting herself down, and her intense loneliness? Together, could we create a vision of her that encompasses all of these emotions, as well as those that are helping to kill her spirit because they are absent? Would we be able to invite her to live, without pushing her sorrow underground? Could we forge a process that helps Lydia respect herself and love herself enough to passionately protect and cherish her own life?

References

Alexie, S. (2008). What you pawn, I will redeem. In J. Kelly (Ed.), *The Seagull reader stories* (pp. 8–29). New York: W. W. Norton & Company.

Arieti, S., & Bemporad, J. (1978). *Severe and mild depression*. New York: Basic Books.

Bonime, W. (1982). Psychotherapy of the depressed patient. *Contemporary Psychoanalysis*, *18*, 173–189.

Buechler, S. (1995). Emotion. In M. Lionells, J. Fiscalini, C. H. Mann, & D. B. Stern (Eds.), *Handbook of interpersonal psychoanalysis* (pp. 165–188). Hillsdale, NJ: Analytic Press.

Buechler, S. (1999). Searching for a passionate neutrality. *Contemporary Psychoanalysis*, *35*, 213–227.

Buechler, S. (2004). *Clinical values: Emotions that guide psychoanalytic treatment*. Hillsdale, NJ: Analytic Press.

Buechler, S. (2008). *Making a difference in patients' lives: Emotional experience in the therapeutic setting*. New York: Routledge.

Buechler, S. (2010). No pain no gain? Suffering and the analysis of defense. *Contemporary Psychoanalysis*, *46*, 334–355.

Buechler, S. (2012). *Still practicing: The heartaches and joys of a clinical career*. New York: Routledge.

Buechler, S. (in press). My personal Interpersonalism: An essay on Sullivan's one genus postulate. *Contemporary Psychoanalysis*.

Casey, N. (2001). Wish you were here. In N. Casey (Ed.), *Unholy ghost: Writers on depression* (pp. 270–280). New York: HarperCollins.

Dickens, C. (1996). *Great expectations*. London: Penguin Classics.

Dorman, L. (2001). Planet no. In N. Casey (Ed.), *Unholy ghost: Writers on depression* (pp. 229–242). New York: HarperCollins.

Ferenczi, S. (1929). The unwelcome child and his death instinct. In *The final contributions to the problems and methods of psychoanalysis* (pp. 102–107). London: Hogarth Press.

Freud, S. (1917). Mourning and melancholia. In J. Strachey (Ed. & Trans.), *The standard edition of the complete psychological works of Sigmund Freud* (Vol. 14, pp. 237–258). London: Hogarth Press.

Hawthorne, N. (1952). The minister's black veil. In M. Crane (Ed.), *Fifty great short stories* (pp. 494–500). New York: Bantam Dell.

Izard, C. E. (1977). *Human emotions*. New York: Plenum Press.

Mairs. N. (2001). On living behind bars. In N. Casey (Ed.), *Unholy ghost: Writers on depression* (pp. 181–213). New York: HarperCollins

Munro, A. (1991). Dulce. In *The moons of Jupiter* (pp. 36–60). New York: Vintage.

Oates, J. C. (1999). Where are you going, where have you been? In J. Updike & K. Kenison (Eds.), *The best American short stories of the century* (pp. 652–670). New York: Houghton Mifflin Company.

O'Leary, J. (2008). Putting it together while falling apart: A personal view on depression. *Contemporary Psychoanalysis*, 44, 531–551.

Solomon, A. (2008). Depression, too, is a thing with feathers. *Contemporary Psychoanalysis*, 44, 509–531.

Stringer, L. (2001). Fading to gray. In N. Casey (Ed.), *Unholy ghost: Writers on depression* (pp. 105–114). New York: HarperCollins.

Styron, R. (2001). Strands. In N. Casey (Ed.), *Unholy ghost: Writers on depression* (pp. 126–137). New York: HarperCollins.

Styron, W. (1992). *Darkness visible*. New York: Vintage Books.

Styron, W. (2001). From Darkness visible. In N. Casey (Ed.), *Unholy ghost: Writers on depression* (pp. 114–126). New York: HarperCollins.

Tyler, A. (2002). Teenage wasteland. In A. H. Bond (Ed.), *Tales of psychology: Short stories to make you wise* (pp. 254–267). St. Paul: Paragon House.

Chapter 9

Generative Aging

Willa Cather's story "Neighbor Rosicky" (1992) tells us something about the potential satisfactions and sorrows that aging can bring. Anton Rosicky and his wife, Mary, raised five boys and one girl. Both hard-working farmers, Mary is 15 years younger. At 65, Anton is warned by his doctor that his heart is bad and he should avoid hard labor. But, at first, this feels to Anton rather like avoiding being the only self he knows. As he puts it, he can accept that he is getting to be an old man, but not that he is getting to be an old woman!

Anton reminisces and comes to the realization that what matters most to him is that his sons continue to farm the land. But why is this crucial? There is something he so desperately wants to pass on. He has a gift for them, but will they take it? When he himself is not sure why he needs this so badly, can he make them understand?

As he reflects, Anton grasps that his greatest legacy would be to communicate that life can have an organic quality, and this wholeness renders life beautiful. Anton expresses the yearning of a man who can, at last, understand his life's work, but doesn't know whether or not he will be granted the time to achieve it.

The poignant yearning of this man, the joy he feels in understanding his life's meaning, mingles with sorrow. Nothing can keep his life from slipping through his fingers. He is losing Mary, the farm, his children, the future, his body and its aches and pleasures. He has achieved some wisdom, but is it too late? Will his heart break before he has a chance to bestow his greatest gift? The end of the story, while ambiguous, seems optimistic to me. Rosicky dies while his physician, Doctor Ed, is away. Doctor Ed returns, visits Rosicky's grave, and is startled by a new perception: "For the first time it struck Doctor Ed that this was really a beautiful graveyard. He thought of city cemeteries; acres of shrubbery and heavy stone, so arranged and lonely and unlike anything in the living world" (p. 326). In contrast, this place was open and free, a square of living grass stirred by an enlivening wind. It was a place of ongoing life: "Nothing could be more undeathlike than this place; nothing could be more right for a man who had helped to do the work of great cities and had always longed for the open country and had got to it at last. Rosicky's life seemed to him complete and beautiful" (p. 326). By dying in the setting he loved best, Rosicky communicated his wholeness, and left a legacy that endures.

In her story "Little Selves" (1999), Mary Lerner also portrays the joys and sorrows of aging, but with a different emphasis. Lerner highlights the potential meaning in remembering our younger selves as we let go of life. Margaret O'Brien is 75, a great aunt, devout, and clearly dying. She feels weary enough to be ready to die, and yet, she seems to have one last purpose. Even in the midst of company, her eyes turn inward, and she struggles mightily to remember her earliest days. In her words, "I must be getting back to the beginning" (p. 9). She strives to recover earlier and earlier memories, straining backward, reaching for her earliest conscious awareness of herself.

Margaret is astonished at the little selves she retrieves: "How full of verve and life were all those figures! That glancing creature grow old? How could such things be!" (p. 13). It *is* amazing how supple skin yields to wrinkled old age. At last, Margaret captures her prey: the touchstone memory of herself. She is 9 or 10, and her mother has bought her a new red coat in a large size so it will last for a while. But Margaret wants a more stylish fit. So, secretly, she sews until it takes a form-fitting shape. Her mother is aghast, until a neighbor remarks that Margaret has done an excellent job. Everyone has a good laugh, and the child escapes punishment and gets her way. Remembering this little self brings old Margaret O'Brien great joy: "With its fullness of detail, it achieved a delicious suggestion of permanence, in contrast to the illusiveness of other isolated moments. Margaret O'Brien *saw* all those other figures, but she really *was* the child with the red coat" (p. 15).

Margaret's final wish is to tell her niece, Anna, about her little selves so that they may be remembered and live on. She is afraid Anna will laugh at her, but Anna fully comprehends and replies, "'Tis a thought I've often myself, let me tell you,' she admitted. 'Of all the little girls that were me, and now can be living no longer'" (p. 16). Margaret is overjoyed at Anna's compassionate understanding. She confesses that she sometimes hears her little selves in her head, pleading not to be forgotten. With sudden sorrow, she realizes that these little girls are "all the children I ever had. My grief! that I'll have to be leaving them! They'll die now, for no man lives who can remember them any more" (p. 16). But Anna promises to sit beside Margaret every night, so Margaret can acquaint her with all the "lasses." Anna's mother had already told her stories from that earlier time, so she reassures Margaret that her mind is well-prepared to receive the little girls. She vows to call them up often after Margaret is gone. So the old woman "had her heart's desire. She recreated her earlier selves and passed them on, happy in the thought that she was saving them from oblivion" (p. 16). When she dies the young American priest thinks Margaret's radiance comes from religious ardor, but Anna alone understands its source. And, true to her word, Anna slips into the magic circle of her aunt's memories.

This lyrical story is equal parts joy and sorrow. In its balance of heartache and unexpected pleasure, it exemplifies life. We are reminded of how much it can mean to remember, to be recognized, to be heard, and to pass on something deeply felt.

Aging transforms a much less sympathetic character in Benjamin Rosenblatt's story, "Zelig" (1999). Zelig is a miser. Convinced to leave his homeland in Russia, he comes to America because his only son is dying there, and he regrets the move every day. His sole wish is to save enough money to return. When his wife begs him for money for medications or a doctor to try to save their son, he refuses. The son dies of tuberculosis that night, leaving Zelig and his wife to care for their little grandson, who suffers from his father's malady. Zelig refuses to pay for the boy's treatment or education. His wife explodes, but he remains adamant. That night, Zelig can't sleep and stands gazing at his sleeping grandson's emaciated body. He notices the boy's sunken cheeks and still wet tears. He bends over the figure of his grandson, whispering that, tomorrow, he will give him money for school.

Zelig's greed is supremely cruel, not out of a motive to injure, but out of passionate, single-minded self-interest. But, at the end, something breaks through his adamancy. What, exactly, manages to evoke a spark of human kindness in this stubborn old man? At the story's end, it seems as though Zelig is discovering his grandson's longstanding suffering for the first time. As the child literally turns his body away from his grandfather, Zelig becomes afraid that the boy will hate him and turn against him emotionally. The last line of the story, after Zelig promises the money, reads, "You hate to look at granpa; he is your enemy, eh?" (p. 6).

Zelig has always been a passionate man, but until now, his passion has been spent for himself and his beloved Russia. In his single-minded determination, he could only see the boy as a potential obstacle. Somehow, at the end, he begins to see the child as a person, with his own pain, purpose, and, perhaps, determined hate. As I read between the lines, I imagine that Zelig understands, at long last, that if his grandson hates him, he will truly die in enemy territory. Zelig has found a new way home.

In "The Middle Years" (1992), Henry James explores the ravages of premature aging and also hints at what can modulate its pain. Dencombe is a middle-aged successful writer whose most recent book, *The Middle Years*, has just appeared in print. He is convalescing at a health resort as a result of a recent bout of a debilitating illness. He has just received a copy of his new book from his publisher and realizes, to his great dismay, that he doesn't remember what he wrote. He sits on a bench, struggling to understand this mysterious blankness. What does it mean about the functioning of his mind, at present and in the future?

James immediately raises profound questions about bearing the passage of time. As Dencombe puts it, "He should never again, as at one or two great moments of the past, be better than himself. The infinite of life was gone, and what remained of the dose a small glass scored like a thermometer by the apothecary" (p. 171). Tears fill Dencombe's eyes as he reflects that for him

> something precious had passed away. This was the pang that had been the sharpest during the last few years—the sense of ebbing time, of shrinking opportunity; and now he felt not so much that his last chance was going as that it was gone indeed. He had done all he should ever do, and yet hadn't done what he wanted. (p. 173)

What comes to my mind here is the distinction between grief and depression that I explored in chapters 7 and 8. As is true of grief, losses are part of the territory of aging. Opportunities *are* shrinking, at least in some senses. But aging, like grief, does not have to become depression. Sorrow is inevitable, since, realistically, there are losses to bear. But perhaps reprieve is also possible. Rosicky, Margaret, and Zelig (see above) find solace that leavens their pain. Can Dencombe?

As Dencombe begins to read his own book, he is dazzled by its brilliance. As I see it, the balance of his feelings begins to shift, from sorrow laced with regret and rage to sorrow softened by joy and pride. It is still sorrow, but it sits lighter. This is so despite the continuing presence of painful yearning: "Ah for another go, ah for a better chance" (p. 174).

In the distance, Dencombe spots a young man (Doctor Hugh) who, amazingly, is also absorbed in reading a brand new copy of Dencombe's book, in the company of an older dowager (the Countess) and her young paid companion (Miss Vernham). Dencombe begins to speculate about the relationships among these three strangers. In a beautifully succinct sentence, James lets the reader know how such imaginings have always lifted Dencombe's spirits: "He already felt better of his melancholy; he had, according to his old formula, put his head at the window" (p. 176). Why do these speculations have such a positive effect? Is it a reminder, to Dencombe, that he is still Dencombe, with his accustomed habits of mind, despite the changes wrought by aging? Is it merely a pleasant distraction? Does it put his situation in some kind of perspective? That is, does it lift Dencombe to a higher level of abstraction, looking *at* the scene instead of merely being one of its participants?

One factor in Dencombe's change of heart is the sheer, amazing coincidence of meeting this young admirer. If life can surprise him, perhaps invigorating literary challenges still await him. He had tried to renounce the hope that there was more work to be done. As I see it, a jolt to his belief in his own predictive power told him that, perhaps, his gloomy despair was unwarranted. He didn't expect to meet this young admirer, so, maybe, life can still present him with other unexpected opportunities.

What happens next seems like a disaster. Dencombe faints and has to be carried back to the hotel. Doctor Hugh learns his real identity as the author of the book he so admires. Dencombe severely berates himself for causing his own collapse by staying out too long and over-taxing himself. It is as though he accuses himself of being Icarus and reaching for more life than is his portion. Fainting becomes, in Dencombe's mind, his deserved punishment for hubris. He is brought back down to despair. It is as though he begs life for more time, arguing that it wouldn't be fair for him to die just when he is fully realizing his talents but, then, repents his greed.

In their increasing intimacy, Doctor Hugh asks Dencombe why he is so alone, and Dencombe replies that, as often happens with age, he has lost everyone. Doctor Hugh imagines that Dencombe's achievements must comfort him and soften the effect of his losses. But Dencombe replies with renewed despair that this was not the case; he had wasted time and ripened too late and is filled with painful regret. Doctor Hugh suggests that Dencombe needs to have more vanity, but Dencombe replies that what he really needs is more time.

I think the wording of this reply is particularly meaningful. Dencombe pleads for an "extension." James is such an exacting, careful writer that I believe this choice of words must convey great meaning. I take it to imply that Dencombe feels as though there is an authority judging whether or not he is worthy of getting a special favor and having another chance to fully realize his genius. Talking to Doctor Hugh gives Dencombe the inspiration to flesh out what he would still like to write and how it would be the culmination of his career. The act of explaining himself to this intensely interested listener allows Dencombe a great leap in creative self-knowledge. But, just at that moment, Miss Vernham catches Dencombe and reprimands him for distracting Doctor Hugh and causing him to lose the Countess's favor (and her fortune). Dencombe is crushed. He feels he must leave the resort at once to save Doctor Hugh's prospects. He bars Doctor Hugh from visiting him, hoping that this will encourage the young man to attend to the Countess. But, along with discharging Doctor Hugh, Dencombe feels he has lost his last hope of an "extension," and the escalation of his illness is rapid. Doctor Hugh comes back for a last visit, bringing with him favorable notices of Dencombe's book. But the author is not pacified, saying that his next book would have deserved these glowing reviews if only he had been granted the time to write it. He learns that Doctor Hugh has lost the Countess's favor by neglecting her in order to spend time with Dencombe.

Dencombe recognizes that the idea of a second chance was born of illusion. Each of us gets only one chance. Doubts, frustrations, and imperfections are part of every life. The good news, and the terrible news, is that they pass. But, just before dying, Dencombe comes to yet another realization: His real "glory" is having gotten Doctor Hugh to care about him so much. That will not pass, as Dencombe's life ends.

The pain of yearning for more time is heart-wrenching in Thom Jones' aptly titled story, "I Want to Live" (1999). Mrs. Wilson struggles to comprehend the wild proliferation of her advancing cancer. Although it deals with devastating illness, this story captures the poignant longing for more time and the belated appreciation of everyday life that aging can evoke. Looking back on her youth, Mrs. Wilson remembers, "It had been a great, wide, wonderful world in those days, and no matter what, an adventure lay ahead, something marvelous" (p. 674). She asks herself where all the time went. How did all her dreams fall away?

As Mrs. Wilson grapples with a devastating diagnosis, as she struggles to bear relentless chemotherapy, she mourns her youth, replete with "[g]ood looks, a clean complexion, muscle tone, a full head of hair—her best feature, although her legs were pretty good, too. Strength. Vitality. A happy kid with a bright future" (p. 674).

At first, she can grab precious moments of forgetting about her pain and terror by playing with her little granddaughter. She is momentarily grateful that "[a]fter a year of sheer hell, in which all of the good stuff added up to less than an hour and four minutes total, there was a way to forget" (p. 678). Although tongue in cheek, this assessment of the shifting balance between sadness and joy seems apt. For many, advancing age brings a lopsided tally, with sorrows outweighing increasingly infrequent pleasures.

Mrs. Wilson does have one lucky break; she spends her last days with her daughter and son-in-law. He combines practical intelligence with a rare talent for living: "The son-in-law worked swing shift and he cheered her in the morning when he got up and made coffee. He was full of life. He was real. He was authentic" (p. 679). Although never given a name other than "the son-in-law," this compassionate man teaches Mrs. Wilson to be less compliant with the doctors' strict orders about her use of pain killers, bending the rules as her suffering escalates. This leads her to reflect that she had always believed in the rules, and tried to leave the world a better place than she had found it: "She had been a good person, had always done the right thing—this just wasn't right. It wasn't fair. She was so . . . angry!" (p. 679).

Unbearable pain can challenge longstanding but unformulated beliefs. It smokes out our fairy tales. Do I think a handsome prince will save me in the end if I am very good? Do I hold onto some stubborn fantasy that we get what we deserve? If I cling to hopes such as these, it may be more likely that my suffering will be tinged with outrage at the sudden confrontation of cozy idealizations by stark reality.

As each body part begins to fail, Mrs. Wilson longs for "zilch." But there is real relief in her son-in-law's ability to truly accompany her. He doesn't flinch from her body or her grief. He really wants to know what she is feeling, no matter what it is. He is a miracle. And he introduces her to her last surprise, Schopenhauer. One afternoon, she comes upon this passage in his copy of the philosopher's writing: "In early youth, as we contemplate our coming life, we are like children in a theater before the curtain is raised, sitting there in high spirits and eagerly waiting for the play to begin. It is a blessing that we do not know what is really going to happen" (p. 681).

Is it? Mrs. Wilson is cheered by the resonance with her experience. Finally, here is someone willing to be honest. But she regrets that she found Schopenhauer and his truths so late. She reflects that

> Schopenhauer got right into the heart of all the important things. The things that really mattered. With Schopenhauer she could take long excursions from the grim specter of impending death. In Schopenhauer, particularly in his aphorisms and reflections, she found an absolute satisfaction, for Schopenhauer spoke the truth and the rest of the world was disseminating lies! (p. 682)

In Mrs. Wilson's self-contradictions, we can see some of the profound puzzles aging brings. She asserts that "the truth was worthwhile. It was more important than anything, really" (p. 683). She grieves that she didn't meet Schopenhauer earlier, and yet agrees with him that it is a blessing that we live so long in ignorance of what the endgame is really like. She yearns for more life, to look at snowflakes again, to walk down "the sunny side of the street" or, at least, to sing in the rain. Anything, she seems to beg. Just give me another chance. And yet, she also longs to "simply push a button and never have been born" (p. 683). Wisely, the author does not try to resolve the contradictions, but just lets them wash over us.

Like Margaret in "Little Selves" (above), Mrs. Wilson returns to early childhood as she is really dying. She sees her farm, her pet rooster, and her mother. She smells the bacon, the coffee, and her Ovaltine. And with these memories comes, perhaps, her deepest regret. If only she had been more like the rooster! If only she had walked the earth feeling entitled to any "hen" she laid her eyes on! What a different life she might have had. But it is too late.

Those last sentences, that she ached to express, couldn't be uttered. Too late, Mrs. Wilson yearns to reassure her daughter that she loves her, despite a lifetime of being unable to speak the words. She should have been more demonstrative when she had the chance. After all, that was what it was all about. Or was it? In confusion, in sorrow, in longing, in profound regret, Mrs. Wilson dies.

In "Mrs. Cross and Mrs. Kidd" (1991), Alice Munro gives us a portrait of how the bonds of friendship can soften our sorrows as we age. Mrs. Cross and Mrs. Kidd met in kindergarten, 80 years ago. They now find themselves in Hilltop Home, a facility for the aging that caters to people with widely varying disabilities.

Munro helps us see how differences in their characters shape their approaches to the challenges of life at Hilltop. Mrs. Kidd has always found comfort in a wide array of books, whereas Mrs. Cross is everlastingly a people person. At first, their friendship with each other fills their otherwise empty days with card games and conversation. But as the story progresses, strains challenge the relationship.

Munro reflects on the picture Mrs. Kidd's three adult children need to have of their mother. They have fixed their image of her, preferring to view her as unchanged from her 40-year-old self. They send her books she would have been eager to get at that earlier point. They insist on seeing her as an unusually curious, roving, middle-aged mind, rather than as a woman in her eighties who has trouble concentrating.

In contrast, Mrs. Cross's six grown children have less need to distort their picture of their mother, since she is as interested in other people as ever. Unlike Mrs. Kidd, who needs to shield her eyes from the most infirm residents, Mrs. Cross befriends them. So she immediately makes contact with a newcomer named Jack, a 59-year-old stroke victim who was a journalist but now cannot speak, write, hold himself straight, or move the left side of his body.

I don't know whether the author intends to educate clinicians, but she certainly provides ample lessons for us in this story. When Mrs. Cross tries to engage Jack in conversation, Scrabble, or cards, his feeble attempts are followed by frustrated weeping. Mrs. Cross's tough love approach has been shaped by her experience as a mother. Early in their relationship, Jack tries and fails to wipe his own tears.

Mrs. Cross "remembered what you do when children cry; how to josh them out of it. 'How can I tell what you're saying if you're going to cry? You just be patient. I have known people that have had strokes and got their speech back. Yes I have'" (p. 167).

Mrs. Cross's unquenchable hope and empathy take the form of an unending series of experiments to find ways of communicating with Jack. What doesn't work informs her about what to try next. Like a brilliantly inventive clinician, she learns from her interpersonal mistakes. Asking him questions only increases his helpless sorrow, since he can't answer. In Munro's words, "That was the beginning of Mrs. Cross's takeover of Jack. She got him to sit and watch the card game and to dry up, more or less, and make a noise which was a substitute for conversation (an-anh) rather than a desperate attempt at it (anh-anh-*anh*)" (p. 168). Wanting Jack to be able to tell her what town he is from, she searches for an atlas so he can point to it but fails to find one. But when Jack points to a picture on the wall, she uses this as a basis for guessing and figures it out.

Mrs. Cross realizes that, in her efforts to help Jack, she is entirely alone. Mrs. Kidd does not want to hear about them, feeling that Jack has taken her friend from her. And the other residents have, for the most part, sunken into their own miseries: "Nobody cares about anybody else's misfortunes in here, she thought. Even when somebody dies they don't care, it's just me, *I'm still alive, what's for dinner?* The selfishness" (p. 171).

When Mrs. Cross tries the experiment of asking Jack to write instead of talk, he fails and cries. Mrs. Cross takes the onus, declaring that if she were smarter she could help him more. With irony, she observes that she can express anything she thinks, but her mind is limited, whereas Jack's mind is full, but he can't express any of his thoughts. Subtly, she has re-framed the situation so it is a mutual problem facing two human beings with different limitations. No seasoned clinician could do better!

What Mrs. Cross does next, while seemingly commonplace, is a "stroke" of genius, if you will pardon the pun. She invites Jack to have coffee with her and invents the game of asking him questions that can be answered with "yes" or "no." Through adroit guesses, she discovers the name of the woman he has always loved. Jack, we learn, has had experiences of helplessness even before his stroke. Each night, Mrs. Cross goes over her interactions with Jack, learning as much as possible from them. To my mind, she is the consummate clinician, eager but not too impatient, loving but never sentimental or maudlin, open about her own failings, secure enough not to have to deny her own limitations, infinitely curious about people, and intensely invested in life itself.

In a final, extremely moving scene, Mrs. Kidd tells Mrs. Cross the secret of her worst moments of utter helplessness: when she fell over and blacked out, before she came to Hilltop Home. Mrs. Kidd needs to deny the terror she still feels when she remembers this awful episode, making a joke of it. Meanwhile, exhausted from helping Jack, Mrs. Cross is without her wheelchair and doesn't know if she has the strength to get back to her room. She accepts help from Mrs. Kidd, who wheels her back in her own chair. Mrs. Kidd hides how much the physical exertion is costing her. Each trying to spare the other, they make their way to Mrs. Cross's room. For the moment, at least, love, friendship, compassion, and sheer willpower, triumph. While Mrs. Kidd and Mrs. Cross have brought different character structures, different strengths and weaknesses, to the task of aging, they find common ground in friendship, in the effort to retain something of their former selves, and in their empathy for each other. In the other, each sees mirrored her own courageous struggle not to go too gently into the good night waiting for us all.

With great delicacy, Munro has contrasted two very different characters, as they each bear the challenges of aging. As I see it, Mrs. Cross's strengths are holding up better than Mrs. Kidd's. Mrs. Kidd's reliance on a world of ideas fails to sustain her as her faculties fade. But Mrs. Cross's skills with people still get ample exercise. She can have the sense of *still being her*, coping in *her* distinctive way. I do not mean to suggest any moral difference between them. I am not saying that Mrs. Kidd's abilities are less valuable than Mrs. Cross's. But in a practical sense, they render her less adaptable to changes in her cognitive functioning.

Their differences are poignantly illustrated in a very brief scene when they visit the ward with the most debilitated residents. Mrs. Cross is a bit breezy but interested in the old men and women who are "not running on all cylinders" (p. 164). But Mrs. Kidd can't stand the smell of urine and the sight of a resident with her dress hiked all the way up and a tongue she couldn't stuff back in her mouth. Mrs. Kidd has to leave and never comes back for a second visit.

I suggest that Mrs. Kidd has no way to bear seeing people who, in a sense, are no longer themselves. Some part of each of them has returned to being more like an inanimate object than an aspect of a particular individual. That tongue is, in a way, no longer what it used to be. Now it is a symptom, an obstacle that helps to establish a new definition of its owner. Once, the woman attached to the tongue was a very specific human being with a life story. Of course, looked at from some angles, she is still that person. But it is all too easy to see her as more of a thing than a unique human being. She is a bizarre tongue with a face and body attached to it. I think this is an aspect of what we all fear about aging. As I get older, will I turn into some*thing* grotesque? Will others still see Sandra when they look at me? Will I? Alice Munro deftly demonstrates how character can make a difference in our ability to cope with the anxieties of growing old. While there can be no guarantees, no matter what happens to Mrs. Cross, she is as likely to remain as much herself as it is possible to be.

Character Magnified

One of my longstanding beliefs is that, for many of us, rather than mellowing as we age, we become more entrenched in our defensive styles and character issues. The challenges of aging can strengthen our need for the defenses we have cultivated all our lives. I think it is not infrequent that the schizoid become more isolated, the obsessive more exacting, the hysteric more preoccupied with their bodies, the depressed more gloomy, the paranoid more fearful, and, perhaps above all, the narcissistic more vulnerable to self-esteem injuries. I see aging as the ultimate test of character. What are our resources for coping with psychic and bodily changes? What (and who) have we invested in?

Unlike the other chapters, this one will not conclude with a section on treatment. I think it is clear that aging in itself does not warrant therapy. While this section touches on the voluminous literature on aging, it does not review it. But I would like to illustrate some of the specific difficulties of aging that spring from the character patterns discussed in the previous eight chapters. There are some physical, cognitive, and emotional challenges we all face, but their outcome is affected by the character-driven strengths and limitations we bring to the last phase of our lives.

I suggest that each of the character patterns discussed in previous chapters poses a significant challenge as we get older. For example, for the person who has always relied on obsessive defenses, remembering details and keeping things "perfect" can become more difficult. The deeply entrenched "conform versus rebel" issue can take on new and problematic meanings. In adolescence, it may have been expressed in anti-establishment rebellions. The core identity may have been forged in opposition to those in authority. What happens to these tendencies as aging advances? Of course, there are many possibilities. Some may find sublimations that help them adapt (for extensive discussion of this, see the work of Erikson, 1978, and Vaillant, 1977, 1993). But, more problematically, I think that with aging obsessive patterns often morph into a tendency toward fruitless protests. We can well imagine that Clarence Day's (1952) father (chapter 6) becomes an increasingly cantankerous old man, as his sense of being in charge slips away. The sad fate of Henry James' (1952) character Brooksmith, and the equally tragic plight of Melville's (1994) Bartleby, illustrate how obsessive defenses ill-prepare us for growing older. (see chapter 6 for further discussion).

I. B. Singer's (1999) character Bessy (discussed in chapter 2 on paranoia) beautifully illustrates how the price of some defensive styles rises with age. As her own physical, cognitive, and emotional equipment deteriorates, the world seems more and more alien and threatening. In a sense, aging upsets the balance between her strength and the strength she needs in order to cope. Life becomes a series of trials that can easily feel like they are deliberately inflicted by malicious predators.

What of those with hysteric tendencies to convert the psychological into the physical, as discussed in chapter 5? As the body develops creaks, as faculties diminish, it seems to me that conversion symptoms are likely to become more prominent. From another angle, what happens to the hysterical bargain? Having bartered away one's sense of autonomy in exchange for care, how does aging treat the hysteric? It is not hard to imagine dire endings. Elisa, the protagonist in John Steinbeck's story "The Chrysanthemums" (1952) (discussed in chapter 5), can serve as an example. As she realizes more clearly what her "deal" with her husband has cost, she truly loses heart.

Aging can pose extreme challenges for those with narcissistic issues, as will be discussed further below. But, briefly, whether we tend toward the more grandiose end of the spectrum or suffer from a lifelong sense of deficiency, those with self-esteem issues seem unlikely to be well-equipped to deal with the narcissistic injuries that can accompany the aging process.

Of course, losses (of significant relationships, among other forms of loss) accumulate. While this seems to me to mean there are more and more opportunities for grief, I don't think these have to become triggers for depression. As discussed in chapters 7 and 8, I believe that the relative health of the sense of self plays a major role in determining whether or not depression develops.

All in all, it seems as though dependence on any specific set of defenses and character patterns makes us more vulnerable as we age. Another way to say this is that, increasingly, we need our superego to operate as a real friend, softening self-criticisms and leavening regrets. I would suggest that those who are able to avail themselves of many defensive styles, as well as many interests, are better equipped. A narrow dependence on one style, or strength, or outlet leaves one at risk. As James' (1952) character Brooksmith so pithily expresses it, the loss of his old position, "c'est la fin de tout" (p. 59).

Some of the Challenges of Aging

Maintaining and Modifying Identity

> Still, it is like a long, hopeless homesickness my missing those young days. To me, they're like my own place that I have gone away from forever, and I have lived all the time since among great pleasures but in a foreign town. Well, OK. Farewell, certain years.
>
> Paley (1996, p. 227)

In Grace Paley's story "Distance" (1966), Dolly reflects on the long road she has traveled. Much has happened to Dolly: Her husband has died, her son has married and now has children of his own, and Dolly will never again know the "young days" she so sorely misses. Who is she now?

Dolly is a salty, rough, candid, clear-eyed woman trying to face aging as squarely as she has faced other events in her life. Aware of feeling at a disadvantage, Dolly is a keen observer of how the young react to having the upper hand: "All of a sudden they look at you, and then it comes to them, young people, they are bound to outlast you, so they temper up their icy steel and stare into about an inch away from you a lot. Have you noticed it?" (p. 233).

When Dolly was young, she was, in her own words, a "wild one," sexually and emotionally drunk on freedom (among other things). Looking back, she asks whether there is any satisfaction in getting old. She wonders, "What the devil is it all about, the noisiness and the speediness, when it's no distance at all?" (p. 236).

So, on the one hand, Dolly has left her youth, her "own place," forever, but, on the other, she feels as though she hasn't gotten that far. From my point of view, this succinctly expresses one of life's central challenges. At the points (such as adolescence and older age) when we can get preoccupied with how much we are changing, we struggle with identity issues. Who will we be, if we will never be the same? How much should we fight to stay the same, and how much should we surrender to change?

Many characters in the stories discussed in the first part of this chapter struggle with identity issues. Some, like Zelig in Benjamin Rosenblatt's (1999) story (above), make significant changes. Others (e.g., Mrs. Wilson in Thom Jones', 1999, story, above) better understand who they have been. In Mary Lerner's (1999) story, as she dies, Margaret sees a parade of the "little selves" she has inhabited and doesn't want them to be lost forever. Margaret needs to feel some part of her past will be preserved in the future. Unlike Zelig, she is not engaging in a process of change in the present. But, despite these differences, I think all of these aging characters are focusing on an aspect of their identities that they hope will be remembered, cherished, and, in a sense, kept alive.

Challenges to Self-Esteem

In James' story, "The Middle Years" (1992) (above), the writer, Dencombe, struggles to forgive himself for his limitations as a writer. He feels he has bloomed too late, and, as a result, he will not get the chance to fully realize his talents. He could look at what he *has* been able to accomplish but seems bent on facing his unfulfilled potential. Knowing his impact on Doctor Hugh may make this (just about) bearable. Dencombe's self-esteem is so dependent on his accomplishments as an author that it comes as a surprise that there might be more to life than that.

Through moments of intimacy, Mrs. Kidd (In "Mrs. Cross and Mrs. Kidd" by Alice Munro, 1991, above) is able to triumph over her prideful terror of being helpless. She finds an empathic listener in her old friend, Mrs. Cross. Because of her different makeup, the situation is less dreadful for Mrs. Cross. She is better able to be open about her cognitive and physical failings. Her pride is not as dependent on retaining any one attribute, so it is easier for her to give and receive help.

As I have said previously (chapter 4), time is the enemy of the narcissist. Inevitably, we see the scales tip toward favoring others. As Dolly (in Grace Paley's story "Distance," 1966, above) expresses it, the young have the upper hand, since they will outlive their elders. Elsewhere (Buechler, 2008, 2012), I have discussed the sad, heart-wrenching (rather than competitive, aggressive) side of the Oedipal situation, which flows from the unquestionable circumstance that, as the younger generation comes into its own, the older one is losing its ascendancy. I would stress that, among many other feelings, the *sorrow* that this can generate (in *both* generations) is an inevitable part of life. I think that as we age, this sorrow can be exacerbated by narcissistic grandiosity. Needing to be "the fairest of them all" can make it harder and harder to look in the mirror. It is no accident that many works of art, fiction, opera, and so on have as a theme how a particular character copes with a shift in the balance of power between generations. Each coping pattern can present its own handicaps for dealing with this shift, but, I would suggest, that grandiosity and other self-esteem issues frequently pose the most difficult challenges.

Forging a Sense of Purpose

Dolly (in Grace Paley's story "Distance," above) asks, "What the devil is it all about?" (p. 236). I think that Anton (in "Neighbor Rosicky," by Willa Cather, above) could probably answer her. Before he dies, he wants to communicate to his children that life has an organic quality, and this wholeness lends it beauty. He burns with this purpose, even locating his grave so as to accomplish it.

In Alice Munro's portrayal of Mrs. Cross (in "Mrs. Cross and Mrs. Kidd," above), we have a portrait of a woman with an abiding sense of purpose. She doesn't verbally articulate it, but she lives it. Wherever she is, she exemplifies the power of human connection. She reaches out to Jack, the (relatively) young stroke victim, who despairs about all his losses. Her determination to further his functioning, in whatever way she can, is inspiring. It also gives her days and nights unquestionable purpose. At night, she reflects on what she can learn from her experiments with Jack, so she can do better with him the next day.

Dencombe (in James' story "The Middle Years," above) also feels a fierce sense of purpose, but his purposes change over the course of the story. At first, he is determined to wrest from life an "extension" of time so that he can better fulfill his potential in his next book. Gradually, as he accepts that this hope will not be realized, his purpose also becomes more interpersonal as he recognizes the value of his impact on Doctor Hugh. As we age, we may feel a greater urgency about fitting our purposes to our true capacities, since the tally is soon to be final.

The Final Tally

Many have studied the role generativity can play in older age. I like Vaillant's (1993) way of defining it: "Generativity means assuming sustained responsibility for the growth and wellbeing of others" (p. 150). Of course, that sense of responsibility can be expressed in numerous ways. Whether we care for a community or a toddler makes no difference, in this understanding of the term. Generativity is one way we can gain balance, in more than one sense. Its joys can offset some of our losses. Several of the stories in this chapter illustrate this idea. Anton, in Willa Cather's story "Neighbor Rosicky," and Mrs. Cross, in Alice Munro's story "Mrs. Cross and Mrs. Kidd," portray it clearly. Each gets profound pleasure from leaving a legacy for those they love. We can approach an understanding of this from many angles. Generativity can be seen in emotion theory (Buechler, 2004, 2008; Izard, 1977) terms, as providing positive feelings that balance negative affects. Or, from another angle, generativity can give us a sense of purpose and lend greater meaning to our lives. Life's "glass" becomes a little more than half full, so to speak. I think of generativity as one way to resolve self-esteem problems that can complicate aging.

My lifelong patterns of relating interpersonally and functioning intrapsychically will affect what aging means to me. More specifically, these patterns, along with many other factors, will help shape how much I can still feel like myself, regardless of the changes aging brings. In addition, my coping patterns will affect the degree to which I can develop passionate generativity. Whatever form they take, these passionate investments can shift my focus. With generativity, the ground I have lost is balanced by the ground I am gaining. Through it I become a means to an end, as well as an end in myself. I become an instance of life.

References

Buechler, S. (2004). *Clinical values: Emotions that guide psychoanalytic treatment.* Hillsdale, NJ: Analytic Press.
Buechler, S. (2008). *Making a difference in patients' lives: Emotional experience in the therapeutic setting.* New York: Routledge.
Buechler, S. (2012). *Still practicing: The heartaches and joys of a clinical career.* New York: Routledge.
Cather, W. (1994). Neighbor Rosicky. In A. W. Lidz (Ed.), *Major American short stories* (pp. 301–326). New York: Oxford University Press.
Day, C. (1952). Father wakes up the village. In M. Crane (Ed.), *Fifty great short stories* (pp. 315–321). New York: Bantam Dell.
Erikson, E. H. (1978). *Adulthood.* New York: W. W. Norton & Company.
Izard, C. E. (1977). *Human emotions.* New York: Plenum Press.
James, H. (1952). Brooksmith. In M. Crane (Ed.), *Fifty great short stories* (pp. 53–70). New York: Bantam Dell.
James, H. (1992). The middle years. In J. C. Oates (Ed.), *The Oxford book of American short stories* (pp. 171–190). New York: Oxford University Press.
Jones, T. (1999). I want to live. In J. Updike & K. Kenison (Eds.), *The best American short stories of the century* (pp. 671–687). New York: Houghton Mifflin Company.
Lerner, M. (1999). Little selves. In J. Updike & K. Kenison (Eds.), *The best American short stories of the century* (pp. 7–18). New York: Houghton Mifflin Company.
Melville, H. (1994). Bartleby the scrivener. In A. W. Lidz (Ed.), *Major American short stories* (pp. 135–167). New York: Oxford University Press.
Munro, A. (1991). Mrs. Cross and Mrs. Kidd. In *The moons of Jupiter* (pp. 160–181). New York: Vintage.
Paley, G. (1966). Distance. In J. Moffett & K. R. McElheny (Eds.), *Points of view: An anthology of short stories* (pp. 227–236). New York: New American Library.
Rosenblatt, B. (1999). Zelig. In J. Updike & K. Kenison (Eds.), *The best American short stories of the century* (pp. 1–7). New York: Houghton Mifflin Company
Singer, I. B. (1999) The key. In J. Updike & K. Kenison (Eds.), *The best American short stories of the century* (pp. 493–503). New York: Houghton Mifflin Company.
Steinbeck, J. (1952). The chrysanthemums. In M. Crane (Ed.), *Fifty great short stories* (pp. 337–348). New York: Bantam Dell.
Vaillant, G. (1977). *Adaptation to life.* Cambridge, MA: Harvard University Press.
Vaillant, G. (1993). *The wisdom of the ego.* Cambridge, MA: Harvard University Press.

Index

Agee, J.: *A Death in the Family* 5, 98
aging 2; challenges to self-esteem 66, 135–6, 137; character magnified 132–4; in fiction 6–7, 124–32; forging a sense of purpose 136; generativity 136–7; maintaining and modifying identity 134–5
Aiken, C.: "Impulse" 36–7; "Silent Snow, Secret Snow" 4, 32–3
Alexie, S.: "What You Pawn I Will Redeem" 6, 115–16
analysis *see* treatment
Anderson, S.: "Death in the Woods" 4, 50–1
Arieti, S. 119
attention 55–6
Auden, W. H.: "Musée des beaux arts" 99
autobiography 51–2, 98, 101, 103–5, 114–15

Ball, L. 71–2
Bayley, J. 104–5
Beckett, S.: "Molloy" 5, 83, 92
Bellow, S.: "A Father-To-Be" 45–7, 50; "A Silver Dish" 105
Bemporad, J. 119
Bollas, C. 80
Bonime, W. 119, 120
Bowles, J.: "A Day in the Country" 63–4
Breuer, J. 71
Bromberg, P. 110
Buckley, S. 2
Buechler, S. 26, 97, 116, 119, 120, 121, 135

Carver, R.: "A Small, Good Thing" 106–7, 110
Casey, N. 121
Cather, W.: "Neighbor Rosicky" 7, 124, 136; "Paul's Case" 4, 62

Chopin, K.: "The Story of an Hour" 101
clinicians: attitudes to hysteria 78–9; clinical values 3; confidence 38; countertransference 24, 25, 65–6, 93–4; emotional intensity 109; engagement 56; gender 38–9; humility 37, 40–1; the "invisible court" 41–2; loneliness 24; as objects of scrutiny 40; obsessive devices 93–6; personhood 2–3, 42; role 96; self-acceptance 38; self-esteem 65–7; shame 65–7; *see also* treatment
Crowley, R. 14
cultural contexts 76, 102–3

Dark, A. E.: "In the Gloaming" 100
Day, C.: "Father Wakes Up the Village" 5, 90, 91, 133
De Maupassant, G.: "Looking Back" 3, 15–16
depression 4, 5–6; and anger 119; in fiction 113, 115–18; and grief 99, 106, 107, 113–15, 116, 119; and narcissism 58–9, 60, 64–5, 66; schizoid depression 10, 15, 17–19; self-destructive impulses 115–18; and self-esteem 114–15, 117; shame 6, 114, 115, 118, 120, 122; treatment 119–22
diagnosis 1
Dickens, C.: *Great Expectations* 6, 113; *Hard Times* 94
Didion, J.: "The Year of Magical Thinking" 103–4
Donley, C. 2
Dorman, L. 113
Dostoevsky, F.: *The Idiot* 84; "Notes from the Underground" 1, 3, 13–15; "The Meek Girl" 4, 52–3

Eliot, T. S.: "East Coker" 5; Prufrock 6–7
emotion theory 99, 120, 136
emotional intensity 109

Farber, L. 78
Ferenczi, S. 119
fictional characters 1–2
Freedgood, S.: "Grandma and the Hindu Monk" 70–1, 80
Freeman, M. E. W.: "A New England Nun" 3, 11; "Luella Miller" 64–5
Freud, S. 6, 71, 99, 105, 110, 113, 114

gender 38–9, 76, 105–6
generativity 136–7
Gide, A.: "My Mother" 49–50
Gilman, C. P.: "The Yellow Wallpaper" 4, 29–30, 72–3
Gogol, N.: "The Diary of a Madman" 4, 30–2
grandiose posturing: and aging 134, 135–6; characteristics 57, 60; depression 58–9, 60, 64–5, 66; in fiction 4, 57–65; insecurity 59–60, 62–3, 64; purpose 67–8; self-esteem 60–1, 65, 134; shame 61, 66; treatment 65–8; *see also* humiliated suffering
grief 2, 5; and aging 134; autobiographical accounts 98, 101, 103–5; and depression 99, 106, 107, 113–15, 116, 119; in fiction 5, 98–9, 100–3, 105–8; shame 99, 100, 111; treatment 109–11
guilt 99
Guntrip, H. 12, 14–15, 17

Hawthorne, N.: "The Minister's Black Veil" 5–6, 113
Hoffman, I. 53
Horwitz, A. V. 99, 104
humiliated suffering 44; characteristics 47; in fiction 4, 44, 45–51, 52–3; inattention 55; self-analysis 51–2; shame 44–5, 47, 50–1, 54–5; treatment 53–6
hysterical bargaining: and aging 133; cultural context 76; in fiction 4–5, 70–7; theories 71–2, 75–6; treatment 29–30, 77–81

I Love Lucy 71–2
Icarus myth 4
insecurity 27, 45, 52; and narcissism 59–60, 62–3, 64

introversion 14
Iyer, P. 109
Izard, C. E. 99

James, H.: "Brooksmith" 90–1, 133, 134; "The Middle Years" 7, 126–8, 135, 136; "The Tree of Knowledge" 12–13
Jones, T.: "I Want to Live" 128–30, 135
Joyce, J.: "Araby" 45

Kafka, F.: "Letter to His Father" 51–2
Kanwal, G. S. 1
Khan, M. R. 75
Kohut, H. 57–8, 59, 66

Lansky, M. 66
Lardner, R.: "Liberty Hall" 83–4
Leavitt, D.: "Gravity" 100–1
Lerner, M.: "Little Selves" 7, 125, 135
Levenson, E. 2
Lewis, H. B. 66
Lindsay-Abaire, D.: *Rabbit Hole* 107
Lionells, M. 71, 75, 78
London, J.: "To Build A Fire" 19–20

McGrath, P. 29
McWilliams, N. 2, 15, 26
Mairs, N. 115
Mann, T.: "A Gleam" 45, 50; "Little Lizzy" 4, 45, 54; "The Blood of the Walsungs" 4, 57–9; "The Dilettante" 4, 59–61, 68; "The Hungry" 44
Mason, B. A.: "Shiloh" 13
Maugham, W. S.: "The Outstation" 88–90
McCullers, C.: "The Sojourner" 20–1
Melville, H.: "Bartleby the Scrivener" 5, 86–8, 133; *Moby-Dick* 86
Mitchell, S. W. 73
Moore, L.: "You're Ugly, Too" 64
Morrison, A. 66
mourning 42–3, 99, 105, 119
Mukherjee, B.: "The Management of Grief" 102–3
Munro, A.: "Bardon Bus" 105–6; "Dulse" 118, 122; "Labor Day Dinner" 76–7; "Mrs. Cross and Mrs. Kidd" 130–2, 135, 136; "Visitors" 16–17
Murdoch, I. 104–5

narcissism *see* grandiose posturing

Oates, J. C.: "Where Are You Going, Where Have You Been?" 116–17
obsessive controlling: and aging 133; characteristics 92–3; in fiction 5, 82–91; language 83–4, 92, 93, 94–5, 96; perfectionism 90–1; power struggles 86–90, 93; rationalization 84–6, 92; rigidity 83; shame 96; treatment 92–7
O'Connor, F.: "Everything That Rises Must Converge" 82–3
Oedipus 135
O'Leary, J. 120, 121
Orange, D. M. 66
Ovid: *Metamorphoses* 67

Paley, G.: "Distance" 134–5, 136
paranoid processing 2, 27, 28–9; and aging 133; "allergy" to blame 28, 39–40; certainty 28, 38–9; characteristics 28–9; in fiction 3–4, 27, 29–37; the "invisible court" 41–2; projection 28, 39, 40; treatment 37–43
Parker, D.: "A Telephone Call" 76
patients 3
perfectionism 90–1
Phillips, A. 2, 42
plays 5, 101–2, 107
poems 5, 27–8, 67, 99
Porter, K. A.: "Flowering Judas" 62–3; "Theft" 98–9
psychotherapy *see* treatment

Rattigan, T.: *In Praise Of Love* 101–2
regret 99
Rich, C. M.: "My Sister's Marriage" 72
Rilke, R. M. 23
Rosenblatt, B.: "Zelig" 126, 135

Sartre, J-P.: "The Room" 34–6; "The Wall" 3, 17–19
schizoid relating: characteristics 10–11, 13–15; compromise 11–13, 16–17, 20–3; defense 17, 19–20; depression 10, 15, 17–19; in fiction 3, 10, 11–14, 15–23; treatment 23–6
Schopenhauer, A. 129
self-esteem 4; and aging 66, 135–6, 137; and depression 114–15, 117; and narcissism 60–1, 65, 134; *see also* humiliated suffering
self-worth 55–6

Seneca 65
Shabad, P. 55
Shakespeare, W.: *King Lear* 5, 86
shame 99; of clinician 65–7; in depression 6, 114, 115, 118, 120, 122; in grief 99, 100, 111; in humiliated suffering 44, 45, 47, 50–1, 54–5; in narcissism 61, 66; in obsessive controlling 96
Shapiro, D. 2
Shaw, I.: "Main Currents of American Thought" 3, 21–2
short stories 1–2
Singer, I. B.: "Gimpel the Fool" 84–6; "The Key" 2, 3, 27, 28, 42–3, 133
Solomon, A. 121
Steele, W. D.: "How Beautiful With Shoes" 3, 10–11
Steinbeck, J.: "The Chrysanthemums" 4, 73–4, 133
Stern, D. 28
Stringer, L. 6, 109, 114
styles of coping 2–3
Styron, W.: *Darkness Visible* 6, 113–15
Sullivan, H. S. 77, 83, 92, 93, 95, 96, 111

Tan, A.: "The Joy Luck Club" 107–8
Taylor, E.: "A Red Letter Day" 48–9
terminology 2, 3
Tolstoy, L.: "The Death of Ivan Ilych" 22–3
Tomkins, S. 54
treatment 2, 3; depression 119–22; grandiose posturing 65–8; grief 109–11; humiliated suffering 53–6; obsessive controlling 92–7; paranoid processing 37–43; schizoid relating 23–6
Tyler, A.: "Teenage Wasteland" 117

Updike, J.: "The Lucid Eye in Silver Town" 47–8, 50

Vaillant, G. 136

Wakefield, J. C. 99, 104
Wharton, E.: "Roman Fever" 57; "The Other Two" 4–5, 74–5
White, E. B.: "The Door" 4, 33–4
Will, O. A. 37

Yeats, W. B.: "The Second Coming" 27–8